RTI
for
Diverse
Learners

RTI

for

Diverse
Learners

MORE THAN

200

**INSTRUCTIONAL
INTERVENTIONS**

CATHERINE COLLIER

CORWIN
A SAGE Company

For information:

Corwin
A SAGE Company
2455 Teller Road
Thousand Oaks, California 91320
(800) 233-9936
Fax: (800) 417-2466
www.corwin.com

SAGE India Pvt. Ltd.
B 1/I 1 Mohan Cooperative
   Industrial Area
Mathura Road,
   New Delhi 110 044
India

SAGE Ltd.
1 Oliver's Yard
55 City Road
London EC1Y 1SP
United Kingdom

SAGE Asia-Pacific Pte. Ltd.
33 Pekin Street #02-01
Far East Square
Singapore 048763

Printed in the United States of America

Library of Congress Cataloging-in-Publication Data

Collier, Catherine.
RTI for diverse learners : more than 200 instructional interventions / Catherine Collier.
      p. cm.
Includes bibliographical references and index.
ISBN 978-1-4129-7162-1 (pbk.)
   1. Remedial teaching. 2. Slow learning children—Education. 3. Learning disabled children—Education. I. Title.

LB1029.R4C61 2010
372.4'3—dc22   2009047363

This book is printed on acid-free paper.

11   12   13   14   10   9   8   7   6   5   4   3

Acquisitions Editor:	Jessica Allan
Associate Editor:	Sarah Bartlett
Production Editor:	Amy Schroller
Copy Editor:	Codi Bowman
Typesetter:	C&M Digitals (P) Ltd.
Proofreader:	Ellen Howard
Indexer:	Judy Hunt
Cover Designers:	Scott Van Atta and Michael Dubowe
Graphic Designer:	Scott Van Atta

Contents

Acknowledgments

Corwin gratefully acknowledges the contributions of the following individuals:

Julie Esparza Brown, Assistant Professor in Special Education
Portland State University
Portland, OR

Margaret Gallego, Professor of Teacher Education
San Diego State University
San Diego, CA

Nicole Gritters, Special Education Consultant
Area Education Agency 267
Cedar Falls, IA

Kevin McRae, Special Education Consultant
Area Education Agency 267
Cedar Falls, IA

Al Rabanera, Teacher
Fullerton Joint Union High School District
Fullerton, CA

Deborah Rhein, Assistant Professor of Communication Disorders
New Mexico State University
Las Cruces, NM

About the Author

 **Catherine Collier** is a specialist in the emerging field of bilingual/cross-cultural special education, and she has worked directly with a small cadre of nationally recognized professionals in establishing this field of study. She has extensive experience as a classroom teacher with nonnative English learners as well as teacher preparation and research. She taught as a bilingual special educator with culturally diverse learners in Alaska, Arizona, Colorado, and New Mexico. Dr. Collier is currently on the faculty of Western Washington University, the director of a national professional development program funded by the Federal Office of English Language Acquisition. There is a current interview with Dr. Collier featured at the Colorín Colorado Web site (http://www.colorincolorado.com).

Introduction

Framework for Instructional Intervention With Diverse Learners

The biggest mistake of past centuries in teaching has been to treat all children as if they were variants of the same individual, and thus to feel justified in teaching them the same subjects in the same ways.

—Howard Gardner (in Siegel & Shaughnessy, 1994)

Culturally and linguistically diverse (CLD) students, including those who are learning English as an additional language, face tremendous challenges in our schools as do the educators who teach them. Students must overcome culture shock, acquire basic communicative competence in English, master academic language for each subject area, deal with shifts in family roles and language use in the dominant culture, and negotiate problematic concerns of identity in a social climate that is often hostile to difference. Teachers face the challenge of finding ways to ensure the academic success of these students whose educational backgrounds, home cultures, and languages are, in the majority of cases, different from their own. Most teachers are not prepared, by either their experiences or their teacher-preparation programs, to respond to the diversity they find in public schools. Although significant advances have been made in our understanding of effective teaching for CLD students, the transfer of the research to practice remains scant. This is particularly true for English language learners (ELL) with learning and behavior problems and has been magnified by the introduction of response to intervention models in most school districts in the United States.

The use of response to intervention (RTI) as an alternative means of identifying students with specific learning disabilities was made part of the 2004 reauthorization of the Individuals With Disabilities Education Improvement Act. Although RTI is not mandated, states are authorized to choose a more effective way to identify specific learning and behavior disabilities than the older discrepancy and checklist screening (Bradley, Danielson, & Doolittle, 2005). Because of this legislation, many states have quickly begun to move toward implementation of some form of response to intervention.

WHAT IS RESPONSE TO INTERVENTION?

RTI is the current paradigm for the instructional intervention process discussed as part of problem solving. As currently practiced in the majority of school districts, it goes beyond a focus on learning disabilities to problem solving for various learning and behavior issues arising in the classroom setting. RTI is usually described as a multistep approach to providing services to struggling students. Bender and Shores (2007) cite research related to this model going back to the 1960s, but the RTI process remains new for most teachers and parents. E. Johnson, Mellard, Fuchs, and McKnight (2006) define the RTI process as a student-centered assessment model using problem-solving and research-based methods to identify and address learning difficulties in children. Teachers provide instruction and interventions to these challenged and challenging students at increasing levels of intensity. They also monitor the progress students make at each intervention level and use the assessment results to decide whether the students need additional instruction or intervention in general education or referral to special education.

Although few education professionals disagree with the general concept of RTI and the theories behind it, some fear the implementation of RTI as currently carried out may shortchange children with disabilities as well as those with diverse language needs (Tomsho, 2007). As noted by Tomsho, the push for RTI is the latest chapter in a long-running battle over just how far schools should go to educate disabled and challenged students in regular classrooms. Some educators think RTI could boost mainstreaming to unprecedented levels by shifting resources away from separate special education programs and requiring regular-education teachers to tackle tougher learning challenges in their classrooms.

In many places, RTI is being directed at children with specific learning disabilities (SLD). Created under federal law, this fast-growing category includes dyslexia and other processing disorders that are manifested in an imperfect ability to listen, think, speak, read, write, spell, or do mathematical calculations. SLD students account for approximately 46% of the nation's 6.1 million special education students, up from less than a quarter in the 1970s. Finally, the number of students identified for SLD services has increased 200% since 1977, creating concern in the field about misdiagnoses (Vaughn, Linan-Thompson, & Hickman, 2003), such as false positives including overidentification of students with high IQs and average achievement, and false negatives such as underidentification of students with lower IQs and below-average achievement (Kavale, 2005; Semrud-Clikeman, 2005). Meanwhile, there are no standards for what the RTI process should look like or how long the various tiers of intervention should last.

RTI supporters call the traditional SLD identification of discrepancy between achievement and ability a wait-to-fail approach. They maintain that many children now in special education are simply victims of poor instruction and wouldn't need expensive special education services if they had received extra help as soon as their problems surfaced.

Under RTI, children are generally considered for special education only if they don't respond to a gradually intensifying series of closely monitored interventions. As noted by Reschly (2005), RTI is both more humane and more cost-effective to screen for problems early and intervene at younger ages than it is to attempt to treat problems after they are firmly established. Many of us who work with CLD students with various learning and behavior problems have welcomed the move away from prereferral protocols toward intensive problem solving as more responsive to our students' diverse learning needs.

Thus, RTI is commonly seen as a process that involves problem solving, progress monitoring, and ongoing evaluation of children's responsiveness to instruction and/or evidence-based interventions as a guide for instructional and eligibility decisions. The greatest benefits of RTI for limited English proficient and CLD students may come from its utility as a framework for guiding service delivery for those with unmet needs. The 2004 reauthorization of the Individuals with Disabilities Education Act (IDEA) provides a legal basis for RTI. IDEA ensures educational services to children with disabilities on a national level and regulates how states and public agencies administer these services to more than 6.5 million children with disabilities in the United States (U.S. Department of Education, n.d.). With the reauthorization, the law now reads that schools can "use a process which determines if a child responds to a scientific, research-based intervention" as a mechanism for identifying (and subsequently serving) those with learning and behavior problems, including ELLs and those with specific learning disabilities. RTI models have several components in common. Bradley et al. (2005) and Bender and Shores (2007) identify several core components including high-quality classroom instruction, universal screening, continuous progress monitoring, research-based interventions, and fidelity or integrity of instructional intervention. RTI uses tiers of instructional intervention for struggling students, relies on a strong core curriculum and instruction prior to intervening with individual students, incorporates problem solving to determine interventions for students, requires regular monitoring of students, and can be used to predict at-risk students and to intervene with all students who have academic and behavioral difficulties.

RTI models differ in the number of tiers or levels, who is responsible for delivery of the interventions, and whether the process is viewed as a problem-solving process that is an end in itself or as a standard protocol (i.e., a prereferral) leading to a formal evaluation for eligibility. Sometimes the process itself serves as the eligibility evaluation (Fuchs, Mock, Morgan, & Young, 2003).

An additional shift in the current application of RTI and other problem-solving models is the expansion of the model to include progress monitoring of response to instruction (RTII) as well as intervention. These RTI and RTII models are becoming more popular as the limits of RTI are being felt, particularly in districts with large emerging numbers of CLD learners.

Current RTI and RTII models are based on three or four tiers. Generally, in all models, both three and four tiers, at Tier 1, general education teachers provide instruction within the core curriculum to all students in the school. In RTI and RTII models, progress monitoring begins with measuring how students are doing in response to the general content core curriculum with particular attention paid to students identified at entry as at-risk or coming from CLD backgrounds. It is assumed that about 80% of students in a school will be successful in the benchmarked curriculum and will not need intensive further assistance (Philip Chinn, personal correspondence, August 2004). In some models, differentiation of instruction including language support is included as part of Tier 1, particularly where dual-language and two-way bilingual transition models are implemented. In others, specific differentiation for learning and behavior, particularly language transition and behavior adaptation support for students experiencing culture shock, is provided in Tier 2 (both Kansas and Pennsylvania have variations of this model). In all multitier models, Tier 2 is generally seen as the point at which focused, small group assistance begins, based on some emerging need identified through the progress monitoring done during Tier 1 instruction and intervention. It is here that reading specialists, English as a second language (ESL) instructors, and other content area assistance may be provided to struggling students in small group pullout or push in situations. In most schools with bilingual transitional or dual-language programs, English literacy development (ELD) is not seen as a specific intervention but as an essential core curriculum component of Tier 1. Emerging issues such as unusual delays in language acquisition or unresolved culture shock and transition issues would call for moving the student into a more focused Tier 2 setting for intervention.

Figure I.1 Example of the Three-Tier Model illustrates the basic three-tier RTI or RTII model and the percentage of students considered appropriate to be served at that level. Most state programs have some sort of version of this basic model. However, there is great variation in these applications.

Figure I.1 Example of the Three-Tier Model

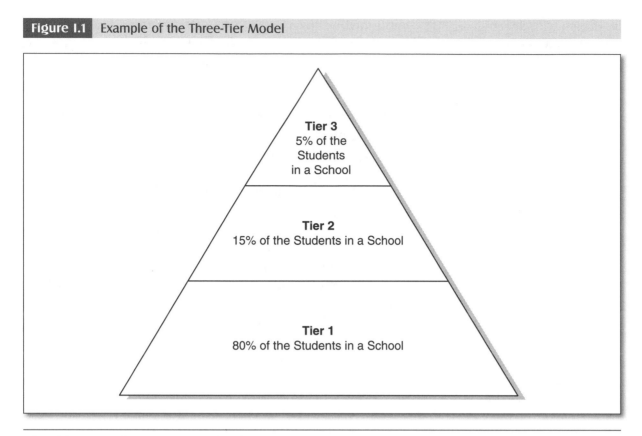

Adapted from National Association of State Directors of Special Education (2005).

In other programs, there are more levels or tiers within each tier although the common is three or four tiers. In both the four-tier and three-tier models, when students fail to respond to small group and intense, individualized interventions, they are referred for special education. Special education teachers may help develop interventions and/or plan assessments for students receiving instruction and interventions in Tiers 1 and 2. They may not provide instruction to students until Tier 3 or 4, when the student could be referred and identified for special education. In the four-tier model, Tier 4 is generally seen as the most individualized and intensive level of instruction and intervention and usually includes students on individualized education plans (IEP) and other special education or related service provisions.

Figure I.2 Example of the Four-Tier Model illustrates a four-tier RTII problem-solving model for CLD students. As students are served at the various tiers, the intensity of intervention and instruction increases as illustrated by the arrows going up the left side of the pyramid. As services move up the pyramid and intensity increases, the number of students served at each tier decreases. This is shown by the arrows going up the right side of the pyramid. In some school districts, students will be moved up until their needs are met and then moved back down to the lower tier to solidify this problem resolution. Not all students return entirely to Tier 1 but need to continue some form of Tier 2 differentiation their entire school career.

Some advocates of the problem-solving approach disagree with illustrating repeated response to instruction and intervention with a triangle, which seems to imply movement in only one direction. They prefer to use a circle to show that movement of the student and intervention process is continuous. This is shown in Figure I.3 Continuous Problem-Solving Model.

Figure I.2   Example of the Four-Tier Model

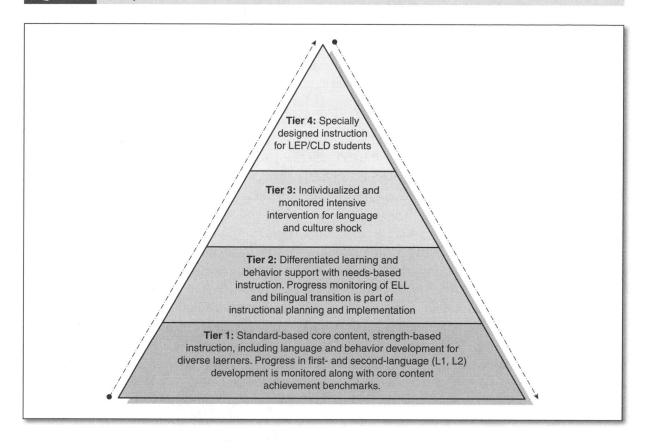

Figure I.3   Continuous Problem-Solving Model

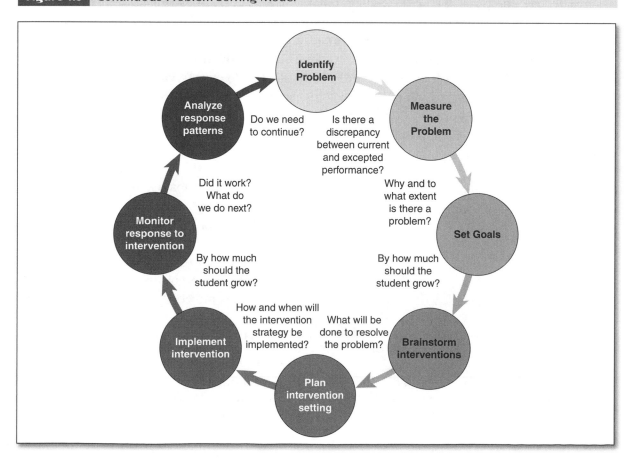

The difference between the process depicted in the triangles (Figures I.1 and I.2) versus the circles (Figure I.3) highlights an issue in the use of these models with diverse learners mentioned earlier (i.e., the idea of a standard protocol or set of prescribed steps to follow in resolving one or more learning or behavior problems versus a problem-solving model that works to resolve a continuing series of problems with no end point as part of the process). Teachers have told me of their frustration with specific aspects of both models when working with challenging CLD students.

Typically, in the RTI standard protocol, lists of interventions and instructional procedures are provided to classroom personnel to follow until the student meets target benchmarks of response to the prescribed activities. Often, a specific timeline is given in which a response is to be achieved. These are often expansions from a previously implemented prereferral process and classroom personnel are given specific workbooks or reading kits, checklists, or other guidelines to follow in the application of prescribed numbers and types of interventions to use. The materials and procedures are designed to address specific learning disability areas of concern. I have heard teachers call this "RTI in a box" along with their common frustration in following a fixed set of procedures that they see as inappropriate or ineffective with CLD learners. The strategies presented in this book are specifically designed to work "out of the box" for school personnel frustrated with prepackaged RTI interventions and provide teachers with expanded, research-based RTI and RTII options.

Although less frequent, I have also had teachers express dissatisfaction with the circular, continuous problem-solving model when used with CLD students with learning and behavior problems. On the one hand, problem solving can be out of the box and focus on actual presenting problems, including a variety of language transition and behavior adaptation issues. However, teachers have expressed frustration with what appears to be recycling or a never-ending cycle of problem solving. They have told me their ELL/CLD students with continuing learning and behavior problems never get out of the circle of problem solving into service resolution. Therefore, I recommend a blend of dynamic problem solving in a tiered RTII model and not a static triangle.

- The way I propose looking at problem solving for ELL/CLD students is to think of a pyramid of instruction and intervention comprised of many specific strategy blocks: a three-dimensional RTII structure without a fixed number of tiers per se. Each block represents a specific strategy cluster or approach designed to build on the strengths or address the needs of an individual ELL/CLD student, and each level represents a degree of intensity of focus. As various instructional and strategic approaches are used with each individual student, they fill in that particular tier of the pyramid. The complete pyramid of resiliency and intervention strategies model is illustrated in Figure I.4 Pyramid of Resiliency, Instruction, Strategies, Intervention, and Monitoring (PRISIM) for diverse learners (C. Collier, 2009).

Figure I.4 Pyramid of Resiliency, Instruction, Strategies, and Intervention Monitoring

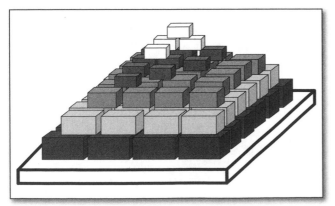

- The principal elements of PRISIM are the myriad strategies that comprise the building blocks. This book contains my current recommended set of strategies with the research base necessary under today's RTI/RTII structures. As new problems with diverse learners arise, I recommend teachers keep their strategy and intervention toolboxes open, as new approaches will become necessary.

- A pyramid is only as strong as its foundation, so the more comprehensive and complete the information gathering, teacher preparation, curricula, and system support can be, the stronger and more effective the instructional program of the school will be for ELL/CLD students, including those with special needs. The foundation of personnel, system, curricula, and comprehensive data provide a solid foundation on which the building blocks of learning are firmly established. Each block represents a cluster of strategies, core content, and settings that may be differentiated for specific strengths and/or needs of learners.

A teacher may end up using all of these strategies, but differentiate them for different student needs and issues. The instructional strategy set at Tier 1 in the PRISIM version of the RTII model will be comprehensive and geared to the larger group process and based on facilitating resiliency and learning readiness of all students. As teachers see that some students need more intensive differentiation and present some unresolved learning or behavior problems, they may move the instructional focus to smaller group interventions for particular ELL/CLD students. At Tier 2 of the PRISIM version of the RTII model, teachers may use several different approaches, of which many will be successful for the majority of ELL/CLD students. However, some of the more challenging ELL/CLD students will need even more individualization and some students will require assistance from other education personnel. At this point, students may be moved into more intensive problem solving, whether this is termed Tier 3 of an RTI or RTII model or whether it is an individualized application in the continuous problem-solving model. At these more structured points in problem-solving or tiered intervention, the student is more tightly monitored with more intensity in individual intervention.

During this entire RTI or RTII process, it is extremely important that specific cultural and linguistic issues be addressed as well as the specific learning and behavior that are part of the teacher's concern. Before school personnel can move to formally evaluate and consider placement in special education services, they must document that the presenting problems are not principally because of language and culture issues. They must document that the primary cause of the presenting problem is not because of the student's English proficiency or level of culture shock. Language and culture issues will always be part of serving an ELL/CLD student, but under the reauthorized IDEA of 2004, the team must document the extent to which these are part of the presenting problem and that they are not the most significant determining factor.

Asking the Right Questions

These issues frequently appear in school settings as questions asked by concerned school personnel. "He has been here for more than two years, so isn't his lack of academic achievement a sign of a possible disability?" "Is this communication problem a language difference or is it a language disability?" "She was born here, so can't we rule out culture shock and language development issues?" Although illustrative of the good intentions and heartfelt concern about these students by education professionals, it is more productive to ask what information do we need and how will we use it.

What Information Do We Need?

The information to be gathered answers specific questions critical to separating difference from disability (SDD) considerations.

- **Education:** Has the student been in school before? Are there gaps in the student's education experiences? Sufficient intensity of instruction?

- **Home language**: Are languages other than English spoken in the student's home? What languages other than English does the student speak? Is the student maintaining an ability to communicate with his or her family members?
- **Language proficiency**: What is the student's language proficiency and literacy? Is the student developing the home language at a normal rate?
- **English**: Does the student need assistance with learning English? Is the student acquiring English at a normal rate?
- **Achievement:** What is the student's level and rate of academic achievement? Is this normal for the general student population in your district/school? Specific population of the student?
- **Behavior**: Is the student's emotional stability developmentally and culturally appropriate? Are there individual or family circumstances that may explain the observed behavior?
- **Adaptation:** What is the student's level of acculturation? Is the student at risk for culture shock? Is the student adapting to our school at a normal rate?

How Should We Use the Information?

Information about students is not valuable if it is not instructionally meaningful and does not lead to a course of action for the student's benefit.

- **Education**: Prior experience in school, whether in the United States or another country, facilitates transitional instructional models. Thus, knowing that the student has received schooling elsewhere tells school personnel they can focus on transition from one academic language foundation to English academic language (V. P. Collier & Thomas, 2007). If the student has never had a formal education experience, school personnel must start by building an understanding of school culture, rules, expectations, and basic school interaction language in the student's most proficient language before transitioning to English.

SDD concern: If the student shows little progress with adapting to school expectations and continues to struggle with acquiring school interaction language in the home language, he may have an undiagnosed disability and a full evaluation may be needed.

- **Home language:** Students who are raised in homes where English is infrequently or only one of the languages used come to us with unique strengths that can become the foundation of instruction. Research shows that they have cognitive and linguistic capacities that can facilitate learning (Baca & Cervantes, 2003). Additionally, psychological well-being is built on quality family communication and interactions (Padilla, Padilla, Morales, Olmedo, & Ramirez, 1979).

SDD concern: If the student has not acquired a developmentally appropriate proficiency in a language other than English, it may be because of family circumstances or the presence of an undiagnosed disability. In either case, this can delay English acquisition. A structured, intensive intervention in the primary home language would show whether the student has the ability to develop language and communication. If the student's communication does not improve under intervention, then a referral for a full evaluation might be warranted.

- **Language and literacy**: The student's proficiency and background in a language other than English assists in deciding the most effective instructional communicative models. It is critical to assess to the extent possible the student's proficiency in her home language/communication mode. As there are not standardized tests available for every language or communication mode, alternative measures are frequently needed (Baca & Cervantes, 2003). These can be structured sampling and observation, interview, interactive inventories, and other analytic tools (Hoover, Baca, & Klingner, 2007).

SDD concern: A student may score low on a standardized test in the home language because he has never received instruction in the language and has only an oral proficiency. Thus, low primary language and low English may look like there is some language disability. A structured intensive intervention in the primary language including basic literacy readiness would serve to profile the student's proficiency and establish whether the low score is learning based rather than something else. If the student makes little or no progress in the RTI or RTII, a referral for a full evaluation may become necessary.

- **Communication:** The student's language proficiency in English is directly related to eligibility and entry level for ESL instruction. There are many tools available for determining whether a student needs assistance with learning English (Baca & Cervantes, 2003). For initial services in English language learning for limited English proficient (LEP) speakers, school personnel should select instruments that are quick, nonbiased, and focus on speaking and listening skills. Including a literacy screening would be instructionally meaningful only for students who have received prior instruction in English.

SDD concern: Some students speak enough English to not qualify for ELL/LEP services but have such a limited classroom language foundation that they look like students with learning disabilities. Thus, English screening for ELL/LEP services must include screening for cognitive academic language proficiency and not just social language. A structured, intensive intervention in English including basic phonemic awareness, phonics, vocabulary, fluency, comprehension, and other reading and writing readiness would serve two purposes: (1) profile the ELL/LEP student's proficiency and (2) establish whether the low score is learning based rather than something else. If the student makes little or no progress in the RTI or RTII, a referral for a full evaluation is necessary. Additionally, if the child has a disability, is receiving special education services, and is an ELL/LEP student, the IEP should list the ELL/LEP accommodations as part of related services. This could be bilingual assistance or specially designed assistance in English (Freeman & Freeman, 2007) in the special education setting or some other appropriate monitored intervention with specific objectives related to acquiring English. In many cases, the disabling condition is such that it seriously impacts the acquisition of English, and thus, special education personnel and ELL/LEP personnel must work together on realistic outcomes. These modified language outcomes need to be included in the IEP.

- **Cognition:** All children can learn but they learn at different rates and in different manners. All children can learn but they enter and exit at different points. A challenge of today's standards-based education models is that students who do not fit the scope and sequence of a particular school system are frequently placed in alternative instructional settings that may or may not be appropriate to their needs (Baca & Cervantes, 2003).

SDD concern: If a student is not meeting the benchmarks established by a school system even when given learning support, she may be referred to special education as having a learning disability of some sort. Sometimes special education is the only instructional alternative available in the building. It is not appropriate to place students who do not have a disability in special education even when it is the best alternative instructional setting available. Programs should be restructured to include differentiated instructional environments where any student can enter a lesson at his or her entry point and learn to the maximum of his or her abilities. A structured intensive intervention in fundamental learning strategies would establish whether the low score is learning based rather than something else. If the student makes little or no progress in the RTI or RTII, a referral for a full evaluation may be necessary.

- **Behavior:** Family and community events can be a contributing factor, and it is critical to effective instruction to explore both school and nonschool environments and their relationship to the student's presenting problem. Whether the behavior problem is because of an innate disorder, biochemical dysfunction, or a temporary response to trauma or disruption in the student's home or school environment, the student needs effective and immediate intervention and assistance.

SDD concern: Although the student needs assistance with managing or controlling his behavior, special education is not the appropriate placement if the etiology of the problem is culture shock or an event or chronic stressors in the student's home or school environment (C. Collier, Brice, & Oades-Sese, 2007). An intensive instructional intervention that facilitates self-monitoring and control in a supportive and safe environment should always be implemented first. If the problem does not appear to decrease in frequency or intensity, or if the student makes little or no progress, a referral for a full evaluation might become necessary.

- **Adaptation:** The level and rate of acculturation and accompanying degree of culture shock must be addressed in the instructional environment. All students must adapt to the school environment regardless of if they speak English; students who come into your school from homes or communities very different from the school will experience greater degree of culture shock (C. Collier et al., 2007).

SDD concern: The manifestations of culture shock look a lot like learning and behavior disabilities and unaddressed acculturation and adaptation needs can concatenate into serious learning and behavior problems later in the education experience. An intensive instructional intervention that mitigates culture shock and facilitates adaptation and language transition should always be implemented, particularly for newcomers. Most students will respond within weeks to this intervention. This positive response does not mean that culture shock may not reappear, as culture shock is cyclical and a normal part of our adaptation to anything strange to us. However, a positive response to acculturative assistance lets school personnel know that the presenting problems are because of a normal adaptive process, acculturation, which responds over time to instructional intervention. Students should have their level of acculturation measured at entry into your school system and their rate of acculturation monitored annually to assure the student is making normal progress in your school. If the student's rate of acculturation is not within normal range, it is an indication either that the program is not adequately addressing his transition needs or that there may be an undiagnosed disability of some sort that is depressing the rate of acculturation.

Although RTI and RTII are generally thought of as referring to academic intervention, most programs (93.3% according to Berkeley, Bender, Peaster, and Saunders, 2009) also incorporate behavioral intervention in the RTI and RTII model or use a similar multitiered approach to address the behavioral needs of students. All but one of the programs examined by Berkeley et al. use tiered approaches to address behavior in addition to academics. In conclusion, while RTI and RTII are seen as a positive development in assisting all learners, our principle concern is that typical RTI/RTII programs are designed for native English-speaking students with learning and behavior problems and need to be expanded and adapted for use with ELL and CLD students.

Providing Some Context

Up to this point, I have described what is current practice or what research has established as best practice in typical K–12 schools including serving students with various learning and behavior problems. These problem-solving programs can be effective for all learners with specific modifications for use with ELL/CLD students. Problem-solving programs with progress monitoring are particularly helpful with ELL/CLD students when expanded to include instructional

What RTI/RTII for ELL/CLD Students Is and What It Is Not	
RTI/RTII Is	**RTI/RTII Is Not**
An initiative that supports general education school improvement goals for all diverse learners	A stand-alone special education initiative
Intended to help as many CLD students as possible meet proficiency standards without special education	A means for getting more ELL/CLD students into special education
A method to unify general and special education to benefit CLD students through greater continuity of services	A method for increasing or decreasing special education numbers
Focused on effective instruction to enhance CLD student growth	Focused primarily on learning disability determination among CLD students and documented through a checklist

strategies and instructional interventions directly addressing their unique learning and behavior needs (Baca & Cervantes, 2003; C. Collier, 2009). As my goal with this book is to provide direct pragmatic suggestions for implementing instructional interventions in classroom settings with ELL/CLD, I will provide examples from my teaching experience. Specific examples will precede the list of recommended interventions for each RTI/RTII level or tier of instruction and intervention. These recommended interventions are not a substitute for other content intervention that research has shown to be effective with ELL/CLD students but are to be used in conjunction with research-based academic strategies and interventions typically used with all students exhibiting learning and behavior problems. There is nothing magic about these instructional and intervention strategies; they all take extra effort and focus on the part of instructional personnel. Some teachers will be familiar with many of these but may not have thought about using them as part of an intensive, focused instructional strategy or intervention process. They are particularly effective with ELL/CLD students who are in integrated classrooms with non-ELL/CLD students of mixed ability level but are also beneficial in ELL and special education pullout settings.

Prior to becoming a special education teacher, I was a primary teacher and a beginner teacher. Beginner was the term used for students who had never been in school before and who did not speak English. These students were assigned to my classroom until they tested as able to participate in a classroom with their grade-level peers. Thus, I had mixed ages, mixed abilities, and mixed language proficiency in my classroom, and I was responsible for instructing all of my students in the core curriculum detailed in our school's scope and sequence guidelines.

Over the years, specific students with very challenging learning and behavior problems passed through my classroom doors. I will use these students' stories to illustrate the instructional intervention process.

Tier 1 Interventions

1

INTRODUCTION TO TIER 1 INSTRUCTIONAL FOCUS

For all response to intervention (RTI) and response to instruction and intervention (RTII) problem-solving models, the first tier consists of general education instruction in the core curriculum and content interventions, including some implemented in differentiated instructional settings administered classwide or to struggling students who are identified through universal screening and/or benchmark assessments. Instructional strategies at this level are intended to build on student strengths and create a foundation for further learning and achievement. Instruction at Tier 1 is also a time during which, as described by Esparza Brown & Doolittle (2008), baseline data through universal screening are gathered for all students and achievement is monitored regularly. Problem-solving RTI/RTII systems rely on the use of evidence-based curricula that is taught in a consistent manner (treatment integrity). It is assumed that effective and research-based instruction already occurs in the general education classroom for all students. For instruction to be effective and appropriate for culturally and linguistically diverse (CLD) and English language learner (ELL) students, as discussed earlier, assessment as well as instruction must be both linguistically and culturally appropriate and effective. That is, the teacher who wants to teach ELL/CLD students appropriately and effectively must know their levels of language proficiency in their first language (L1) and second language (L2) when planning assessment and instruction and provide culturally relevant curricula that reflect the background and experiences of the students (Delpit, 1995; Gay, 1985; Macedo & Bartolomé, 1999). Appropriate instruction for ELL/CLD at Tier 1 requires that teachers embrace pedagogy that is "rooted in the cultural capital of [their students] and have as its point of departure the native language and culture" (Freire & Macedo, 1987, p. 151). In other words, a child's language and culture are never viewed as liabilities but rather as strengths on which to build an education. Tier 1 instruction should always be based on the strengths that students bring with them to school and instructional strategies selected that promote learning while creating a learning environment that is designed to minimize or prevent the development of counterproductive learning behaviors and practices.

When ELL/CLD students enter the school program, the comprehensive benchmarked curriculum in which they are instructed, including heritage language development and support and ESL instruction, become part of their Tier 1 instruction. During Tier 1 instruction, if concerns arise about ELL/CLD students' progress, the instructional program itself must be examined to determine the match between the demands of the curriculum and the child's current level of proficiency in the language of instruction. It is important to examine the achievement of the student's peers (similar language proficiencies, culture, and experiential background) to see if they are excelling or not. If similar culture and language peers are struggling, this is an indication that the instruction is less than optimal for that group of students. A typical instructional strategy at Tier 1 for ELL/CLD students is primary language instruction to strengthen their literacy readiness (e.g., Spanish phonics, reading readiness, primers in Spanish).

Esparza Brown and Doolittle (2008) recommend that once instruction is adjusted to meet each student's individual or personalized needs at Tier 1, progress should be closely monitored and decisions made as to whether students are meeting predetermined targets or benchmarks. They further suggest that instruction in the child's home language or more proficient non-English language be part of the ELL/CLD student's instruction at Tier 1. Only if the ELL/CLD student does not make targeted gains after this and other instructional modifications should a move into Tier 2 more intensive instruction and intervention be considered.

PROGRESS MONITORING AT TIER 1

Although there are varying levels of intensity in intervention required during the RTI and RTII process, according to Berkeley, Bender, Peaster, and Saunders (2009), all programs require progress monitoring. Progress monitoring increases in intensity and frequency throughout the tiers in the RTI/RTII models. At Tier 1, the expectations are regular classroom monitoring with annual achievement testing. At Tier 2, the expectations are approximately monthly measuring of the student's performance in the small group activities plus the regular assessments in the classroom. At Tier 3, the monitoring is individualized with daily/weekly measures of the individual interventions, depending on what concepts and behaviors the teacher is focusing on during this period. At Tier 4, the monitoring is continuous measurement for the objectives outlined in an individualized education plan (IEP). Specific minimum requirements include universal screening at least three times a year with progress monitoring occurring in the range of two to four times per month at Tiers 2 and 3.

Generally at Tier 1 and frequently at Tier 2, teachers with ELL/CLD students in their classroom will be addressing more than one issue at a time with specific instructional strategies and interventions. For example, at Tier 1, the classroom teacher will be working with the whole classroom on the core curriculum in reading, writing, mathematics, science, social studies, and with academic language development in these content areas, supporting English acquisition, facilitating the adaptation of ELL/CLD students to their new learning environment, as well as juggling a wide range of behavior and learning abilities and prior learning experiences.

For example, suppose a student of concern has been identified as having an unusually high level of distractibility and failure with task completion, enough so that attention deficit disorder is suspected by some of the teachers working with him. By addressing attention issues at Tier 1 of the RTI/RTII process, the teacher is working to accommodate normal ranges of ability and experience by facilitating better attending and listening by all students in the general education classroom as well as addressing specific difficulties with attending and completing tasks by particular students. Modifications in the instructional setting, teaching strategies, and the presentation of specific content are selected to address general issues as well as specific ones, such as presenting lessons in such a way as to facilitate better attention to task and core content task completion for all students including the particular student they are concerned with. First, the teachers identify the normal expectation for level of attention and task completion and establish criteria for measuring student performance. They then select one of the intervention strategies that will best facilitate students responding appropriately while learning core content lessons.

The targeted intervention strategy is previewed with all of the students and the teacher working with the class begins the intervention as part of the daily or weekly instructional practice. At the beginning, the strategy used for intervention is usually conducted daily. If the intervention selected is effective and students improve their responses by showing measurable increase in attention to task and in task completion, the teacher would then gradually broaden the application to monitoring specific students of concern. They would monitor the application in all instructional settings including specific core content lessons. If the intervention was a success (i.e., the target students improve their attention and task completion to the target goal), then the teacher can add that strategy to the regular teaching repertoire as a successful tool. Table 1.1, Progress Monitoring at Tier 1, illustrates what the monitoring chart might look like for the attention intervention described while at the same time monitoring the target student's success in learning to spell 100 English words. Pictures, stories, putting words onto charts, tracing words in sentences, and other language development strategies are used to teach the vocabulary words.

If the intervention was not a success (i.e., the student only achieved staying on task when the aide touched the student's shoulder and immediately reverted to off-task behavior when the aide moved away), then the teacher might need to consider more drastic measures. This could include intensifying the intervention by moving the student into a Tier 2 small group or individual work setting.

Table 1.1 Progress Monitoring at Tier 1

Setting: Whole class	Week 2	Week 4	Week 6	Week 8	Week 10
(Strategy 1) Stepped proxemics	Aide walking around	Aide standing by desk	Aide touching shoulder	Aide standing by desk	Aide walking around
Response to strategy	On task 30% of the time	On task 60% of the time	On task 90% of the time	On task 100% of the time	On task 100% of the time
Content goal: Correctly use and spell 100 new English words	Student listens and reads 10 new words each week	Student correctly uses, copies, and reads 40–50 words	Student uses, reads, and spells 50–70 words; adds 10 new words each week	Student uses, reads, and spells 70–90 words; adds 10 new words each week	Student uses, reads, and spells 90–100 words

SO WHAT DO I DO WITH AN ELL STUDENT AT TIER 1?

Example From Classroom Practice

One year my primary classroom had 30 students in it. These students were all diverse learners but their language proficiency in their home languages and in English varied considerably. Although all of my students were from homes where someone spoke a language other than English, not all were proficient in the home language; some were English proficient, and most were proficient in their home language and not proficient in English. We used an integrated bilingual instructional approach in the classroom (i.e., ESL in the content areas with guided assistance in the home language every day with home-language literacy activities twice a week). Five students were particularly a challenge for me: Tommy, Justin, Clarence, Irving, and Mary. One of the common issues they presented to me was that it was extremely difficult to get them to stay on task, to pay attention during instruction, and to get them to hand in their work on time. As this is something all learners need to be able to do in our classrooms, I began by having the whole class practice the steps needed to pay attention, including having everyone *role-play* (described in Strategy 14 under Communication Issues at Tier 1) paying attention and discussing why it was important to pay attention and to get their assignments done for each lesson. As part of this preview, I walked around the room in an exaggerated manner, stopping and *modeling* (Strategy 4, Tier 1) touching students on the shoulder and asking them to show me what they were doing. After this initial introduction of the strategy, I proceeded with our usual lessons in the content areas. Referred to next as *proximity*, periodically, I would move next to various students, including my target students, and see if they were working on their assignments. I charted my target students' responses as I moved closer and stayed longer in their vicinity. All target students responded to this strategy by increasing their attention to task, but only Mary and Tommy seemed to be able to sustain their focus without my near presence.

The following are strategies and instructional practices that facilitate learning and building cognitive academic proficiency for ELL/CLD students in mixed language and ability classrooms. I have organized these strategies by the issue they primarily address, giving their purpose, a brief description of how to implement the strategy, the research base for the strategy, and a brief discussion of considerations that must be made for CLD issues when using these with ELL/CLD students. Teachers using these strategies can enter this information into their intervention log, RTI/RTII form, or other required format for progress monitoring and as part of their documentation regarding intervention and assistance the student may qualify for after the intervention is complete.

READINESS AND RESILIENCY ISSUES AT TIER 1

1. PROXIMITY (PROXEMICS)

Purpose of the Strategy

1. Increase students' time spent on task

2. Redirect attention for distracted learners

3. Reassure frustrated students

How to Do It

1. At Tier 1, this strategy is done in the whole classroom group. The teacher and/or other students are strategically positioned to provide support and to prevent or minimize misbehaviors.

2. For example, the teacher circulates throughout the classroom during group or independent activities, spending more time next to particular students.

3. This can also be done with an assistant who moves closer to distracted students to redirect attention back to task. The assistant may gradually end up sitting next to the target students and sometimes gently touching them on the shoulder to redirect them to their assignment.

Research Base

Etscheidt, Stainback, S. B., & Stainback, W. C., 1984

Evertson & Weinstein, 2006

Gunter & Shores, 1995

Marable & Raimondi, 1995

What to Watch for With ELL/CLD Students

1. All cultures have guidelines about how close or how far away to stand or sit next to another person. These are mostly unspoken and learned through being raised in the culture and community where the proximity to another person is seen and remarked on by those around you.

2. These space relations are also affected by whether someone is standing over or sitting under another person. These relative positions convey power and control relationships, which vary from culture to culture.

3. Teachers must familiarize themselves with the proximity rules of the various cultures represented in their classrooms before expecting to use proxemics strategically to promote learning.

2. REDUCED STIMULI

Purpose of the Strategy

1. Enhance ability of students to focus on learning

2. Encourage questioning and exploration of new learning

3. Reduce response fatigue

4. Reduce culture shock

5. Develop personal control of situations

How to Do It

At Tier 1, this strategy can be done with the whole classroom or large groups. Teachers start rooms with relatively blank walls and empty spaces, also monitoring the use of music and other auditory materials. Teachers do not display or use visual/auditory materials until students have been introduced to the content or have produced the materials themselves. Visual, tactile, and auditory experiences are introduced gradually and with demonstration.

Research Base

P. Nelson, Kohnert, Sabur, & Shaw, 2005

Wortham, 1996

What to Watch for With ELL/CLD Students

1. Newcomers may become overly stimulated by lots of bright, new, unfamiliar, and strange objects, signs, sounds, and miscellany in their new classroom. They do not know what is important to attend to and what is not important. It is all new and exciting.

2. This is also going to impact students with undiagnosed neurological conditions that they have not yet learned to accommodate.

3. It is better to start out with less and add as students become comfortable and familiar with what is in the classroom.

3. REST AND RELAXATION TECHNIQUES

Purpose of the Strategy

1. Enhance ability of students to learn new things

2. Develop self-monitoring skills

3. Reduce anxiety and stress responses

4. Reduce culture shock side effects

How to Do It

At Tier 1, this strategy is done with the whole classroom. Relaxation techniques are shown in video or demonstration form with an explanation in home and community language when possible. Students discuss when they might need to use these techniques.

Research Base

Allen & Klein, 1997

Page & Page, 2003

Thomas, 2006

What to Watch for With ELL/CLD Students

1. Heightened anxiety, distractibility, and response fatigue are all common side effects of the acculturation process and attributes of culture shock.

2. ELL and CLD students need more time to process classroom activities and tasks. Building in rest periods will provide thinking and processing breaks in their day.

4. MODELING

Purpose of the Strategy

1. Reduce code-switching

2. Develop cognitive academic language

3. Build transfer skills

4. Develop content knowledge foundation

How to Do It

At Tier 1, this strategy can be done with the whole classroom. Teachers act out what is to be done. This can include behavior as well as academic responses and expectations. The situation is explained in home and community language when possible, and each response and expectation is modeled. Students then practice each response and interaction until comfortable and successful.

Research Base

Cole, 1995

Tovani, 2000

What to Watch for With ELL/CLD Students

1. Remember that some ELL and CLD students have had very little experience with school or with being with people outside of their family or culture. They may not know what action you are modeling if it is something they have never experienced or seen.

2. The desired action and response need to be explained in the students' most proficient language.

5. CONCURRENT LANGUAGE DEVELOPMENT/ ACQUISITION SESSIONS FOR STUDENTS AND PARENTS

Purpose of the Strategy

1. Build awareness of appropriate communication behaviors for school language and rules

2. Improve confidence in home, community, school culture interactions

3. Build on the diverse language foundations of students and parents

4. Strengthen school/parent partnerships

How to Do It

At Tier 1, this strategy is an effective way to improve readiness among students while building communication with their parents. Classes for both parents and their children are provided at a time selected by the parents. Parents participate in English as a second language instruction in one room with a bilingual instructor while their children receive home and community language instruction (when possible) and academic content support in another room. After the formal class period, the groups reunite and parents practice bilingual educational games that they can play at home with their children.

Research Base

Brownlie & King, 2000

Cole, 1995

Law & Eckes, 2000

What to Watch for With ELL/CLD Students

1. This is most effective with large communities of one language and more difficult to implement where there are separate families or small groups speaking various and diverse languages.

2. In multilanguage family communities, focus can remain on English as a second language with first-language support offered for as many languages as you have access to bilingual personnel.

6. FAMILY-CENTERED LEARNING ACTIVITY

Purpose of the Strategy

1. Build awareness of academic expectations

2. Build awareness of appropriate school language and rules for academic and social behaviors

3. Build on family language and culture

4. Strengthen school-parent partnerships

How to Do It

1. At Tier 1, this strategy is useful in building family involvement in school as well as strengthening the support at home for student learning. Evening learning activities are offered to families centered on specific content areas.

2. For example, family math, family computer, and family literacy nights, offering several interactive activities, provide an educational and fun setting for all. Parents benefit from home and community language explanations, when possible, about education outcomes and how they can help students at home.

3. These activities can be done bilingually or in the family language. If the family speaks Spanish, you can tie into the existing Spanish language computer, math, science, and language materials available online from National Council for Lifelong Learning and Work Skills (Consejo Nacional de Educacion para la Vida y el Trabajo [CONEVyT]).

Research Base

D. C. Garcia, Hasson, Hoffman, Paneque, & Pelaez, 1996

Sink, Parkhill, Marshall, Norwood, & Parkhill, 2005

What to Watch for With ELL/CLD Students

1. It is important to tie these extracurricular activities into general classroom content areas. These can be a point of academic content support by offering the activities in the home language of participants as well as having bilingual personnel available.

2. The Mexican government offers free materials and textbooks that can supplement these activities for Spanish-speaking families. Contact the Mexican embassy or consulate closest to you to find out more. An example of what the Mexican government offers is CONEVyT. CONEVyT was created in 2002 in Mexico to provide primary and secondary education and training to adults (15 and older) with low educational levels in that country as well as migrant populations living in the United States. Through an online portal and a network of Plazas Comunitarias where direct instruction, assessment, and varied materials can be found, both the U.S. and Mexican governments make educational support available for anyone willing to learn or to teach. For more information go to www.conevyt.org.mx.

7. GUIDED MEMORIES

Purpose of the Strategy

1. Build transfer skills

2. Facilitate discussion about new learning

3. Strengthen school-parent partnerships

How to Do It

At Tier 1, this strategy is done in general education and integrated classrooms where all students participate in the activity. The teacher selects the events or length of time to cover (e.g., two years, five years, or such as appropriate to the age and developmental level of the students). The teacher gives the students an event in time or a length of time as a framework. The students research and then tell about their personal or family history during this event or length of time. Students may create booklets about their memories, their families, and the like.

Research Base

Carrigan, 2001

What to Watch for With ELL/CLD Students

1. Students may be reluctant to describe or discuss what happened to their family during a specific time or specific event. Very difficult or painful things may have occurred for this student or family.

2. The teacher must be prepared to deal with sensitive information, should it arise, and know when not to push further for information. Only elicit information that the student is comfortable sharing at that particular point in time.

3. Students may share more as they become more comfortable in the classroom or more trusting that the information will not be used against them or their family.

8. PEER/SCHOOL ADAPTATION PROCESS SUPPORT

Purpose of the Strategy

1. Build awareness of adaptation process

2. Strengthen ability to discuss what is happening

3. Reduce anxiety and stress

How to Do It

1. At Tier 1, primary grade level, this strategy is most effective where there are more than a few diverse learners at each grade level and where some of these students have been in the school for more than a year or two. Successful older students in the upper grades assist younger students around the school building and during lunch and play times. This can be used in conjunction with and as a supplement to a peer buddy system in individual classrooms.

2. At Tier 1, intermediate level, this strategy works well with facilitating adaptation and communication. A peer support group is established and given time to meet regularly. The support group discusses their experiences with school adaptation and how they are dealing with culture shock. Successful students from the secondary level may assist as peer support models.

3. At Tier 1, secondary level, this strategy works well with facilitating adaptation and communication and may assist as students prepare to transition out of school into the work environment. A peer support group is established and given time to meet regularly. The peer support group discusses their experiences with school adaptation, how they are dealing with culture shock, and specific language and learning transition issues. This may be paired with a college mentor program.

Research Base

Carrigan, 2001

What to Watch for With ELL/CLD Students

1. Students may wish to discuss their struggles only in the home language and with peers from similar backgrounds. With first-generation refugee and immigrant groups, the teacher must be careful about pairing students of similar language background without also considering cultural and class differences that may exist.

2. Teachers must be prepared to deal with prejudice between populations where language is the same but culture, class, or racial issues may impede comfort and communication. American all togetherness may come in time, but teachers must proceed slowly and not push.

3. Students may interact more as they become more comfortable in the classroom or more trusting that they are accepted and valued.

COMMUNICATION ISSUES AT TIER 1

9. BILINGUAL AIDE/ASSISTANT

Purpose of the Strategy

1. Build on existing language strengths of student

2. Develop cognitive academic language

3. Build transfer skills

4. Build awareness of appropriate academic behavior

5. Strengthen knowledge of academic content

How to Do It

At Tier 1, this strategy is done in the general education classroom with a bilingual adult working in coordination with the classroom teacher. An instructional assistant or aide fluent in both English and the native or home language of ELL students is available in the classroom to assist ELL and limited English proficient (LEP) students when possible, regarding content instruction, academic behavior, and communication. The bilingual instructional assistant coordinates with the teacher in presenting content area instruction to all students. The aide must be trained in providing bilingual assistance and must plan lessons with the teacher.

Research Base

Cole, 1995

E. E. Garcia, 2005

Kovelman, Baker, & Petitto, 2008

What to Watch for With ELL/CLD Students

1. When this strategy is used for sequential translation (i.e., the teacher speaks and then the aide speaks), ELL/LEP students may become dependent on the bilingual aide and remain unengaged while the teacher speaks in English, waiting for the interpretation and explanation by the bilingual aide.

2. Better use would be for the aide to prepare the ELL/LEP students for the English lesson by reviewing key vocabulary words, explaining what will be occurring, and discussing what the teacher's expectations will be for the students' performance. This would then be followed by the teacher presenting the lesson in English. Students would be given the opportunity to ask for specific clarification only during the lesson.

3. Students could work on their projects subsequent to the English lesson with the assistance of the bilingual aide, as needed. Content discussion and clarification should be in the students' most proficient language while they are preparing their task or project for presentation in English with the rest of the class.

10. BILINGUAL PEERS

Purpose of the Strategy

1. Build on existing language strengths of student

2. Develop cognitive academic language

3. Develop basic interpersonal communication

4. Build transfer skills

5. Develop content knowledge foundation

How to Do It

1. At Tier 1, this strategy is done by pairing students in an integrated classroom. Home and community language peers who are more proficient in English assist home and community language students in specific content area lessons and activities. The peer assistants are given training in being tutors, with guidelines about how to facilitate learning without doing another's work, how to translate appropriately, and how to monitor for understanding.

2. This can be part of a general classroom buddy system where students are matched up with partners of differing skills for specific activities.

Research Base

Cole, 1995

E. E. Garcia, 2005

Kovelman et al., 2008

What to Watch for With ELL/CLD Students

1. With specific first-generation refugee, indigenous, migrant, and immigrant groups, teachers must be careful about pairing students based on their perceptions of them coming from similar language backgrounds. There can be cultural and class differences that will make the partners uncomfortable with one another.

2. Teacher must be prepared to deal with prejudice between populations where language is the same but culture, class, or racial issues may impede comfort and communication. American all togetherness may come in time, but teachers must proceed slowly and not push.

3. Students may interact more as they become more comfortable in the classroom or more trusting that they are accepted and valued.

11. BILINGUAL TEXTS

Purpose of the Strategy

1. Build on existing language skills of students

2. Develop cognitive academic language

3. Build home- and community-language-to-English transfer skills

4. Strengthen knowledge of academic content

5. Develop confidence in academic interactions

How to Do It

1. At Tier 1, this strategy is facilitates understanding content area instruction in the integrated general education classroom. Duplicate or parallel texts are available in English and the home or community language of students for all content areas.

2. Reference texts are available in English, bilingual, or home and community language format. Students are shown how and when to access the texts.

3. One source for bilingual materials in Spanish is the Colorín Colorado Web site and organization, http://www .colorincolorado.org.

4. Another source is the CONEVyT. CONEVyT was created in 2002 in Mexico to provide primary and secondary education and training to adults (15 and older) left behind in education in that country as well as migrant populations living in the United States. Through an online portal and a network of Plazas Comunitarias where direct instruction, assessment, and varied materials can be found, both U.S. and Mexican governments make educational support available for anyone willing to learn or to teach. For more information go to www.conevyt.org.mx.

Research Base

Cole, 1995

E. E. Garcia, 2005

Hu & Commeyras, 2008

Kovelman et al., 2008

Ma, 2008

What to Watch for With ELL/CLD Students

1. Not all ELL/CLD students are literate in their home or community language.

2. Picture dictionaries with bilingual words and definitions are usually the most practical reference to use with younger, less educated students.

12. BILINGUAL VIDEOTAPES ABOUT NORTH AMERICAN SPEECH

Purpose of the Strategy

1. Build on existing language strengths of student

2. Build awareness of appropriate social and academic language

3. Build transfer skills

4. Develop confidence in school language and rules for academic and social interactions

How to Do It

1. At Tier 1, this strategy is used in the general education and ELL classroom.

2. This can also be done during parent nights or outside of the school day when it would be possible to include ELL parents and families.

3. Groups of students and/or their families view videos developed locally or available from Intercultural Press and other publishers about North American idioms, communication structures, and expectations. Best shown when an experienced bilingual facilitator is available.

Research Base

Cole, 1995

C. Collier, 2003

What to Watch for With ELL/CLD Students

1. There are many dialects of spoken English and differences of opinion about what is the proper dialect to use as the model for ELL/CLD students.

2. The teacher should be aware of the diversity of reaction to specific dialects of spoken English in North America and be prepared to address expressions of prejudice or value judgments about certain speakers shown on the videotapes.

3. The most practical way to deal with this is to prescreen the videos and select segments that most closely represent the dialects common in your local communities, plus a few as examples of the diversity that exists in our country.

13. CROSS-CULTURAL COMMUNICATION STRATEGIES

Purpose of the Strategy

1. Build transfer skills

2. Build awareness of appropriate communication behaviors for school language and rules

3. Develop confidence in school language and rules for academic and social interactions

How to Do It

1. At Tier 1, this strategy facilitates the transition of ELL/CLD students from their primary language base to bilingualism and helps with their interaction with all students in the general education classroom.

2. The teacher models cross-cultural communication strategies such as reflection, proxemics, latency, and active listening. Reflection is positioning yourself in an almost mirror image to the posture of the other person, using similar rate of speech. Proxemics is paying attention to how close you are to the other speaker and latency is the culturally learned length of time between one speaker's turn and the next speaker's turn to speak. Active listening is showing that you are paying attention and responding in culturally appropriate ways to indicate your attention. This may include repeating some portion of what was said.

3. The teacher has the students practice using these strategies in a variety of interactions.

Research Base

Croom & Davis, 2006

Gibbons, 2002

Trudeau & Harle, 2006

What to Watch for With ELL/CLD Students

1. All cultures have different mores about how close you can stand or sit next to another person (proxemics), who or what you may touch, how much time should elapse before you speak after another person (latency), and the like. The teacher should become familiar with these differences regarding the students in this classroom.

2. The strategy of reflection can look like mockery and mimicry if not done with sensitivity. The goal is to reflect—not imitate—the mode of the speaker.

14. GUIDED PRACTICE AND PLANNED INTERACTIONS WITH DIFFERENT SPEAKERS

Purpose of the Strategy

1. Build transfer skills

2. Build awareness of appropriate school language and rules for communication behaviors

3. Develop confidence in school language and rules for academic and social interactions

4. Develop cognitive academic language

5. Develop personal control of situations

6. Reduce anxiety in social/academic interactions

7. Reduce response fatigue

How to Do It

1. At Tier 1, this strategy facilitates the transition of ELL/CLD students from their primary language base to bilingualism and helps with their interaction with all students in the general education classroom.

2. A peer or a specialist demonstrates how to act or speak in a given school culture situation. The situation is explained in the home and community language when possible, and each part of the situation is modeled.

3. Representatives of the mainstream school language and rules who are familiar to the learners come into the classroom and act out the situation with the instructor. Students then practice each part of the interaction with these familiar participants until comfortable with the interaction.

Expansion: Students select new interactions they wish to learn.

Research Base

Cole, 1995

Haneda, 2008

Reggy-Mamo, 2008

Ross, 1971

What to Watch for With ELL/CLD Students

1. It is important to have the example speakers be people with whom the students are familiar and comfortable.

2. This can be paired with role-play of school interactions.

LITERACY ISSUES AT TIER 1

15. BILINGUAL TEXTS

Purpose of the Strategy

1. Build on existing language skills of students

2. Develop cognitive academic language

3. Build language transfer skills

4. Strengthen knowledge of academic content

5. Develop confidence in academic interactions

How to Do It

1. At Tier 1, this strategy is facilitates understanding content area instruction within the integrated general education classroom. Duplicate or parallel texts are available in English and the home or community language of students for all content areas.

2. Reference texts are available in English, bilingual, or home and community language format. Students are shown how and when to access the texts.

Research Base

Cole, 1995

E. E. Garcia, 2005

Hu & Commeyras, 2008

Kovelman et al., 2008

Ma, 2008

What to Watch for With ELL/CLD Students

1. Not all ELL/CLD students are literate in their home or community language.

2. Picture dictionaries with bilingual words and definitions are usually the most practical reference to use with younger, less educated students.

16. GUIDED READING AND WRITING IN HOME AND COMMUNITY LANGUAGE

Purpose of the Strategy

1. Improve motivation

2. Minimize behavior problems

3. Build transfer skills

4. Develop confidence in school language and rules for academic and social interactions

5. Reduce code-switching

6. Develop cognitive academic language

How to Do It

1. At Tier 1, this strategy facilitates the transition of ELL/CLD students from their primary language base to bilingualism and helps with their interaction with all students in the general education classroom.

2. Teachers direct advanced-fluency students to lead a guided reading or writing activity in the home and community language. Students can reread parts of a story in pairs after the directed reading activity. Students then write summaries of what they have read. Writing can be in either the home and community language or English. During this time, the students have a chance to help one another. Advanced-fluency students can dramatize and create dialogue to illustrate the action.

Research Base

Cole, 1995

Haneda, 2008

Reggy-Mamo, 2008

Ross, 1971

Strickland, Ganske, & Monroe, 2002

What to Watch for With ELL/CLD Students

1. Not all ELL/CLD students are literate in their home or community language.

2. Picture dictionaries with bilingual words and definitions are usually the most practical reference to use with younger, less educated students.

17. WRITING STRATEGIES—TOWER

Purpose of the Strategy

1. Build awareness of learning

2. Develop personal control of situations

3. Develop thinking and planning skills

4. Improve access to prior knowledge

5. Reduce off-task behaviors

6. Strengthen language development

How to Do It

1. At Tier 1, this strategy is done in the general education classroom with mixed groups of students. The TOWER writing strategy framework provides a structure for completing initial and final drafts of written reports.

2. It may be used effectively with the COPS proofreading strategy structure.

3. The steps in COPS are

Capitalization
Overall appearance
Punctuation
Spelling

4. To help the students remember the steps in TOWER, the teacher can provide the students with a printed form with the letters T, O, W, E, R down the left side and their meaning next to each letter.

5. The steps students follow in TOWER are

Think
Order ideas
Write
Edit
Rewrite

Research Base

Cole, 1995

Ellis & Colvert, 1996

Ellis & Lenz, 1987

Goldsworthy, 2003

What to Watch for With ELL/CLD Students

1. Newcomers will need to have the TOWER steps modeled and explained in their most proficient language before they can proceed independently.

2. Students can be paired with partners who are slightly more bilingual than they are to facilitate their learning this process.

18. READING STRATEGY—FIST

Purpose of the Strategy

1. Assist students to actively pursue responses to questions related directly to materials being read

2. Improve reading comprehension

How to Do It

1. At Tier 1, this strategy is done in the general education classroom with mixed groups of students. The FIST analysis strategy framework provides a structure for understanding reading and building reading comprehension.

2. Students follow the steps in the FIST strategy while reading paragraphs in assigned readings. To help the students remember the steps, the teacher can provide a checklist of the steps with the letters F, I, S, T down the side and their meaning next to each letter.

3. The steps in FIST are

First sentence is read

Indicate a question based on first sentence

Search for the answer to the question

Tie question and answer together through paraphrasing

Research Base

Allington & Cunningham, 2002

Cole, 1995

Moore, Alvermann, & Hinchman, 2000

Tovani, 2000

What to Watch for With ELL/CLD Students

1. Newcomers will need to have the FIST steps modeled and explained in their most proficient language before they can proceed independently.

2. Students can be paired with partners who are slightly more bilingual than they are to facilitate their learning this process.

19. RETENTION STRATEGY—PARS

Purpose of the Strategy

1. Build retention of information and learning

2. Reduce distraction

3. Strengthen focus on task

How to Do It

1. At Tier 1, this strategy is done in the general education classroom with mixed groups of students. This strategy is for retention of content.

2. The PARS retention strategy framework provides a structure for understanding what is being learned and retaining the information for later application.

3. PARS is recommended for use with younger students and with those who have limited experiences with study strategies. Students can create cue cards or use posters to remind themselves of the steps.

4. The steps in PARS are

Preview

Ask questions

Read

Summarize

Research Base

Cole, 1995

Law & Eckes, 2000

What to Watch for With ELL/CLD Students

1. Newcomers will need to have the PARS steps modeled and explained in their most proficient language before they can proceed independently.

2. Students can be paired with partners who are slightly more bilingual than they are to facilitate their learning this process.

20. ADVANCED ORGANIZERS

Purpose of the Strategy

1. Build language transfer skills

2. Build awareness of the appropriate content language in English culture/language

3. Develop confidence in academic interactions

How to Do It

1. The teacher or assistant previews the lesson content in students' first language when possible, outlining key issues, rehearsing vocabulary, and reviewing related prior knowledge.

2. May use analogy strategy described next to teach one or more of the advanced organizer tools (e.g., KWL+, W-star, graphic organizer, mind map, and the like). Students implement strategy with a specific task or lesson.

3. KWL+ is done by asking the students to discuss the following questions before beginning the lesson: What do you already *know* about this content? What do you *want* to know about this content? What will we *learn* about this? Why should we learn this? And how will we learn this content? This may be done on a chart.

4. W-star is done by asking the students to brainstorm before beginning a reading: Who do you think this story/event is about? Where do you think the story/event is located? When do you think the story/event occurs? How do you think the story/event turns out? The answers are written onto the points of a star diagram, each point of which represents one of the W questions.

5. Mind mapping has various forms, but the basic idea is to put the central concept or vocabulary word related to what will be in the lesson in a circle on the board or on a piece of paper. Students then generate other words or concepts related to that main idea and connect them to the center like spokes on a wheel. For each of these ideas or words, another set of connections may be made outward from the center concept.

6. When applying the advanced organizer strategy, students work through problems or tasks using a sequence of ordering, sequencing, and connecting techniques. Suppose you want your students to write a short personal reflection about the story *Everybody Cooks Rice* by Norah Dooley (1991), which the class has just finished reading together. You would start by having your students work in small groups of similar ability level. You would show a copy of a graphic organizer form outline (Strategy 163) on the overhead projector or drawn on the whiteboard. Each group would be assigned two or three of the boxes in the graphic organizer. For example, you might assign the most challenged group to fill in the box about title, author, location, and country. Another group would be responsible for the main and supporting characters. Another

group would be responsible for identifying the sequence of events in the story and a summary statement about these. Another group could be assigned to identify the main problem faced by the main character. After reading the story through the first time, the groups complete their tasks and you or they write down their answers on the large or projected graphic organizer. Now as a group, you ask about how this main problem (finding Anthony) was resolved, the barriers to resolution that Carrie faced, and things in the story that helped Carrie solve her problem. The class can now discuss the final resolution (everyone is home for dinner) and what the moral of the story might be, in their perspective. You can expand this activity by comparing and contrasting the story with others like it or with happenings in the students' lives.

7. You might now step back from the lesson and discuss the metacognitive learning that you have provided students, the learning to learn lesson that is represented by the strategy you had them use.

Research Base

Harwell, 2001

Heacox, 2002

Moore et al., 2000

Opitz, 1998

What to Watch for With ELL/CLD Students

1. There are cultural differences in cognitive/learning style and some ELL/CLD students may not respond to the "brainstorming" construct behind most advanced organizers.

2. By keeping the graphic design of the advanced organizer as close as possible to the illustrations in the text or some aspect of the lesson, the teacher can more tightly connect the concepts being studied with the what/who/where questioning that precedes the lesson.

3. This is another activity that works best with preparation in the students' most proficient language and relevance to their culture before proceeding.

21. ANALOGY

Purpose of the Strategy

1. Develop higher tolerance

2. Facilitate access to prior knowledge

3. Build transfer skills

4. Develop categorization skills

How to Do It

1. At Tier 1, this strategy can be done in the general education classroom with all students participating. Students may be paired with culture and language peers at first and then mixed pairs of diverse students as they become comfortable with the strategy.

2. Students each share something they already know about the lesson topic, something that is meaningful to them. They go through the steps of analogy in pairs, as they share their items/ideas with one another. Steps for students to follow in implementing this analogy strategy

    a. What do I already know about this item or concept?

    b. How does what I already know about this idea or item compare with the new idea or item?

   c. Can the known idea or item be substituted for the new item or idea and still make sense?

   d. How can I elaborate on these comparisons through analogies?

   3. For example, students are shown an object that looks familiar, such as a metal rod used to connect two wheels on a toy car. They generate words describing the rod such as "long," "shiny," "manufactured," "connects," and "an axle." They then are shown another metal rod that is unfamiliar to them. They generate more words describing the new object. Some of the words will be similar, some different. Example words might be "long," "shiny," "threaded ends," "connects something," "pointy," "heavy," and "metallic." They may actually try to substitute the new rod for the toy axle, or they may make guesses about substitution and conclude that it could be done but would not work exactly. They generate sentences such as "The axle is smaller than the new rod;" "The new rod is larger than the axle of the toy car;" "The new rod has threaded ends while the axle does not;" "The axle is to a car as the new rod is to something else;" and "The axle is as shiny as the new rod."

Research Base

Cole, 1995

Tovani, 2000

What to Watch for With ELL/CLD Students

   1. Be sure students are matched with peers with whom they can communicate comfortably while they are all learning the strategy and steps in the process.

   2. After students learn the process and steps, posters or cards with reminder illustrations and the words of the steps can be put up around the room.

   3. Once students can use analogy without prompting, they can be paired up with nonbilingual peers for more applications.

22. EXPERIENCE-BASED WRITING/READING

Purpose of the Strategy

   1. Build transfer skills

   2. Develop cognitive academic language

   3. Develop content knowledge foundation

   4. Facilitate analogy strategies

How to Do It

   1. At Tier 1, this strategy can be done in the general education classroom with all students participating. Students may be paired with culture and language peers at first and then mixed pairs of diverse students as they become comfortable with the strategy.

   2. At the primary grades, the teacher guides students to illustrate specific experiences in which students have participated. Activity may be paired with field trips or other shared experiences, or it may be in reference to prior life experiences of ELL/LEP students. Community members may make presentations about events significant to students' families. The teacher then has students tell what their illustrations depict and write down verbatim what the students say. Students then read back to the teacher what has been written.

   3. For intermediate and secondary grades, the teacher guides students to illustrate and write stories about their experiences. These stories can be put into collections and bound for use by other students. Stories can be kept in the classroom, library, or media center.

Research Base

Cole, 1995

What to Watch for With ELL/CLD Students

1. Some shared experiences will be very novel for particular cultural members of a group, more than for other members. Be sure to give those who have never seen something before extra preparation time and explanations of what they are going to see or do during the field trip or experience.

2. Be sure students are matched with peers with whom they can communicate comfortably while they are all learning the strategy and steps in the process.

3. Be sensitive to cultural mores about certain experiences and businesses. You may need to spend extra time discussing what is going to be seen and heard or, in some cases, be prepared to have some students participate in a related but separate activity.

23. GUIDED READING AND WRITING IN HOME AND COMMUNITY LANGUAGE

Purpose of the Strategy

1. Improve motivation

2. Minimize behavior problems

3. Build transfer skills

4. Develop confidence in school language and rules for academic and social interactions

5. Reduce code-switching

6. Develop cognitive academic language

How to Do It

1. At Tier 1, this strategy facilitates the transition of ELL/CLD students from their primary language base to bilingualism and helps with their interaction with all students in the general education classroom.

2. The teacher directs advanced-fluency student to lead a guided reading or writing activity in the home and community language. Students can reread parts of a story in pairs after the directed reading activity rather than have one student read while the others all listen. Students then write summaries of what they have read. Writing can be in either home and community language or English. During this time, the students have a chance to help one another. Advanced-fluency students can dramatize and create dialogue to illustrate the action.

Research Base

Cole, 1995; see pages 150–152

Haneda, 2008

Reggy-Mamo, 2008

Ross, 1971

Strickland et al., 2002; see page 217

What to Watch for With ELL/CLD Students

1. Not all ELL/CLD students are literate in their home or community language.

2. Picture dictionaries with bilingual words and definitions are usually the most practical reference to use with younger, less educated students.

24. LANGUAGE GAMES

Purpose of the Strategy

1. Develop cognitive academic language

2. Develop basic interpersonal communication

3. Build transfer skills

4. Develop content knowledge foundation

How to Do It

1. At Tier 1, this strategy can be done in the general education classroom with all students participating. Students may play in groups with culture and language peers at first and then mixed groups of diverse students as they become comfortable with the games activities.

2. Students play language games that reinforce specific content. The games are structured to reinforce and elaborate on content knowledge while developing home and community language and English language skills including turn taking; asking questions; giving appropriate responses; giving directions; and other game, communication, and interaction skills.

3. Examples of game structures are memory games like Concentration, rummy games such as Go Fish, and matching games such as Old Maid.

4. The content topics of the games can be chosen and developed to match a specific topic or lesson in the classroom and to reinforce the vocabulary words of that lesson. Some examples might be terms from the rainforest, historical events, types of animals, mathematical equations, visits to community locations, and workers in the community.

5. These are also useful in illustrating second-language learning strategies. All of the three basic games, sets, pairs, and memory, can be played to reinforce receptive and expressive language, visual and auditory memory, or content literacy.

6. The games can be played periodically during the school year to provide a review of foundation concepts when making a transition to a new topic or subject matter. The cards may also be used individually as flashcards to review the vocabulary words and language content.

7. The games may be used as an alternate assessment process. By watching the students play the card games, especially when a lot of expressive and receptive language is required, the teacher will be able to observe the extent to which individual students have acquired the learning concepts and content or how well they have retained previously presented information.

8. All of the games can be played to reinforce receptive and expressive language, visual and auditory memory, or content literacy. If students are nonverbal, the games can be played through cognitive visual matching. If students do not speak English or are LEP, the games can be played in their native language or bilingually. They can play using as much English as they have acquired, and eventually be able to play completely in English.

9. For example, the weather game may be used in versatile ways to supplement content lessons at any grade level. It is best used as a review, reinforcement, or assessment tool. Three basic games can be played with these cards: (1) sets, (2) pairs, and (3) memory. Each of the three basic games can be varied according to specific lesson objectives. The cards in the weather game consist of nine sets of four cards per set illustrating common weather conditions in English. These are the weather words most often used in calendar activities in the classroom.

   a. **Players:** Two to six in each group playing.

   b. **Object:** Collect the most sets of four of a kind.

   c. **Deal:** Cards are dealt one at a time. Each player receives five cards. The rest of the pack is placed face down in the center of the table to form the draw pile.

d. **Play:** Have the students choose the first player by names alphabetically, ages, or other devices. Starting with the first player, each player calls another by name and requests cards of a specific type, such as, "David, do you have any sunny days?" The player asking must hold at least one of the type of card requested (sunny day). The player asked must give up the card requested, saying, "Yes, Kala, I have a sunny day." Another variation of this is to have the player ask for a category first. If Kala successfully identifies the picture, cloudy day, then she gets the card. The player asked does not have to say if she has more than one of the set of cards. The player requesting has to ask for each individual card (e.g., "David, do you have another cloudy day?").

If the player asked does not have any cards of the type requested, then she says, "Draw!" and the asker draws the top card from the draw pile. A player's turn to ask continues as long as she is successful in getting the cards requested. If she is told to draw and happens to draw a card of the type requested, the player may show this card, name it, and continue the turn. As soon as any player gets a set of all four cards of one type, he must show them and give the names of the cards aloud, placing them on the table in front of him. If played competitively, the player who collects the most sets by the end of the game wins.

Research Base

Ajibade & Ndububa, 2008

Law & Eckes, 2000; see pages 204–206

Padak & Rasinski, 2008

Wright, Betteridge, & Buckby, 2006

What to Watch for With ELL/CLD Students

1. Be sure to establish consistent game-playing rules and phrases that all students are to use when playing the game. At first, these can be as simple as "Do you have a _____?" "Is this a _____?" "Here are _____."

2. The phrases can become more complex and more natural as students become more comfortable playing the games.

BEHAVIOR ISSUES AT TIER 1

25. ACCOUNTABILITY

Purpose of the Strategy

1. Ensure that students are aware of and responsible for their actions

2. Develop awareness of the connection between their actions and the consequences of these actions

How to Do It

1. At Tier 1, this strategy is done in the general education classroom with mixed groups of students.

2. Establish rewards and consequences for completion of work and appropriate behavior, ensuring that these rewards and consequences are consistently implemented. For example, the teacher assists the student in setting up an agenda or plan of a personalized list of tasks that the student must complete in a specified time.

Research Base

C. A. Tomlinson, 1999

What to Watch for With ELL/CLD Students

1. Particular social groups and cultures have different expectations of adults and children when it comes to being accountable for task completion. This is a learned difference between cultures. The teacher needs to be aware that the expectations in an American school may need to be taught directly to CLD students and should not assume that they are understood.

2. One way to introduce the idea of your classroom rules is to ask students about any rules their parents have for them at home or rules they have learned about crossing the street or playing games. This can then be expanded to the idea of rules for completing tasks and acting appropriately in a classroom.

26. CHOICES

Purpose of the Strategy

1. Facilitate learning

2. Accommodate diverse learning styles

3. Develop task completion

4. Alleviate power struggles between teacher and student

5. Reduce fears associated with assignments

How to Do It

1. At Tier 1, this strategy can be done with all students in a mixed general education classroom. Provide students the opportunity to select one or more activities developed by the teacher.

2. The teacher provides two or more different reading selections of interest to the student, both of which address the same desired objective. Allow the student to choose one of the selections for the assignment. If student does not choose either of the selections, introduce a third selection or ask student to choose a content-appropriate reading selection.

3. The readings can be leveled as well as different takes on the same subject. National Geographic and Hampton Brown have excellent leveled reading materials on a wide variety of topics.

Research Base

Ainley, 2006

Cordova & Lepper, 1996

Flowerday & Schraw, 2003

Flowerday, Schraw, & Stevens, 2004

Kragler & Nolley, 1996

What to Watch for With ELL/CLD Students

1. Some CLD students have had previous schooling in situations where students have no choice and teachers are authority figures who direct every action in the classroom.

2. When the teacher wishes to make choice and student empowerment an instructional goal, this strategy is an excellent direction to take.

3. Demonstrate how the choices as to be made, including color coding or otherwise graphically illustrating the different choices.

4. Some role-play in the process from initial choice to final task completion may be helpful.

27. EXPECTATIONS AWARENESS/REVIEW

Purpose of the Strategy

1. Ensure that each student is familiar with specific academic and behavioral expectations

2. Reduce frustration in students because of unclear expectations

3. Minimize ambiguity in classroom

How to Do It

1. At Tier 1, this strategy is done with the entire general education classroom population.

2. The teacher modifies or breaks down general classroom rules into specific behavioral expectations to ensure that each student knows exactly what is meant by acceptable behaviors.

3. Illustrations and demonstrations of the desired behaviors and rules should be posted around the room.

Research Base

Davis, 2005

J. R. Nelson, Martella, & Galand, 1998

Rubenstein, 2006

What to Watch for With ELL/CLD Students

1. Particular social groups and cultures have different expectations of adults and children when it comes to being accountable for task completion. This is a learned difference between cultures. The teacher needs to be aware that the expectations in an American school may need to be taught directly to CLD students and should not assume that they are understood.

2. One way to introduce the idea of your classroom rules is to ask students about any rules their parents have for them at home or rules they have learned about crossing the street or playing games. This can then be expanded to the idea of rules for completing tasks and acting appropriately in a classroom.

3. Demonstrate all of the desired behaviors and rules. Some role-play may be helpful. Examples of inappropriate behaviors may be used with caution.

28. PARTNERS

Purpose of the Strategy

1. Improve motivation

2. Minimize behavior problems

How to Do It

1. At Tier 1, this strategy is done by pairing up all the students in the general education classroom.

2. With paired oral reading, each student participates either as an interested listener or as reader while the teacher moves from pair to pair listening. Reading can be varied by changing partners. Children can reread parts of a story in pairs after the directed reading activity rather than have one student read while the others all listen. During this time, the students have a chance to help one another.

3. With science and math lessons, different partners may be used matching a successful learner with one just slightly less successful and so on down the line. Problem solutions can be revisited by changing partners and redoing the problem and solution.

Research Base

Kamps et al., 2007

Koskinen & Blum, 1984

Wood & Algozzine, 1994

Wood & Harmon, 2001; see pages 211–217

What to Watch for With ELL/CLD Students

1. Partners must be selected carefully with specific objectives in mind. If competence and understanding of the content is the goal, then similar language skills are necessary.

2. If expansion and transition of learning is the goal, then paring a less proficient with a more proficient bilingual partner will help.

3. If challenging application is the goal, then pairing very differently skilled parties may work.

29. PLANNED MOVEMENT

Purpose of the Strategy

1. Prevent inappropriate moving around the room

2. Minimize behavior problems in the classroom

How to Do It

1. At Tier 1, this strategy is done with the entire classroom.

2. Periodically, provide students opportunities to move about the classroom for appropriate reasons.

3. For example, the teacher allows students to move to a learning center or study booth for part of their independent-work time instead of remaining seated at their desks for the entire period.

Research Base

Evertson & Neal, 2006

Evertson & Weinstein, 2006

Kaufman, 2001

Williams, 2008

What to Watch for With ELL/CLD Students

1. Differences in mobility and movement by children are learned differences among cultures and social groups. In some families children are expected to get up and move around whenever they want to; in others, children are expected to remain seated or in one place unless and until they are given permission to move elsewhere.

2. Some children may have undiagnosed conditions that inhibit their sitting or standing in one place without moving occasionally. Using planned movement and making accommodations for opportunities for students to move facilitates learning for all students.

30. POSITIVE REINFORCEMENT

Purpose of the Strategy

1. Increase the frequency of appropriate responses or behaviors

2. Facilitate students' comfort with learning environment

How to Do It

1. At Tier 1, this strategy is used by the teacher at all times with all students in the classroom.

2. The teacher provides feedback or rewards for completing appropriate tasks or behaving in appropriate ways.

3. For example, teacher provides a student extra free time when the math or reading assignment has been completed.

Research Base

Cole, 1995

Harwell, 2001

Opitz, 1998

What to Watch for With ELL/CLD Students

1. What is rewarding to one person is not necessarily rewarding to another. This is a learned preference.

2. The teacher should use a variety of affirmatives, words, and phrases to denote reinforcement.

3. When using physical rewards, always do some research to identify cultural, developmental, and gender appropriate items.

4. When using extra time or a special activity as a reward, vary these depending on the students' interests.

31. REDUCED STIMULI

Purpose of the Strategy

1. Enhance ability of students to focus on learning

2. Encourage questioning and exploration of new learning

3. Reduce response fatigue

4. Reduce culture shock

5. Develop personal control of situations

How to Do It

1. At Tier 1, this strategy is done at the beginning of the school year and, possibly, at the beginning of each semester depending on the time of year new students seem to enroll.

2. The teacher starts the classroom with relatively blank walls and empty spaces and monitors the use of music and other auditory materials.

3. The teacher does not display or use visual/auditory materials until students have been introduced to the content or have produced the materials themselves.

4. Visual, tactile, and auditory experiences are introduced gradually and with demonstration.

Research Base

P. Nelson et al., 2005

Wortham, 1996

What to Watch for With ELL/CLD Students

1. Newcomers may become overly stimulated by lots of bright, new, unfamiliar, and strange objects, signs, sounds, and miscellany in their new classroom. They do not know what is important to attend to and what is not important. It is all new and exciting.

2. This is also going to impact students with undiagnosed neurological conditions that they have not yet learned to accommodate.

3. It is better to start out with less and add as students become comfortable and familiar with what is in the classroom

32. SELF-REINFORCEMENT

Purpose of the Strategy

1. Build awareness of learning

2. Develop personal control of situations

3. Develop thinking and planning skills

4. Facilitate access to prior knowledge

5. Facilitate language development

6. Improve motivation and response

7. Reduce off-task behaviors

How to Do It

1. At Tier 1, this strategy is done with all of the students in the integrated classroom. The teacher assists students in developing checklists for task completion and appropriate classroom behavior.

2. At first, the teacher stops the class occasionally and points out appropriate learning or behavior taking place, rewarding with points or praise.

3. As students become familiar with what is desired, they can check off points on their checklists.

4. Individual students reward themselves for appropriate behavior and performance at specific check-in points during the lesson. Eventually, each student uses a self-developed checklist and gives reward to self upon completion of tasks.

5. Facilitates language development related to cognitive academic language.

Research Base

C. A. Tomlinson, 1999; see pages 66–68

What to Watch for With ELL/CLD Students

1. ELL students who are LEP may need the process explained in their most proficient language.

2. Points are not intrinsically reinforcing. What is rewarding to one person is not necessarily rewarding to another. This is a learned preference.

3. The points may initially be paired with some more directly rewarding action, and then gradually progress to use of only points.

33. GUIDED PRACTICE AND PLANNED INTERACTIONS WITH DIFFERENT STUDENTS

Purpose of the Strategy

1. Build transfer skills

2. Build awareness of appropriate school language and rules for communication behaviors

3. Develop confidence in school language and rules for academic and social interactions

4. Develop cognitive academic language

5. Develop personal control of situations

6. Reduce anxiety in social/academic interactions

7. Reduce response fatigue

How to Do It

1. At Tier 1, this strategy facilitates the transition of ELL/CLD students from their primary language base to bilingualism and helps with their interaction with all students in the general education classroom.

2. A peer or a specialist demonstrates how to act or speak in a given school culture situation. The situation is explained in the home and community language when possible, and each part of the situation is modeled.

3. Representatives of the mainstream school language and rules who are familiar to the learners come into the classroom and act out the situation with the instructor. Students then practice each part of the interaction with these familiar participants until comfortable with the interaction.

Expansion: Students select new interactions they wish to learn.

Research Base

Cole, 1995

Haneda, 2008

Reggy-Mamo, 2008

Ross, 1971

What to Watch for With ELL/CLD Students

1. It is important to have the example speakers be people with whom the students are familiar and comfortable.

2. This can be paired with role-play of school interactions.

34. GUIDED PRACTICE IN CLASSROOM BEHAVIOR EXPECTATIONS AND SURVIVAL STRATEGIES

Purpose of the Strategy

1. Develop personal control of situations

2. Improve confidence in school interactions

3. Reduce distractibility

4. Reduce acting out behaviors

How to Do It

1. At Tier 1, this strategy is done with the entire general education classroom population.

2. In primary grades, an intermediate student, a peer, or a specialist demonstrates how to act in a given school or school culture situation. The situation is explained, in home and community language when possible, and each stage is modeled. Students then practice each stage of the interaction with familiar participants until comfortable and successful in appropriate behaviors.

3. In intermediate grades, a secondary student, a peer, or a specialist demonstrates how to act in a given school or school culture situation. The situation is explained, in home and community language when possible, and each stage is modeled. Students then practice each stage of the interaction with familiar participants until comfortable and successful in appropriate behaviors.

4. In secondary grades, an older peer or a specialist demonstrates how to act in a given school or school culture situation. The situation is explained, in home and community language when possible, and each stage is modeled. Students then practice each stage of the interaction with familiar participants until comfortable and successful in appropriate behaviors.

Research Base

Davis, 2005

J. R. Nelson et al., 1998

Rubenstein, 2006

What to Watch for With ELL/CLD Students

1. Particular social groups and cultures have different expectations of adults and children when it comes to being accountable for task completion. This is a learned difference between cultures. The teacher needs to be aware that the expectations in an American school may need to be taught directly to CLD students and should not assume that they are understood.

2. One way to introduce the idea of behavior and strategies specific to your classroom is to ask students about how their parents have them behave at home or learned playing games. This can then be expanded to the idea of acting appropriately in a classroom.

3. Demonstrate all of the desired behaviors and strategies. Some role-play may be helpful. Examples of inappropriate behaviors may be used with caution.

35. CLASS BUDDIES/PEERS/HELPERS/PEER TUTORS

Purpose of the Strategy

1. Build transfer skills

2. Develop basic interpersonal communication

3. Develop cognitive academic language

4. Develop content knowledge foundation

5. Develop higher tolerance

6. Develop positive peer relationships

7. Develop thinking and planning skills

8. Ensure learning gains are experienced by both of the students

9. Improve retention

10. Utilize prior knowledge

How to Do It

1. At Tier 1, this strategy is done with all of the students in the general education classroom.

2. Students assist in the classroom by working with other students. Tutors may receive training about objectives, reinforcement, and the like. A student who has mastered a list of sight words or math facts presents these items on flash cards to another student needing assistance in this area. Students help other learners of similar or different ages in the classroom to complete assignments or other responsibilities. This strategy has been shown to provide learning gains for both the tutor and the tutee, and it allows the teacher to work closely with more students. The teacher should always be clear about the objectives of the tutoring session and hold the students accountable for their work.

3. For example, the tutoring student shares his or her report with the tutee. In preparation, the tutor identifies key concepts and vocabulary used in the report and presents these on tag board cards to the tutee. The tutee tells the tutor in his or her own words, what he or she understood from the report.

4. Home and community language peers who are more proficient in English assist home and community language students in specific content area lessons and activities. The peers are given training in being a tutor, with guidelines about how to facilitate learning without doing another's work, how to translate appropriately, and how to monitor for understanding.

Expansion: Peer helpers develop code of ethics and their own guidelines for tutoring.

5. As students become more comfortable, they may be paired with more diverse peers and tutors.

Research Base

Carrigan, 2001

Cole, 1995

What to Watch for With ELL/CLD Students

1. With specific first-generation refugee, indigenous, migrant, and immigrant groups, teachers must be careful about pairing students based on their perceptions of them coming from similar language backgrounds. There can be cultural and class differences that will make the partners uncomfortable with one another.

2. The teacher must be prepared to deal with prejudice between populations where language is the same but culture, class, or racial issues may impede comfort and communication. American all togetherness may come in time, but the teacher must proceed slowly and not push.

3. Students may interact more as they become more comfortable in the classroom or more trusting that they are accepted and valued.

36. PERSONAL TIMELINES

Purpose of the Strategy

1. Develop self-esteem

2. Encourage pride in students' personal history

3. Build transfer skills

4. Facilitate discussion about new learning

5. Strengthen school-parent partnerships

How to Do It

1. At Tier 1, this strategy is done in general education and integrated classrooms where all students participate in the activity.

2. The teacher selects the events or length of time to cover (e.g., two years, five years, or such as appropriate to the age and developmental level of the students). The teacher gives the students an event in time or a length of time as a framework. The students research and then tell about their personal or family history during this event or length of time. Students may create booklets about their memories, their families, and the like.

3. Students make their life timeline and illustrate their life's history to the present. They should be encouraged to see their lives as stories that can be told to others.

Research Base

Carrigan, 2001

What to Watch for With ELL/CLD Students

1. Students may be reluctant to describe or discuss what happened to their family during a specific time or specific event. Very difficult or painful things may have occurred for this student or family.

2. The teacher must be prepared to deal with sensitive information, should it arise, and know when not to push further for information. Only elicit information that the student is comfortable sharing at that particular point in time.

3. Students may share more as they become more comfortable in the classroom or more trusting that the information will not be used against them or their family.

37. USE OF FIRST LANGUAGE

Purpose of the Strategy

1. Build transfer skills

2. Develop confidence in school language and rules for academic and social interactions

3. Develop cognitive academic language

4. Improve motivation

5. Minimize behavior problems

6. Reduce code-switching

7. Build on existing language strengths of student

8. Develop cognitive academic language

9. Build awareness of appropriate academic behavior

10. Strengthen knowledge of academic content

How to Do It

1. At Tier 1, this strategy is done in the general education classroom with a bilingual student, an assistant, or another volunteer working in coordination with the classroom teacher, if the teacher is not bilingual.

2. The teacher directs an advanced-fluency student or a volunteer to lead a guided activity in the home and/or community language.

3. Students can retell parts of a story in pairs after the directed activity rather than have one student speak while the others all listen. Students then write summaries of what they have heard.

4. Writing can be in either home or community language or English. During this time, the students have a chance to help one another. Advanced-fluency students can dramatize and create dialogue to illustrate the action.

Research Base

Carrigan, 2001; see page 191

What to Watch for With ELL/CLD Students

1. The language helper can prepare the ELL/LEP students for an English lesson by reviewing key vocabulary words, explaining what will be occurring, and discussing what the teacher's expectations will be for the students' performance. This would then be followed by the teacher presenting the lesson in English. Students would be given the opportunity to ask for specific clarification in their first language.

2. Students could work on their projects subsequent to the English lesson with the assistance of the bilingual helper as needed. Content discussion and clarification should be in the students' most proficient language while they are preparing their task or project for presentation in English with the rest of the class.

38. CONSISTENT SEQUENCE

Purpose of the Strategy

1. Build academic transfer skills

2. Build awareness of appropriate academic behaviors

3. Improve confidence in academic interactions

4. Reduce distractibility

How to Do It

1. At Tier 1, this strategy is done in the general education classroom with all students.

2. The teacher presents all content lessons with the same instructional language and direction sequence to the extent possible.

3. Posters can be put up around the room with the lesson process and teachers may point to each step as they go through the lesson.

Expansion: Students can role-play giving the directions themselves.

Research Base

Mathes, Pollard-Durodola, Cárdenas-Hagan, Linan-Thompson, & Vaughn, 2007

Vaughn & Linan-Thompson, 2007

What to Watch for With ELL/CLD Students

1. This strategy is consistent with the Sheltered Instruction Observation Protocol (SIOP) model used in many ELL programs.

2. Newcomers who have never attended school may become confused if every lesson and activity occurs in seemingly random patterns. They do not know what is expected of them at various stages of the lesson. They do not know what to attend to and what is less important.

3. This is also going to impact students with undiagnosed attention deficit disorders that they have not yet learned to accommodate.

4. It is better to start out with simple consistent steps and add as students become comfortable and familiar with what is going to happen in the classroom

39. DEMONSTRATION

Purpose of the Strategy

1. Improve confidence in academic interactions

2. Reduce distractibility

3. Build academic transfer skills

4. Develop content knowledge foundation

How to Do It

1. At Tier 1, this strategy can be used in any lesson and in any classroom by teachers, peer tutors, instructional assistants, and volunteers.

2. The teacher, assistant, or peer demonstrates the content of the lesson. The content is explained in the home and community language when possible, and each aspect of the lesson is demonstrated.

3. Students demonstrate their understanding of the lesson and content.

4. Activities and assessment are designed to facilitate demonstration of understanding.

Research Base

Echevarria, Vogt, & Short, 2007

Gibbons, 2006

What to Watch for With ELL/CLD Students

1. This strategy is consistent with both Sheltered Instruction Observation Protocol (SIOP) and the Guided Language Acquisition Design (GLAD) process used in many ELL programs.

2. Students who have never been schooled before will not know what is expected, and they will benefit from concrete direct demonstrations of content elements and activity expectations.

COGNITIVE ISSUES AT TIER 1

40. ADVANCED ORGANIZERS

Purpose of the Strategy

1. Build language transfer skills

2. Build awareness of the appropriate content language in English culture/language

3. Develop confidence in academic interactions

How to Do It

1. The teacher or assistant previews the lesson content in first language when possible, outlining key issues, rehearsing vocabulary, and reviewing related prior knowledge.

2. Teachers may use the analogy strategy described next to teach one or more of the advanced organizer tools (e.g., KWL+, W-star, graphic organizer, mind map, and the like). Students implement strategy with a specific task or lesson.

3. KWL+ is done by asking the students to discuss the following questions before beginning the lesson: What do you already know about this content? What do you want to know about this content? What will we learn about this? Why should we learn this? And how will we learn this content? This may be done on a chart and student answers posted on the chart.

4. W-star is done by asking the students to brainstorm before beginning a reading: Who so you think this story/event is about? Where do you think the story/event is located? When do you think the story/event occurs? How do you think the story/event turns out? The answers are written onto the points of a star diagram, each point of which represents one of the W questions.

5. Mind mapping has various forms, but the basic idea is to put the central concept or vocabulary word related to what will be in the lesson in a circle on the board or on a piece of paper. Students then generate other words or concepts related to that main idea and connect them to the center like spokes on a wheel. For each of these ideas or words, another set of connections may be made outward from the center concept.

6. When applying the advanced organizer strategy students work through problems or tasks using a sequence of ordering, sequencing, and connecting techniques. Suppose you want your students to write a short personal reflection about the story *Everybody Cooks Rice* by Norah Dooley (1991), which the class has just finished reading together. You would start by having your students work in small groups of similar ability level. You would show a copy of a graphic organizer form outline (Strategy 163) on the overhead projector or drawn on the whiteboard. Each group would be assigned two or three of the boxes in the graphic organizer. For example, you might assign the most challenged group to fill in the box about title, author, location, and country. Another group would be responsible for the main and supporting characters. Another group would be responsible for identifying the sequence of events in the story and a summary statement about these. Another group could be assigned to identify the main problem faced by the main character. After reading the story through the first time, the groups complete their tasks, and you or they write down their answers on the large or projected graphic organizer. Now as a group, you ask about how this main problem (finding Anthony) was resolved, the barriers to resolution that Carrie faced, and things in the story that helped Carrie solve her problem. The class can now discuss the final resolution (everyone is home for dinner) and what the moral of the story might be in their perspective. You can expand this activity by comparing and contrasting the story with others like it or with happenings in students' lives.

7. You might now step back from the lesson and discuss the metacognitive learning that you have provided students, the learning to learn lesson that is represented by the strategy you had them use.

8. Steps for teaching advanced organizers

   a. *Inform* the students what advanced organizers are, how they operate, when to use them, and why they are useful. Begin by saying that advanced organizers are a way to help them (the students) plan and remember. They work by previewing or putting information concerning the lesson or assignment they are working on into graphic form. Once they learn how to use advanced organizers, they can use them anytime and with any content or lesson you give them to do.

   b. *Use cues,* metaphors, analogies, or other means of elaborating on a description of advanced organizers combined with visual cues. One way to do this is to have the group look at a blueprint of a house or other building they are familiar with. Have them see how the architect had to plan for everything ahead of time and create a preview or graphic image of what everyone was going to have to do to complete the construction. Explain that almost anyone could help construct the house or building by reading the blueprint and the ability to read and understand these is a special and critical skill that will be useful to them later in life.

c. *Lead group discussions* about the use of advanced organizers. Have students start with talking about a lesson they have just successfully completed. They can go back through the lesson or book using different advanced organizer tools to see how they work and what is required. Encourage them to ask you anything about the learning process they want clarified.

d. *Provide guided practice* in applying advanced organizers to particular tasks. Work directly with student groups demonstrating and modeling how to identify elements. Have students who are more skilled demonstrate for the class.

e. *Provide feedback* on monitoring use and success of advanced organizers. While students use advanced organizers in small groups, you should move around the room listening and supplying encouragement for consistent use of the tools. As students get more comfortable using these tools, you can have them monitor one another in the use of the strategy.

Research Base

Harwell, 2001

Heacox, 2002

Moore et al., 2000

Opitz, 1998

What to Watch for With ELL/CLD Students

1. There are cultural differences in cognitive/learning style and some ELL/CLD students may not respond to the brainstorming construct behind most advanced organizers.

2. By keeping the graphic design of the advanced organizer as close as possible to the illustrations in the text or some aspect of the lesson, the teacher can more tightly connect the concepts being studied with the what/who/where questioning that precedes the lesson.

3. This is another activity that works best with preparation in the students' most proficient language and relevance to their culture before proceeding.

41. EVALUATION

Purpose of the Strategy

1. Build awareness of learning process

2. Develop categorization skills

3. Develop extended time spent on task

4. Develop personal control of situations

5. Strengthen awareness of learning process

6. Develop guidelines for strategy choice

7. Develop field sensitive skills

8. Develop categorization skills

9. Develop higher persistence

10. Lower anxiety levels

11. Reduce confusion in locus of control

How to Do It

1. At Tier 1, this strategy is used in the general education classrooms with all students.

2. The teacher introduces the students to the strategy by explaining that a strategy is a tool to help them learn and evaluation is one of these tools or strategies.

3. The teacher's goals in developing the students' evaluation strategy skills include increasing the students' awareness of what they need to do to complete a given task, providing the students with concrete guidelines for selecting and using appropriate specific strategies for achievement and guiding the students in comprehensive monitoring of the application of the strategy. These goals are accomplished through modeling, demonstrating, and describing the purpose or rationale for using the strategy. This, in turn, assists students to become aware of the types of tasks or situations where the strategy is most appropriate, the range of applications and transferability of the anticipated benefits from consistent use, and the amount of effort needed to successfully deploy the strategy (Pressley, Borkowski, & O'Sullivan 1984).

4. The teacher takes the students through the steps, pointing at a poster or diagram of the four steps. The first step is to think about how to identify what a problem consists of and how it can be measured and completed. The second step is to identify all the components of the problem and all the elements needed to solve it or to complete the task. The third step is to plan ahead for difficulties and to identify where and how to get feedback and assistance. The fourth and final step is to think about ways to generalize the lesson learned and how to apply the information in other settings and contexts.

5. Students use index cards with the steps for the evaluation strategy on them to cue themselves for each step. They select a specific problem or task and use the cards as mnemonics as they proceed through the assignment.

6. Steps for students to follow in implementing the strategy

   a. How will I analyze the problem?

   b. What are the important elements of this problem?

   c. How will I get feedback?

   d. How can I generalize the information?

7. Inform the students what evaluation is, how it operates, when to use it, and why it is useful. Begin by saying that evaluation is a way to help them analyze and monitor their learning. It works by asking and answering a series of five questions concerning a lesson they are working on. Once they learn how to use evaluation, they can use it anytime and with any content or lesson you give them to do.

8. Use cues, metaphors, analogies, or other means of elaborating on a description of evaluation combined with visual cues. One way to do this is to have the group watch a panel discussion or other presentation on television where a group is analyzing a problem or evaluating a proposal to do something. Another is to show a video of scientists working in a laboratory to evaluate whether a substance works effectively. Show how everyone can analyze, monitor, and control learning when going step by step.

9. Lead group discussions about the use of evaluation. Have students start with talking about a science or math lesson they have just successfully solved. They can go back through the lesson or interaction stopping to show how each step

of the lesson can be analyzed and monitored using the evaluation steps to see how they work and what is required. Encourage students to ask you anything about the learning process they want clarified.

10. Provide guided practice in applying evaluation to particular tasks. Here is an example of guided practice as the teacher leads the students through the use of evaluation. Examples of both teacher and student comments are shown.

Teacher: "First, you must analyze the task to determine what it requires. This includes items such as materials, time, space, or types of actions. What is the expected outcome of the task? What steps must you follow to complete the task? Review other completed assignments to determine possible steps you might take to complete this task."

Student: "What do I need to do to complete this task, and do I have all necessary materials and resources? What should the expected outcome look like? What steps must I follow to effectively achieve the expected outcome?"

Teacher: "Second, after you have analyzed the task, you must identify possible strategies that might be used to accomplish the task. Think about strategies you have used in the past to complete similar tasks. One or more of these may be necessary to complete this task."

Student: "What strategies do I know that might be appropriate for this particular task? Why might these be useful in this particular situation?"

Strategy Implementation

Teacher: "Third, prior to using a selected strategy, review the steps in that strategy. Remember that one strategy may be used in several different situations and different situations may require the use of more than one strategy."

Student: "I've selected these strategies for this task. I'll review the process associated with each strategy prior to implementation. I'll use these strategies while I complete this task."

Teacher: "Fourth, you must become aware of how useful it is to use the strategies you have selected. They assist you to complete the task accurately and efficiently. Periodically, reflect on how you are doing and how effective the strategy is for completing the task at hand."

Student: "How useful is this strategy for this particular task? Is this strategy helping me to accurately and efficiently confront the assigned task? Do I need to use a different strategy?"

Teacher: "Finally, think of other previously completed tasks where use of one or more of these strategies would have been beneficial to confronting the tasks. Could you have completed those tasks more efficiently had you used these strategies? Think of other types of tasks or future tasks where you might appropriately use one or more of these strategies."

Student: "Why were these strategies useful to this particular task? In what other types of situations would the use of these strategies be beneficial?"

11. Provide feedback on monitoring use and success of evaluation. While students use evaluation in small groups, the teacher should move around the room listening and supplying encouragement for consistent use of the question and answer steps. As students get more comfortable using this strategy, you can have them monitor one another in the use of the strategy, encouraging one another to ask and/or answer the questions.

12. Provide generalization activities. Have your students use evaluation for a variety of lessons and tasks. You should be sure to identify the strategy by name and point to the poster or visual cues about the strategy whenever you have students use it. Hold enhanced cognitive discussions about the use of evaluation in these different lesson settings, and encourage discussion of how useful or not useful students found this strategy in particular tasks.

Research Base

Brown & Palincsar (1989)

Cole, 1995; see pages 115–116

Opitz, 1998; see page 61

Pressley et al., 1984

What to Watch for With ELL/CLD Students

1. Since these students may have LEP, the monolingual, English-speaking teacher must increase the amount of demonstration and visual cues and rely less on verbal descriptions and cues. If available, bilingual assistance from peers or other education personnel may be useful in translating what is discussed in the classroom. This is especially important to provide explicit information to students concerning the rationale and value of the strategy. In addition, analogy elaboration of the evaluation strategy may be drawn from students' cultural and linguistic backgrounds. This reinforces the validity of students' previous successful learning and increases the ability of the students to make associations that will strengthen their cognitive development.

2. Students who have never been in school before will not know what is expected of them and what measuring, analyzing, and evaluating look like.

3. Some translation and discussion in the ELL students' more proficient language may be necessary to clarify what is to be done and why.

42. REALITY-BASED LEARNING APPROACHES

Purpose of the Strategy

1. Build awareness of learning

2. Reduce confusion in locus of control

3. Reduce off-task behaviors

4. Improve motivation

How to Do It

1. At Tier 1, this strategy is done in general education and integrated classrooms where all students participate in the activities.

2. Teachers provide students with real purposes and real audiences for reading, writing, and speaking.

3. Teachers provide students with real audiences and real application situations for presenting mathematical and scientific hypotheses or calculations.

4. When students write and speak to intended purposes and audiences, they are more likely to be motivated and to obtain valuable feedback on their efforts.

Research Base

Cole, 1995; see pages 25–26

What to Watch for With ELL/CLD Students

1. In some societies and cultures, children are actively discouraged from speculation and make-believe and are encouraged to stay focused on real-life, real objects, and real interactions.

2. It is not always apparent when your students come from homes where make-believe and fantasy are not supported. Always introducing new content by giving real examples and real applications will assist students in accessing and comprehending the content of the lesson.

3. The teacher can begin introducing make-believe examples and applications as students become comfortable with the general learning process. Teachers should always make it clear when something is nonfiction and when something is fiction.

43. INTERDISCIPLINARY UNIT

Purpose of the Strategy

1. Build transfer skills

2. Develop thinking and planning skills

3. Facilitate connections between known and new

4. Improve access to prior knowledge

5. Strengthen language development

How to Do It

1. At Tier 1, this strategy is a way of organizing curricular elements that cuts across subject-matter lines to focus upon comprehensive life problems or broad areas of study that bring together the various segments of the curriculum into meaningful association.

2. Teachers use thematic, interdisciplinary teaching to help students connect what they learn from one subject to another, to discover relationships.

3. In primary grades, students plan a trip to the grocery store. They set up schedule, timing, measuring, counting, reading, identifying, describing, comparing, assessing, and budgeting activities in relation to their trip.

4. In intermediate grades, students plan the same trip to the grocery store, but they add spatial orientation, nutrition, and considerations of the quality of life.

5. In secondary grades, students study the social impact of a given scientific or technological development at the same time that they are becoming acquainted with the science or technology itself.

6. Bondi (1988) recommends the following steps in designing interdisciplinary units.

   a. *Select a theme together.* Brainstorm together possible themes. Look for themes that relate to district/school goals and that interest students. Expand or narrow your theme as appropriate to reflect the teaching situation in which you are involved. Appoint a team leader for the duration of the development of the unit.

   b. *Work independently.* Identify topics, objectives, and skills from within your subject area that could be developed in this unit.

   c. *Meet together to define objectives for the unit.* Share all topics, objectives, and skills and combine them into a manageable package.

   d. *Meet together or select activities.* Match these activities to your goals in individual subjects. Stretch a little, if need be. Look for activities that provide student options and exploratory activities.

   e. *Brainstorm resources.* Consider both material resources and people resources.

   f. *Develop your activities* (individually and collectively). Divide the responsibility among the team to order, collect, and contact.

   g. *Schedule your unit.* This includes not only setting the dates for when to teach it but also scheduling the use of rooms, speakers, and so on.

   h. *Advertise your unit.* Do whatever you can to excite student and parent interest in the unit. Advertise in the school newsletter. Put up a "Coming Attraction" bulletin board. Wear slogans on your lapel.

   i. *Implement your unit.* Have fun and do not expect everything to be perfect.

Research Base

Bondi, 1988

Cole, 1995

What to Watch for With ELL/CLD Students

1. This is an excellent strategy for making content relevant to the lives of diverse learners. Be sure to include real activities related to the specific communities that your students come from.

2. For newcomers and beginning-level ELL students, the teacher should assign a bilingual peer helper or partner as the unit is explained.

44. LEARNING CENTERS OR STATIONS

Purpose of the Strategy

1. Build confidence in independent work

2. Reinforce content lessons

3. Improve access to prior knowledge

4. Expand comprehension

How to Do It

1. At Tier 1, this strategy is part of the general education classroom and worked into the layout of the classroom with use of furniture and other means of demarking specific learning areas.

2. The teacher creates areas or locations in the classroom where students work on various tasks simultaneously.

3. These areas can be formal or informal and can be distinguished by signs, symbols, or colors. Centers differ from stations in that centers are distinct content locations while stations work in concert with one another. For example, there may be a science center, math center, writing center, and reading center in the classroom, each with its special furniture, equipment, and materials. Assignments or tasks specific to each center or station activity are either handed out before the activity begins or available at each location.

Research Base

Ashworth & Wakefield, 2004

Movitz & Holmes, 2007

C. A. Tomlinson, 1999

What to Watch for With ELL/CLD Students

1. ELL/CLD students should not go to separate learning centers for primary instruction in a content lesson or task. They need direct instruction in the content or task including key vocabulary and guided practice in what is expected of them at each learning center.

2. After the ELL/CLD students have been prepared for the learning centers and shown how to use the materials or equipment at each center, they can join in the activities at each center just as the rest of the class does.

3. Learning centers are a good way to reinforce content knowledge and allow students to become engaged in applications of this new knowledge.

45. THEMATIC INSTRUCTION (INTERDISCIPLINARY UNITS)

Purpose of the Strategy

1. Build transfer skills

2. Develop thinking and planning skills

3. Facilitate connections between known and new

4. Improve access to prior knowledge

5. Strengthen language development

How to Do It

1. At Tier 1, this strategy is a way of organizing curricular elements that cut across subject-matter lines to focus on comprehensive life problems or broad areas of study that bring together the various segments of the curriculum into meaningful association.

2. The teacher uses thematic, interdisciplinary teaching to help students connect what they learn from one subject to another, to discover relationships.

3. In primary grades, students plan a trip to the grocery store. They set up scheduling, timing, measuring, counting, reading, identifying, describing, comparing, assessing, and budgeting activities in relation to their trip.

4. In intermediate grades, Students plan the same trip to the grocery store, but they add spatial orientation, nutrition, and considerations of the quality of life.

5. In secondary grades, students study the social impact of a given scientific or technological development at the same time that they are becoming acquainted with the science or technology itself.

6. Bondi (1988) recommends the following steps in designing interdisciplinary units.

   a. *Select a theme together.* Brainstorm together possible themes. Look for themes that relate to district/school goals and that interest students. Expand or narrow your theme as appropriate to reflect the teaching situation in which you are involved. Appoint a team leader for the duration of the development of the unit.

   b. *Work independently.* Identify topics, objectives, and skills from within your subject area that could be developed in this unit.

   c. *Meet together to define objectives for the unit.* Share all topics, objectives, and skills and combine them into a manageable package.

   d. *Meet together or select activities.* Match these activities to your goals in individual subjects. Stretch a little, if need be. Look for activities that provide student options and exploratory activities.

   e. *Brainstorm resources.* Consider both material resources and people resources.

   f. *Develop your activities* (individually and collectively). Divide the responsibility among the team to order, collect, and contact.

   g. *Schedule your unit.* This includes setting the dates for not only when to teach it but also scheduling the use of rooms, speakers, and so on.

   h. *Advertise your unit.* Do whatever you can to excite student and parent interest in the unit. Advertise in the school newsletter. Put up a "Coming Attraction" bulletin board. Wear slogans on your lapel.

   i. *Implement your unit.* Have fun and don't expect everything to be perfect.

Research Base

Bondi, 1988

Cole, 1995; see pages 26–27

What to Watch for With ELL/CLD Students

1.   This is an excellent strategy for making content relevant to the lives of diverse learners. Be sure to include real activities related to the specific communities that your students come from.

2.   For newcomers and beginning-level ELL students, the teacher should assign a bilingual peer helper or partner as the unit is explained.

46. ACTIVE PROCESSING

Purpose of the Strategy

1.   Build awareness of learning

2.   Develop academic language

3.   Develop personal control of situations

4.   Facilitate access to prior knowledge

5.   Reduce off-task behaviors

6.   Reduce impulsivity

How to Do It

1.   At Tier 1, this strategy is done with all students in the general education setting. *Caution:* It can become quite noisy in a large classroom, so be prepared.

2.   When applying the active processing strategy, students work through problems or tasks using the sequence of self-monitoring questions given here. For example, your students must prepare for the state-administered achievement tests required at this grade level, but several of your diverse learners have never taken such tests before and they are unfamiliar with this type of evaluation. They have heard stories of something scary that happens to schoolchildren every year and are bracing themselves to endure this external event. You could modify your preparation for this event by integrating the active processing strategy into the lessons before the testing period. Start by having the students in your class speak aloud with one another in small groups about the content and process of lessons they are learning following the steps in active processing. Do this in every content area until the students are familiar with the process itself. Then a few weeks before the state assessments, introduce the concept of standardized achievement tests to your class. Have your students discuss how group and norm measures differ from individual and curriculum based assessments and the implications of this for each participant (Step 1 of active processing, "What is my task?"). Have the groups discuss what they will need to have with them and what the setting is like. Have those students who have taken tests like this describe the process and what it was like for them. Talk about the expectations of test administrators regarding notes, whispering, looking at others, pencils, calculators, and so on (Step 2 of active processing, "What do I need to do to complete my task?"). Discuss what an acceptable performance might be for various levels of completion and knowledge. Explain some of the test strategies that help successful test takers even when they are unsure of the answer. Clarify the expectations of parents, teachers, and others about the test activity (Step 3 of active processing, "How will I know my task is done correctly?"). Provide suggestions for relieving stress during the test and ideas for self-monitoring their progress through the different sections of the test (Step 4 of active processing, "How will

I monitor the implementation?"). Discuss how timekeepers work and what the timelines will be on this test. Discuss ways to identify when it is time to move to another section and what to do when they are finished with the test (Step 5 of active processing, "How do I know the task is completed?").

3. Students work through a task aloud, naming each step and asking themselves the appropriate questions for the task. Steps for students to follow in implementing this strategy

    a. What is my task?

    b. What do I need to do to complete my task?

    c. How will I know my task is done correctly?

    d. How will I monitor the implementation?

    e. How do I know the task is correctly completed?

4. For example, suppose you want your students to complete a new unit in language arts about bears in fact and fiction. Some of your diverse learners are not familiar with the concept of fact versus fiction as used on our society and have no words in their native language for this distinction; also, several of them have little or incomplete prior schooling. You could modify your preparation for this unit by integrating the active processing strategy into the lessons. Begin having the students in your class speak aloud about what they know about bears and other animals with one another in small groups using the active processing steps. Do this within the context of reinforcement and review of prior content the students have successfully accomplished until the students are familiar with the active processing process itself. Then introduce the concept of fact versus fiction to your class. Have them discuss how these differ using real-life experiences from their homes or communities. Use visual and physical examples of the concept, such as a photograph of a car and a sketch or drawing of a car, a realistic portrait of a child and an abstract painting of a child, a picture of astronauts on the moon and a picture of children playing on the moon, and the like to ensure that students are aware of what is involved. Have students discuss examples from their communities or lives. Discuss how to tell the difference and what is involved in the process (Step 1 of active processing, "What is my task?"). Have the groups discuss what they will need to compare and contrast fact from fiction and what actions are involved. Have those that are more successful describe the process and what it was like for them to learn it. Talk about the importance of learning this skill and discuss the steps involved. Have your students work in groups to develop a set of rules outlining the steps to follow (Step 2 of active processing, "What do I need to do to complete my task?"). Discuss what an acceptable performance might be for various levels of skill and knowledge. Explain some of the strategies that help students be successful at separating fact from fiction. Discuss how to check for the accuracy and the steps involved (Step 3 of active processing, "How will I know my task is done correctly?"). Provide suggestions for relieving stress during the lesson and ideas for self-monitoring their progress through the different steps of the process (Step 4 of active processing, "How will I monitor the implementation?"). Discuss ways to identify when it is time to move to another question or example and what to do when they have finished each set of comparisons (Step 5 of active processing, "How do I know the task is completed?").

5. The strategy preparation can be done in the native language or dialect of the students to assure their understanding of your expectations and their task prior to carrying the assignment out in English or other communication mode.

6. Using active processing reduces impulsive tendencies and naturally illustrates how a student can use reflection in answering questions and completing tasks.

Research Base

Cole, 1995

Tovani, 2000; see pages 26–29

What to Watch for With ELL/CLD Students

1. The strategy preparation can be done in the native language or dialect of the students to assure their understanding of your expectations and their task prior to carrying out the assignment in English or other communication mode.

2. Students who are less proficient in English will need guidance in using the steps of active processing; the process can be explained and practiced in the students' most proficient language before going on in English.

3. Active processing can be used in any language of instruction and in any content area or age level.

47. ANALOGY

Purpose of the Strategy

1. Develop higher tolerance

2. Facilitate access to prior knowledge

3. Build transfer skills

4. Develop categorization skills

How to Do It

1. At Tier 1, this strategy can be done in the general education classroom with all students participating. Students may be paired with culture and language peers at first and then mixed pairs of diverse students as they become comfortable with the strategy.

2. Students each share something they already know about the lesson topic, something that is meaningful to them. They go through the steps of analogy in pairs as they share their items/ideas with one another. Steps for students to follow in implementing this analogy strategy.

   a. What do I already know about this item or concept?

   b. How does what I already know about this idea or item compare with the new idea or item?

   c. Can the known idea or item be substituted for the new item or idea and still make sense?

   d. How can I elaborate on these comparisons through analogies?

3. When applying the analogy strategy, students work through problems or tasks using the previous sequence of self-monitoring questions. Let us suppose that you are about to have your students begin a new unit in social studies about immigration nationally, in your state, and your local community. You have several students who are newcomers to your community, from different parts of the world and from CLD backgrounds. You could modify your usual instructional approach by building in an opportunity for your students to compare and contrast their personal experiences with current immigration and refugee policies and procedures with those in their past experience. You would have them first discuss the difference between immigrant, colonist, settler, emigrant, and refugee using examples from current news stories on television. You could also have them see videotapes or actually visit an INS office or a center where particular groups of newcomers to America receive services. You then have them share what they know about these terms and services from their personal, current experience (Step 1 of analogy, "What do I know about things like this?"). They could then share how these experiences are similar to others they are familiar with or others in the classroom (Step 2 of analogy, "How is what I know similar to this new thing?"). Then they would discuss the differences between their personal or familiar experiences and what is new to them about the policies, procedures, services, and experiences (Step 3 of analogy, "How is this new thing different from what I know?"). The students could explore how different people's experiences might change if certain elements of their circumstances were substituted for another (Step 4 of analogy, "Can I substitute

what I know for this new thing?"). Now the students would be ready to expand this knowledge to identifying ways to improve current models of service and how they might help other newcomers to the community (Step 5 of analogy, "How can I elaborate on this?"). Discussions will naturally rise out of these lessons about comparing and contrasting based on high- versus low-tolerance characteristics.

4. For example, students are shown an object that looks familiar, such as a metal rod used to connect two wheels on a toy car. They generate words describing the rod such as "long," "shiny," "manufactured," "connects," and "an axle." They then are shown another metal rod that is unfamiliar to them. They generate more words describing the new object. Some of the words will be similar, some different. Example words might be "long," "shiny," "threaded ends," "connects something," "pointy," "heavy," and "metallic." They may actually try to substitute the new rod for the toy axle or they may make guesses about substitution and conclude that it could be done but won't work exactly. They generate sentences such as "The axle is smaller than the new rod;" "The new rod is larger than the axle of the toy car;" "The new rod has threaded ends and the axle does not;" "The axle is to a car as the new rod is to something else;" and "The axle is as shiny as the new rod is."

Research Base

Cole, 1995

Tovani, 2000

What to Watch for With ELL/CLD Students

1. Be sure students are matched with peers with whom they can communicate comfortably while they are all learning the strategy and steps in the process.

2. After students learn the process and steps, posters or cards with reminder illustrations and the words of the steps can be put up around the room.

3. Once students can use analogy without prompting, they can be paired up with nonbilingual peers for more applications.

48. PROBLEM-SOLVING COPING

Purpose of the Strategy

1. Build awareness of learning process

2. Develop extended time spent on task

3. Develop higher tolerance

4. Develop personal control of situations

5. Develop problem-solving skills

6. Lower anxiety levels

How to Do It

1. At Tier 1, this strategy is taught to an entire classroom of integrated mixed learners in the benchmarked general education program.

2. The teacher has students identify specific problem(s) they want to solve as a group. Each group follows the coping steps as they address their problem, writing down their answers and ideas for each stage of the problem solving.

3. Steps for students to follow in implementing this strategy

    a. What is the problem?

    b. What are possible solutions?

    c. What is my action plan?

    d. Where can I go for help?

    e. When should I start?

    f. How will I deal with setbacks?

    g. What is my outcome?

4. When applying the coping strategy, students work through problems or tasks using the sequence of self-monitoring questions. Let us suppose that you are about to have your students begin a new unit in language arts about the difference between verbs and nouns. You have several students who are new to your community, of limited prior schooling, from a linguistic community that does not use the same tense and plural forms as English, and many of whom are LEP. You could modify your usual instructional approach by building in an opportunity for your students to examine the lesson ahead of time, to identify any problems they may expect to have in successfully completing the lesson, and to understand exactly what they are expected to do in the lesson (Step 1 of coping, "What is the problem?"). The student groups then would identify what they will need to know as a foundation to the lesson and then what they will need to do to successfully complete the lesson (Step 2 of coping, "What are my action steps?"), discussing ahead of time what kind of words they might see and how they might be used. This might include some practice ahead of time in hearing and speaking the words you want them to use later on their own. They identify ahead of time where sources of information and assistance are available to them (Step 3 of coping, "Where can I go for help?") including materials, dictionaries, peers, and adults available to them in the school. During this planning time, students also discuss what might happen to prevent them getting information or achieving parts of your outcomes. They come up with a supportive, group plan for dealing with barriers in accomplishing their tasks (Step 4 of coping, "How will I deal with setbacks?"). Finally, the students create a clear idea in their minds of what exactly an acceptable outcome of this activity will be (Step 5 of coping, "What will my outcome be?"). By following these steps and keeping all of this in mind while working on the lesson you have for them, they will be able to increase their persistence in accomplishing the task and will increase their likelihood of completing the task successfully.

Research Base

McCain, 2005

Reid, Webster-Stratton, & Hammond, 2007

What to Watch for With ELL/CLD Students

1. The strategy preparation can be done in the native language or dialect of the students to assure their understanding of your expectations and their task prior to carrying the assignment out in English or other communication mode.

49. INFORMATION ORGANIZATION STRATEGY—EASY

Purpose of the Strategy

1. Build awareness of learning process

2. Develop extended time spent on task

3. Develop personal control of situations

4. Facilitate organization and prioritization of information

5. Develop focus

How to Do It

1. At Tier 1, this strategy facilitates all students in learning to organize information and identify what is most important to focus on in a lesson.

2. The teacher can create posters with the EASY steps on them and hang them around the room.

3. Students can create cue cards to remember each step. Students follow steps while reading passages or thematic elements. The steps in EASY are

> **E**licit questions (who, what, where, when, why)
> **A**sk self which information is least difficult
> **S**tudy easy content initially, followed by difficult
> **Y**es! Provide self-reinforcement through rewards or points

Research Base

Lapp, Flood, Brock, & Fisher, 2007

Moore et al., 2000

What to Watch for With ELL/CLD Students

1. Much like the other mnemonics provided in these strategy lists, ELL/CLD students need bilingual explanations of the teacher's expectations and guided practice in implementing the steps in the strategy.

2. Newcomers will need to have the EASY steps modeled and explained in their most proficient language before they can proceed independently.

3. Students can be paired with partners who are slightly more bilingual than they are to facilitate their learning this process.

50. ORGANIZATION STRATEGY—SORTING

Purpose of the Strategy

1. Develop analytical skills

2. Develop association skills

3. Develop categorization skills

4. Develop field independent skills

5. Improve mnemonic retrieval

How to Do It

1. At Tier 1, this strategy is done in the general education classroom with all students participating. Teachers may assign students of similar language and ability to either heterogeneous or homogeneous groups depending on their specific goals.

2. The teacher directs work in small groups. The student groups are given bags or boxes of mixed items. Each small group goes through the steps, sorting all the items in the piles into clusters as defined by the teacher. It is best to start with

an open sort (i.e., do not give the categories or attributes to sort but allow students to generate them). After the open sort, students can be given specific attributes or characteristics to use to sort the items into categories. They make lists of their groups of items to share with the class. Steps for students to follow in implementing this strategy

    a. What elements go together and why?

    b. What do I call these groups?

    c. Can I remember the elements by the group?

    d. How can I generalize this information?

3. When applying the organization strategy, students work through problems or tasks using the sequence of self-monitoring questions. For example, you are going to have a new unit about rocks and minerals (i.e., igneous, sedimentary, conglomerate, and so on). Many of your students are unfamiliar with these ways of grouping natural materials that they consider generically as rocks. One group of students comes from a culture where rocks are grouped by hard versus soft, another from a culture that groups rocks by whether they can be used to produce something in the home. You might introduce your class to the lesson by having actual examples of the rocks to be studied present to handle or take the class on a field trip to the museum or a local mine or industrial area to observe them. You could also show pictures or videos of chemists interacting with the materials. Have the students look for patterns in appearance, use, environment, chemical reactions, and so on. They could chart the attributes and characteristics of the rocks and minerals on a graph or in Venn diagrams (Step 1 of organization, "What elements go together?"). Now they should look for distinctive patterns of commonality between rocks and minerals that shows whether they go together (Step 2 of organization, "What attribute of these am I using to group them?"). Ask the students what they would name the group of rocks and minerals based on the major attributes. Now introduce them to the common English name of the group (Step 3 of organization, "What name do I give to each group?"). Discuss how the materials in each group share certain common characteristics, and then discuss the characteristics that all rocks and minerals share in common as rocks and minerals (Step 4 of organization, "How are the groups similar to one another?"). Discuss how the rocks in each group might differ from one another, how each group of rocks and minerals differ from the other groups, and how rocks differ from nonrocks (Step 5 of organization, "How are the groups different from one another?"). Finish the unit with a discussion of how to find patterns in anything you are studying (Step 6 of organization, "What organization patterns do I see?").

4. You might now step back from the lesson and discuss the enhanced cognitive learning that you have provided students, the learning to learn lesson that is represented by the strategy you had them use. At this point, you would discuss how everything in the world is composed of various elements that need to be identified to understand the whole thing being studied (field independence) and that when all the parts are put together the meaning of the whole thing results (field sensitive).

Research Base

Ferris & Hedgcock, 2005

Iachini, Borghi, & Senese, 2008

What to Watch for With ELL/CLD Students

1. The strategy preparation can be done in the native language or dialect of the students to assure their understanding of your expectations and their task prior to carrying the assignment out in English or other communication mode.

2. Understand that all cultures have different ways of thinking of common attributes of a group of similar objects. What constitutes the criteria to pay attention to will vary based on cultural values and learning practices. Although it seems obvious to one group that the predominant surface color of a set of objects is what links them together as a set of objects, to another group it might be that surface texture or size is more important as an attribute for sorting out similarity and difference.

51. RECIPROCAL QUESTIONING

Purpose of the Strategy

1. Improve reading comprehension

2. Use discourse techniques

3. Use an inquiry approach

4. Improve mnemonic retrieval

5. Improve retention

6. Develop thinking and planning skills

How to Do It

1. At Tier 1, this strategy is done in the integrated classroom in any content area.

2. The teacher and students ask one another questions about a selection. Students modeling of teacher questions and teacher feedback are emphasized as the learner explores the meaning of the reading material.

Research Base

Cole, 1995

Moore et al., 2000; see pages 141–142,

What to Watch for With ELL/CLD Students

1. Provide initial setup in the student's most proficient language.

2. Students can practice reciprocal questioning with one another in their native language and then proceed with English proficient students.

52. COGNITIVE STRATEGIES IN HOME AND COMMUNITY LANGUAGE

Purpose of the Strategy

1. Improve motivation

2. Minimize behavior problems

3. Build transfer skills

4. Develop cognitive academic language

5. Reduce code-switching

How to Do It

1. At Tier 1, this strategy facilitates the transition of ELL/CLD students from their primary language base to bilingualism and helps with their interaction with all students in the general education classroom.

2. Teachers working with student peers or assistants discuss the academic language of learning and of the classroom in both English and in the home and community language, when possible. Bilingual posters and signs about cognitive academic language proficiency are posted and referred to regularly.

Expansion: Periodically, the teacher will stop a lesson in various content areas and ask students to discuss what is being presented and how, and what academic behaviors are expected.

Research Base

Collins Block & Mangieri, 2003

Roessingh, Kover, & Watt, 2005

Strickland et al., 2002

Walter, 2004

What to Watch for With ELL/CLD Students

1. Not all ELL/CLD students are academically fluent in their home or community language.

2. Graphics and illustrations representing the cognitive strategies may be used on posters or individual cue card sets for the students. These can be bilingual.

53. CONSISTENT SEQUENCE

Purpose of the Strategy

1. Build academic transfer skills

2. Build awareness of appropriate academic behaviors

3. Improve confidence in academic interactions

4. Reduce distractibility

How to Do It

1. At Tier 1, this strategy is done in the general education classroom with all students.

2. The teacher presents all content lessons with the same instructional language and direction sequence to the extent possible.

3. Posters can be put up around the room with the lesson process and teachers may point to each step as they go through the lesson.

Expansion: Students can role-play giving the directions themselves.

Research Base

Mathes et al., 2007

Vaughn & Linan-Thompson, 2007

What to Watch for With ELL/CLD Students

1. This strategy is consistent with the Sheltered Instruction Observation Protocol (SIOP) model used in many ELL programs.

2. Newcomers who have never attended school may become confused if every lesson and activity occurs in seemingly random patterns. They do not know what is expected of them at various stages of the lesson. They do not know what to attend to and what is less important.

3. This is also going to impact students with undiagnosed attention deficit disorders that they have not yet learned to accommodate.

4. It is better to start out with simple consistent steps and add as students become comfortable and familiar with what is going to happen in the classroom.

54. CONTEXT EMBEDDING

Purpose of the Strategy

1. Develop content knowledge foundation

2. Develop cognitive academic language proficiency

3. Develop content area skills

How to Do It

1. At Tier 1, this strategy is used with all students in the general education classroom in all content areas at the beginning of every lesson.

2. The teacher presents lessons with concrete, physical models and demonstrations of both content and expected performance. Language is simplified and content focused. Lessons address real-life situations and learning.

3. Students are encouraged to work in small groups on content-focused activities and to discuss lessons in home and community language.

Research Base

Cummins, 1984

Cummins, Baker, & Hornberger, 2001

Donaldson, 1978

Roessingh et al., 2005

What to Watch for With ELL/CLD Students

1. Vocabulary may be previewed with fluent speakers in the students' most proficient language.

2. Some cultures may have strictures against children handling or being too close to certain objects. Always screen items ahead of time with knowledgeable community members.

55. EXPERIENCE-BASED LEARNING

Purpose of the Strategy

1. Build transfer skills

2. Develop cognitive academic language

3. Develop content knowledge foundation

4. Facilitate analogy strategies

How to Do It

1. At Tier 1, this strategy can be done in the general education classroom with all students participating. Students may be paired with culture and language peers at first and then mixed pairs of diverse students as they become comfortable with the strategy.

2. In primary grades, teachers guide students to illustrate specific experiences in which students have participated. Activity may be paired with field trips or other shared experiences or may be in reference to prior life experiences of ELL/LEP students. Community members may make presentations about events significant to students' families. Teachers

then have students tell what their illustrations depict and write down verbatim what the students say. Students then read back to the teacher what has been written.

3. In intermediate and secondary grades, teachers guide students to illustrate and write stories about their experiences. These stories can be put into collections and bound for use by other students. Stories can be kept in the classroom, library, or media center.

Research Base

Beckett, 2002

Beckett & Miller, 2006

Beckett & Slater, 2005

Coelho & Rivers, 2003

Cole, 1995; see page 126

What to Watch for With ELL/CLD Students

1. Some shared experiences will be very novel for particular cultural members of a group, more than for other members. Be sure to give those who have never seen something before extra preparation time and explanations of what they are going to see or do during the field trip or experience.

2. Be sure students are matched with peers with whom they can communicate comfortably while they are all learning the strategy and steps in the process.

3. Be sensitive to cultural mores about certain experiences and businesses. You may need to spend extra time discussing what is going to be seen and heard or, in some cases, be prepared to have some students participate in a related but separate activity.

56. GUIDED READING AND WRITING IN HOME AND COMMUNITY LANGUAGE

Purpose of the Strategy

1. Improve motivation

2. Minimize behavior problems

3. Build transfer skills

4. Develop confidence in school language and rules for academic and social interactions

5. Reduce code-switching

6. Develop cognitive academic language

How to Do It

1. At Tier 1, this strategy facilitates the transition of ELL/CLD students from their primary language base to bilingualism and helps with their interaction with all students in the general education classroom.

2. The teacher directs advanced-fluency student to lead a guided reading or writing activity in the home and community language. Students can reread parts of a story in pairs after the directed reading activity rather than have one student read while the others all listen. Students then write summaries of what they have read. Writing can be in either home and community language or English. During this time, the students have a chance to help one another. Advanced-fluency students can dramatize and create dialogue to illustrate the action.

Research Base

Cole, 1995; see pages 150–152

Haneda, 2008

Reggy-Mamo, 2008

Ross, 1971

Strickland et al., 2002; see page 217

What to Watch For With ELL/CLD Students

1. Not all ELL/CLD students are literate in their home or community language.

2. Picture dictionaries with bilingual words and definitions are usually the most practical reference to use with younger, less educated students.

57. ALTERNATE RESPONSE METHODS

Purpose of the Strategy

1. Facilitate learning

2. Accommodate diverse learning styles

3. Develop task completion

How to Do It

1. At Tier 1, this strategy can be done with all students in a mixed general education classroom. This adapts the mode of response required of students.

2. Students respond to questions in a manner compatible with their needs. Allow students who have difficulty with writing activities to tape-record their answers. Students are allowed to express their understanding of a question or issue in varied ways to meet their individual needs. This practice ensures that students have the best possible chance to show that they have acquired and retained skills and knowledge.

3. For example, students may tape-record their oral responses to questions given in class. For the geography unit, provide the questions in writing for the student to take home and practice responding. Some names of American states are very difficult to pronounce. Provide time for students to work alone or with a peer to write the difficult state names on tag board cards that they can hold up during class discussion rather than say aloud.

4. Keep in mind Howard Gardner's (1993a; 1993b) work on multiple intelligences. What other forms might be available to students to express their understanding? If the topic is westward expansion, the student could find musical examples illustrating the various cultures that came into contact with each other and could make a mixed sound recording to demonstrate the culture clashes and consequences of expansion. The students could draw a map or other illustration supporting the musical representation and their understanding of the geographic concept of the movement of populations from one location to another.

Research Base

Bailey, 1993

Cole, 1995; see pages 34–35

Gardner, 1993a

Gardner, 1993b

Tannenbaum, 1996

What to Watch for With ELL/CLD Students

1. Some CLD students have had previous schooling in situations where students have no choice in their responses and teachers are authority figures who direct every action in the classroom.

2. When the teacher wishes to make student empowerment an instructional goal, this strategy is an excellent direction to take.

3. Demonstrate how the various responses can be made, including color, modeling, illustrating, and the like.

4. Some role-play in the process may be helpful.

58. SUCCESS

Purpose of the Strategy

1. Develop personal control of situations

2. Facilitate student self-concept as a successful person

3. Improve confidence and self-esteem

4. Improve retention

5. Utilize prior knowledge

How to Do It

1. At Tier, 1 this strategy is part of the modus operandi in the general classroom.

2. The teacher ensures that each student successfully completes assigned tasks by initially reducing the level of difficulty of materials and gradually increasing the level of difficulty as easier tasks are met with success. The teacher also reduces the complexity level of vocabulary or concepts in written material to help the student complete a reading task. Through this strategy, learners may read material similar to others in the class without requiring an excessive amount of individual attention from the teacher.

3. For example, the teacher places a transparency over a page of written material, (with a fine-point marker) crosses out the more difficult words, and writes simpler equivalents of those words above or in the margin next to the crossed-out words. As students read, they substitute the simpler words for those marked out.

Research Base

Gibbons, 2003

Krumenaker, Many, & Wang, 2008

Leki, 1995

C. A. Tomlinson, 1999

What to Watch for With ELL/CLD Students

1. The teacher needs information or professional development about all of the diverse learning styles, cultures, and languages in the classroom to design accessible learning activities for all students.

2. There is as much diversity within the ELL and CLD population as there is between the non-ELL and ELL population as a whole.

Tier 2 Interventions

2

INTRODUCTION TO TIER 2 INSTRUCTIONAL FOCUS

In general, Tier 2 intervention involves more intensive, small group interventions with frequent progress monitoring. A major difference at Tier 2 is the way in which interventions are developed. For example, some districts determine interventions at Tier 2 through problem-solving teams that develop specific interventions based on individual student needs. Other districts predetermine a list of research-based interventions that target specific skill deficits and try to maximize efficiency of resources by grouping students who have similar academic needs. There are also differences in Tier 2 regarding who is involved in the problem-solving process and direct instruction. In some districts, Tier 2 instruction is the responsibility of the classroom teacher, special education teacher, speech language pathologist, or other specialists. In other districts, Tier 2 interventions can be provided by any trained staff member under the supervision of a specialist with expertise in the intervention. However, most of these interventions were designed for native English-speaking students, not for CLD or ELL students.

Differentiated instruction is a way of thinking about teaching and learning. It is also a collection of strategies that help the teacher better address and manage the variety of learning needs in the classroom. Differentiated instruction is not a new trend. It is based on what we know about best practices in education. It puts students at the center of teaching and learning. It lets their learning needs direct the instructional planning. Differentiated instruction enhances learning for all students by engaging them in activities that better respond to their particular learning needs, strengths, and preferences. With diverse learners, these needs, strengths, and preferences include accommodations and individualization for diverse culture and language backgrounds as well as differing levels and rates of acculturation. A basic premise of differentiation is that one type of instruction does not necessarily work for all students (i.e., one size does not fit all). Teachers are advised to begin where their students are, with their learning differences and their learning strengths. Instructional personnel are to build on learners' differences and learners' strengths by developing instructional activities based on essential topics and concepts, significant processes and skills, and multiple ways to display learning while providing flexible approaches to content, instruction, and outcomes. It is critical to engage students through different learning styles and use varied rates of instruction as well as respond to students' readiness, instructional needs, interests, and learning preferences. An additional component in differentiation is to meet curriculum standards and individualized education plan (IEP) requirements for each learner while having students compete against themselves rather than others. Guidance to teachers about differentiation also includes the following.

1. Suggesting strategies that provide specific ways for each student to learn

2. Developing challenging and engaging tasks for each learner

3. Providing opportunities for students to work in varied instructional formats

(C. A. Tomlinson, 2003)

Differentiating instruction means changing the pace, level, or kind of instruction the teacher provides in response to individual learners' needs, styles, or interests. Differentiated instruction specifically responds to students' progress on the learning continuum—what they already know and what they need to learn. By using differentiation, teachers can respond to their students' most successful methods of learning, allowing the students to demonstrate what they've learned in ways that capitalize on their strengths and interests. The teacher can differentiate instruction if the curriculum is district mandated, if it is directed by state standards, and even if learning is measured by statewide basic skills exams or performance assessments.

Educators differentiate instruction for students in terms of assessment techniques, general education curriculum accessibility, teaching strategies, technology, universal and physical design accommodations, classroom management techniques, and a wide array of resources and related services based on student needs (Ford, Davern, & Schnorr, 2001; Hitchcock, Meyer, Rose, & Jackson, 2002). An initial step in differentiating instruction is individualizing your curriculum by identifying the concepts, principles, and skills you want to teach (Ford et al., 2001; Watson & Houtz, 1998). Although most students will not require accommodations in curricular goals, the curriculum for other students may need to be personalized by supplementing or changing it to address those students' different learning strengths, challenges, and styles. You can individualize your curricular goals by adding or reducing the material and skills to be learned, varying the levels of difficulty of the content addressed, and having students demonstrate their mastery in different ways (Jitendra, Edwards, Choutka, & Treadway, 2002). Individualized teaching accommodations—changes in the ways information is presented or the ways in which students respond—are essential aspects of differentiated instruction. Stough (2002) offers a continuum for delineating accommodations based on their impact on the individual profiles of students and the level of curriculum mastery expected of students. The first level of the continuum refers to access accommodations. These accommodations provide students with access to the curriculum and instruction and do not affect the level of mastery expected of students. Examples of this type of accommodation include content enhancement, word processing and spell checkers, learning strategies instruction, and peer-mediated instruction.

Another level of differentiation addresses high-impact accommodations that affect curricular expectations of students. These instructional accommodations, sometimes referred to as modifications, alter the content of curriculum as well as the ways in which students are taught, and they require adjustments in the structure and content of the educational program that affect the level of curricular mastery expected of students. Examples of these instructional accommodations include use of multilevel teaching and curriculum overlapping.

PROGRESS MONITORING AT TIER 2

Most programs require that progress monitoring should occur at each tier. Generally, requirements include frequent progress monitoring at Tier 2 and continuous, or even more frequent, progress monitoring at Tier 3. Specific minimum requirements for progress monitoring are similar; for example, most programs require that universal screening occur at least three times a year and that individualized progress monitoring occur in the range of two to four times per month at Tier 2.

To extend the example from Tier 1, suppose a student of concern has been identified as having an unusually high level of distractibility and failure with task completion, enough so that attention deficit disorder is suspected by some of the teachers working with him or her. Before moving the student into a Tier 2 intervention, various interventions at Tier 1 have been implemented in large group settings, for example stepped *proximity* (Strategy 1 in Tier 1). None of the interventions have been successful in addressing the attention issue in a sustainable manner. By moving the students into Tier 2 of the response to intervention (RTI) or response to instruction and intervention (RTII) process, the team of instructional personnel is able to focus the intervention strategy in small group instructional sessions specific to separate elements of the general presenting problem. First, the team identifies a target level of attention and task completion and establishes how far off the student's current performance varies from this goal. They then select one of the intervention strategies that in their judgment will best show them if the student responds appropriately given this intervention.

The targeted intervention is previewed with the student and one of the teachers working with the student begins the intervention in a small group setting. These are usually 30- to 40- minute instructional interactions and may occur in varied settings depending on space available. The interventions are conducted daily at the beginning of the Tier 2. If the intervention selected is effective, and if the student improves his or her response by showing measurable increase in attention to task and in task completion, the team would then gradually broaden the application to monitoring the student in all instructional settings and not just the focus session. If the intervention was a success (i.e., the student improves his or her attention and task completion to the target goal), then the team may cease the Tier 2 sessions and move the student back into classroom Tier 1 level assistance.

Table 2.1　Progress Monitoring at Tier 2

Setting: Small group session	Week 1	Week 2	Week 4	Week 6	Week 8	Week 10
Stepped proxemics in small group setting	Teacher seated facing group of students	Teacher leaning toward target student	Teacher tapping knee of target student	Teacher touching knee of target student	Teacher leaning toward target student	Teacher seated facing group of students
Response	Task done 50% of the time	Task done 70% of the time	Task done 90% of the time	Task done 100% of the time	Task done 100% of the time	Task done 100% of the time
Content goal: Correctly use and spell new English words	Student listens and reads 10 new words	Student correctly uses, copies, and reads 5 words	Student uses, reads, and spells 10 words; adds 5 new	Student uses, reads, and spells 15 words; adds 5 new	Student uses, reads, and spells 10 new words	Student uses, reads, and spells 10 new words

In the example shown in Table 2.1, the strategy of having the teacher sit facing the small group including the target student while directing them at their work on using, reading, and spelling new vocabulary is tried for an entire week. As the student only achieves task completion 50% of the time with this intervention, the strategy is modified by having the teacher lean toward the target student while giving directions to the small group. In the example, this strategy results in the student being able to complete the task 70% of the time; therefore, the strategy is modified again by having the teacher gently tap the student's knee while giving directions. In the example, this strategy results in the student being able to complete tasks 90% of the time, and thus only a slight modification is needed (i.e., having the teacher touch the student lightly on the knee to redirect attention when needed). In the example, the student is now responding to tasks appropriately and is successful in completing tasks with gradually reduced assistance from the teacher.

If the intervention was not a success (i.e., the student only achieved task completion when the teacher touched the student's knee for an extended time and immediately reverted to off-task behavior when the teacher removed her hand), then the teacher might need to consider more drastic measures. Specific strategies (e.g., the intensive touching strategy in vocabulary instruction) should be tried for at least five sessions before further modification or a change of strategy should be made. Although *practice makes perfect*, it does not make sense to continue something that is ineffective. Most RTI/RTII models set specific lengths of time to try specific strategies before moving on to something else. However, if the Tier 2 strategies are not effective, meaning that they do not result in the target student being successful or able to sustain achievement, then something more intensive may be needed. This could include intensifying and individualizing the intervention by moving the student into a Tier 3 individual work setting.

SO WHAT DO I DO WITH AN ELL STUDENT AT TIER 2?

Example From Classroom Practice

Tommy and Mary seemed to respond well in the classroom when I moved nearer to them, and it only took a few reminders of my touching them on the shoulder to get back on task. But Justin, Clarence, and Irving did not respond satisfactorily to this, and I had to move to more structure for them to stay focused on the lesson at hand. Additionally, other behavior and learning problems emerged with all five of these students.

Although Tommy and Mary worked hard and learned to focus on their seatwork, they both struggled to understand and complete assignments satisfactorily. For example, in a lesson on families, Tommy and Mary did not appear able to retain the English vocabulary words (English terms for the family members and their relationship to one another) from week to week. The whole class had heard a story about families and seen a video about different families around the world. They had worked in small groups to make from clay a family of their choice and had given their little people names. They were to label each character and tell or write a short story about their group family. This was part of a larger unit on communities and led to future lessons about jobs, homes, businesses, and the like. The other members of Mary's small group all enjoyed playing with their family and could make up stories using the English vocabulary words. Mary had trouble with remembering father, mother, sister, brother, daughter, son, and so on. I had Mary's group members *model* (Strategy 76), and I had Mary and her group *role-play* (Strategy 146) their characters, emphasizing their different roles in the family. They held up signs with the different terms on them when watching another group role-play their family relationships. The vocabulary words were also given in Mary's *home language* (Strategy 91), and the group discussed in their home language the differences in usage between the way English labels these and how they are labeled in their home language (Strategy 79). We had already had a lesson on same versus different with the whole class.

In the meantime, I moved Justin, Clarence, and Irving into a small group that had the responsibility of building a community base for the other groups' homes and later businesses. In this group, I provided *guided practice* (Strategy 85) with vocabulary and with each step of their assigned tasks. Included in this lesson were quantities and English numbers. They all did better in attending to their assignments when it involved physically making something than when it came to explaining what they had done. Their small group discussed in their home language the tasks and what they were producing and why (Strategy 83). Justin, in particular, seemed to catch on to the larger purpose of the activities and became a sort of "job boss" during the construction phases of our unit. Irving and Clarence remained easily distracted from their tasks and would frequently be found wandering around the room watching what the other students were doing.

ADAPTATION AND DEVELOPMENT ISSUES AT TIER 2

59. GUIDED MEMORIES

Purpose of the Strategy

1. Build transfer skills

2. Facilitate discussion about new learning

3. Strengthen school/parent partnerships

How to Do It

At Tier 2, this strategy is done with small groups. Students tell about their homeland or family history and create booklets about their memories.

Research Base

Carrigan, 2001

What to Watch for With ELL/CLD Students

1. Students may be reluctant to describe or discuss what happened to their family during a specific time or specific event. Very difficult or painful things may have occurred for this student or family.

2. The teacher must be prepared to deal with sensitive information, should it arise, and know when not to push further for information. Only elicit information that the student is comfortable sharing at that particular point in time.

3. Students may share more as they become more comfortable in the classroom or more trusting that the information will not be used against them or their family.

60. MEDIATED STIMULI IN CLASSROOM

Purpose of the Strategy

1. Enhance ability of student to focus on learning

2. Facilitate discussion about new learning

3. Reduce distractibility

4. Reduce resistance to change

How to Do It

At Tier 2, this strategy is done with small groups. The teacher always previews new content, new materials, new sounds, and any new activity with the students. Peers provide home and community language explanations.

Research Base

Echevarria, Vogt, & Short, 2007

Feuerstein, 1986

Feuerstein & Hoffman, 1982

Gibbons, 2002

What to Watch for With ELL/CLD Students

1. Newcomers may become overly stimulated by lots of bright, new, unfamiliar, or strange objects, signs, sounds, and miscellany in their new classroom. They do not know what is important to attend to and what is not important. It is all new and exciting.

2. This is also going to impact students with undiagnosed neurological conditions that they have not yet learned to accommodate.

3. It is better to start out with less and add as students become comfortable and familiar with what is in the classroom

61. ROLE-PLAYING

Purpose of the Strategy

1. Build transfer skills

2. Develop higher tolerance

3. Build awareness of appropriate communication behaviors for school language and rules

4. Build transfer skills

5. Develop cognitive academic language

6. Develop confidence in school language

7. Reduce code-switching

How to Do It

At Tier 2, this strategy is done with small groups. Students identify a number of uncomfortable or uncertain social or formal interactions. Teacher and assistant model the appropriate and inappropriate ways to handle these kinds of interactions. Students take different roles in the interaction and practice with one another and the teacher. The teacher and assistant model the appropriate and inappropriate ways to use basic interpersonal communication and cognitive academic language in various school settings, both in and out of the classroom. Students take different roles in the interactions and practice these with one another and with the teacher. In addition, students may suggest communication situations they want specific assistance with and teacher facilitates role-plays.

Research Base

Cole, 1995; *see pages 65–66, 127–128, 132*

C. Collier, 2003; *see page 183*

J. E. Johnson, Christie, & Yawkey, 1999

Livingstone, 1983

What to Watch for With ELL/CLD Students

1. Many societies and cultures have specific beliefs and understandings about pretending to be something one is not in reality; there are cultural guidelines for make-believe, play, and assuming the role or character of someone or something.

2. Be clear that in public schools and classrooms, we sometimes are like actors in movies or television stories (although understanding that some people may think those are all real) for the purpose of illustrating or demonstrating something.

3. Be clear that they will not become the character or thing and that it is a temporary action to illustrate or demonstrate a particular interaction you want them to learn.

4. It may be easier with some students to start with puppets or drawings and then work up to individual people doing the actions.

62. SHELTERED INTERACTIONS

Purpose of the Strategy

1. Build transfer skills

2. Develop confidence in school culture interactions

3. Develop higher tolerance

4. Facilitate access of prior knowledge

How to Do It

At Tier 2, this strategy is done with small groups. The teacher develops a game or other casual group interaction activity. Teacher or specialist explains in home and community language, when possible, what is going to occur and who the students are going to meet. The home and community culture students are introduced to the school culture students and they engage in the game or activity together.

Research Base

Cloud, Genesee, & Hamayan, 2000

Cole, 1995

Echevarria et al., 2007

Echevarria & Graves, 2006

Garber-Miller, 2006

What to Watch for With ELL/CLD Students

1. It is important to have the example speakers be people with whom the students are familiar and comfortable.

2. This can be paired with role-play of school interactions.

63. TOTAL PHYSICAL RESPONSE

Purpose of the Strategy

1. Build transfer skills

2. Build awareness of appropriate communication behaviors for school language and rules

3. Develop confidence in school language and rules for academic and social interactions

4. Develop cognitive academic language

5. Reduce code-switching

6. Reduce stress for new students

How to Do It

1. At Tier 2, this strategy is done with small groups. A popular and effective way of teaching language that actively involves the students and focuses on understanding the language rather than speaking it is the total physical response (TPR) method. This method asks the students to demonstrate that they understand the new language by responding to a command with an action. At first, the teacher gives the commands and does the actions along with the student. As the student understands the vocabulary, the teacher stops doing the action and has the student do the action alone. Later, the student can give commands to other students or to the teacher.

2. The teacher and assistant model words and phrases in action in various school settings, both in and out of the classroom. For example, teaching the response to a question such as, "What is this?" or "What can you do with this?" by saying and acting out the phrases "This is a pencil," and "This pencil is used for writing on paper."

3. Total physical response begins with simple directions, creating associations between words and actions such as, "I am walking," "She is standing," "Bill is shutting the door."

4. Students take different roles in the interactions and practice these with one another and with the teacher.

Expansion: Students may suggest communication situations in which they would like specific assistance.

Research Base

Asher, 1980

C. Collier, 2003; see page 351

Law & Eckes, 2000; see pages 202–203

What to Watch for With ELL/CLD Students

1. Although this is a common beginner or newcomer strategy for use with ELL students, the teacher must still be cautious about making assumptions about CLD students' understanding of the actions required in the classroom.

2. The teacher must clearly model and act out every action required before asking students to repeat the action.

64. LEVELED ACTIVITIES

Purpose of the Strategy

1. Build awareness of learning process

2. Develop extended time spent on task

3. Develop personal control of situations

4. Improve retention

5. Develop higher tolerance

How to Do It

At Tier 2, this strategy is conducted with small groups. The teacher ensures that students with different learning needs work with the same essential ideas and use the same key skills. For example, a student having difficulty with reading still needs to make sense of the basic concepts and ideas of a story. Simultaneously, a student who is advanced in the same subject needs to find genuine challenge in working with these same concepts and ideas. Leveled activities are used so all students focus on essential understandings and skills but at different levels of complexity, abstractness, and open-endedness. This is conducted by keeping the focus of activity the same but providing routes of access at varying degrees of difficulty.

Research Base

Heacox, 2002

C. A. Tomlinson, 1999

What to Watch for With ELL/CLD Students

1. The key to integrating instruction in mixed-skill classrooms, typical of Tier 2, is the creation of or access to leveled reading, writing, or content materials. Several publishers have excellent leveled materials that can be used as models.

2. An example is books about the ecosystem in a pond. All illustrations are the same and all content is the same, but the reading level of the content in the booklets varies for the ability level of the students (e.g., Level 1, Level 2, Level 3), depending on the classroom needs.

3. For example, National Geographic publishes magazines that are coded in the upper-left corner of the cover for beginner, middle, and advanced readers. They also have topic specific books coded on the back of the cover for levels with one spot, two spots, three spots, or four spots.

65. PEER/SCHOOL ADAPTATION PROCESS SUPPORT

Purpose of the Strategy

1. Build awareness of adaptation process

2. Strengthen ability to discuss what is happening

3. Reduce anxiety and stress

How to Do It

1. At Tier 2, this strategy is done with small groups. Primary-level, successful, older students in the upper grades assist younger students around the school building and during lunch and play times.

2. At Tier 2, this strategy is done with small groups. In intermediate grades, peer support groups discuss their experiences with school adaptation and how they are dealing with culture shock. Successful students from secondary level may assist as peer support models.

3. At Tier 2, this strategy is done with small groups. In secondary grades, peer support groups discuss their experiences with school adaptation and how they are dealing with culture shock.

Research Base

Carrigan, 2001; *see pages 44–45*

What to Watch for With ELL/CLD Students

1. Students may wish to discuss their struggles only in the home language and with peers from similar backgrounds. With specific first-generation refugee, indigenous, migrant, and immigrant groups, teachers must be careful about pairing students based on their perceptions of them coming from similar language backgrounds. There can be cultural and class differences that will make the partners uncomfortable with one another.

2. The teacher must be prepared to deal with prejudice between populations where language is the same but culture, class, or racial issues may impede comfort and communication. American all togetherness may come in time, but the teacher must proceed slowly and not push.

3. Students may interact more as they become more comfortable in the classroom or more trusting that they are accepted and valued.

66. CLASSROOM AND SCHOOL SURVIVAL STRATEGIES

Purpose of the Strategy

1. Build transfer skills

2. Develop personal control of situations

3. Improve confidence in school interactions

4. Reduce distractibility

5. Reduce acting out behaviors

6. Develop confidence in cognitive academic interactions

How to Do It

1. At Tier 2, this strategy is done with small groups. The teacher and the assistant demonstrate how to get around the school and what is expected of students in various school and learning interactions.

2. In primary grades, an intermediate student, a peer, or a specialist demonstrates how to act in a given school or school culture situation. The situation is explained in home and community language, when possible, and each stage is modeled. Students then practice each stage of the interaction with familiar participants until comfortable and successful in appropriate behaviors.

3. In intermediate grades, a secondary student, a peer, or a specialist demonstrates how to act in a given school or school culture situation. The situation is explained in home and community language, when possible, and each stage is modeled. Students then practice each stage of the interaction with familiar participants until comfortable and successful in appropriate behaviors.

4. In secondary grades, an older peer or a specialist demonstrates how to act in a given school or school culture situation. The situation is explained in home and community language, when possible, and each stage is modeled. Students then practice each stage of the interaction with familiar participants until comfortable and successful in appropriate behaviors.

Research Base

Becker & Hamayan, 2008

Brownlie & King, 2000; *see pages 59–74*

Law & Eckes, 2000; *see pages 65–70*

What to Watch for With ELL/CLD Students

1. Particular social groups and cultures have different expectations of adult and children when it comes to learning. This is a learned difference between cultures. The teacher needs to be aware that the expectations in an American school may need to be taught directly to CLD students and not just assume that they are understood.

2. One way to introduce the idea of behavior and strategies specific to your classroom is to ask students about how their parents have them behave at home or how they learned playing games. This can then be expanded to the idea of acting appropriately in a classroom.

3. Demonstrate all of the desired behaviors and strategies. Some role-play may be helpful. Examples of inappropriate behaviors may be used with caution.

67. GUIDED PRACTICE AND PLANNED INTERACTIONS WITH DIFFERENT SPEAKERS

Purpose of the Strategy

1. Build transfer skills

2. Build awareness of appropriate school language and rules with communication behaviors

3. Develop cognitive academic language

4. Develop personal control of situations

5. Reduce anxiety in social/academic interactions

6. Reduce response fatigue

How to Do It

1. At Tier 2, this strategy is done with small groups. A peer or a specialist demonstrates how to act or speak in a given school culture situation. The situation is explained in home and community language, when possible, and each stage is modeled.

2. Representatives of school language and rules who are familiar to the learners come into the classroom and act out the situation with the instructor. Students then practice each stage of the interaction with these familiar participants until comfortable with the interaction.

Expansion: Students select new interactions they wish to learn.

Research Base

Cole, 1995

Haneda, 2008

Reggy-Mamo, 2008

Ross, 1971

What to Watch for With ELL/CLD Students

1. It is important to have the example speakers be people with whom the students are familiar and comfortable.

2. This can be paired with role-play of school interactions.

68. CONCURRENT LANGUAGE DEVELOPMENT/ ACQUISITION SESSIONS FOR STUDENTS AND PARENTS

Purpose of the Strategy

1. Improve confidence in home, community, and school culture interactions

2. Strengthen school/parent partnerships

3. Build awareness of appropriate communication behaviors for school language and rules

4. Reduce culture shock

5. Reduce anxiety and stress

How to Do It

At Tier 2, this strategy can be conducted within small groups. Sessions may be provided at a time selected by parents. Parents and adults participate in English as a second-language instruction in one room while the students receive home and community language instruction (when possible) and academic content support in another room. After the formal class period, the groups reunite and parents practice bilingual educational games they can play at home with their children.

Research Base

Brownlie & King, 2000

Cole, 1995

Law & Eckes, 2000

What to Watch for With ELL/CLD Students

1. This is most effective with large communities of one language and more difficult to implement where there are separate families or small groups speaking various and diverse languages.

2. In multilanguage, family communities, focus can remain on English as a second language with first-language support offered for as many languages as you have access to bilingual personnel.

69. ASSESSMENT

Purpose of the Strategy

1. Measure performance and set goals and objectives

2. Establish baseline performance levels

3. Establish target goals

How to Do It

At Tier 2, this strategy is done with small groups. An example would be for a geography lesson on the United States, determine the individual student's general knowledge of the North American continent, countries bordering the United States, the difference between states and countries, how these boundaries are demarcated, and the like. What does the student know about the geography of his or her country of origin, or city or state? Determine key vocabulary and sentence structures the student needs to master for the lesson, building on structures and vocabulary that the student has already mastered.

Research Base

Shores & Chester, 2009

Walker, Carta, Greenwood, & Buzhardt, 2008

What to Watch for With ELL/CLD Students

1. Non-English speaking or very limited English proficient (LEP) students will need interpreters and lots of modeling and demonstration of how to take a test and how to respond in assessment activities.

2. Explanations and example products should be given in the students' most proficient language before moving into English-only assessment situations. If this is not done, all assessments will become essentially measures of language proficiency and not assessment of content achievement.

70. CROSS-CULTURAL COUNSELING FOR FAMILIES

Purpose of the Strategy

1. Develop personal control of situations
2. Enhance student interaction with family during transition
3. Facilitate family adaptation to new community
4. Reduce anxiety and stress

How to Do It

At Tier 2, this strategy is done with small groups. A specialist with training in cross-cultural stress responses and culture shock provides family counseling and guidance.

Research Base

Brownlie & King, 2000

Carrigan, 2001

Law & Eckes, 2000

What to Watch for With ELL/CLD Students

1. Many cultures have adverse reactions to "official" personnel getting involved with the family and particularly with someone telling them how to raise their children.

2. The specialist facilitating the counseling must be trained not only in cross-cultural techniques but also be familiar with the particular culture and language of the family being assisted.

71. FAMILY-CENTERED LEARNING ACTIVITY

Purpose of the Strategy

1. Build awareness of academic expectations
2. Build awareness of appropriate school language and rules for academic and social behaviors
3. Reduce anxiety and stress
4. Strengthen school-parent partnerships

How to Do It

1. At Tier 2, this strategy is done with small groups. Evening learning activities are offered to families centered on specific content areas.

2. For example, family math, family computer, and family literacy nights offering several interactive activities provide an educational and fun setting for all. Parents benefit from home and community language explanations, when possible, about education outcomes and how they can help students at home.

Research Base

D. C. Garcia, Hasson, Hoffman, Paneque, & Pelaez, 1996

Sink, Parkhill, Marshall, Norwood, & Parkhill, 2005

What to Watch for With ELL/CLD Students

1. It is important to tie these extracurricular activities into general classroom content areas. These can be a point of academic content support by offering the activities in the home language of participants as well as having bilingual personnel available.

2. The Mexican government offers free materials and textbooks that can supplement these activities for Spanish-speaking families. Contact the Mexican embassy or consulate closest to you to find out more. An example of what the Mexican government offers is National Council for Lifelong Learning and Work Skills (CONEVyT). CONEVyT was created in 2002 in Mexico to provide primary and secondary education and training to adults (15 and older) left behind in education in that country as well as migrant populations living in the United States. Through an online portal and a network of Plazas Comunitarias where direct instruction, assessment, and varied materials can be found, both U.S. and Mexican governments make educational support available for anyone willing to learn or to teach. For more information go to www.conevyt.org.mx.

72. GUIDED PRACTICE WITH SERVICE PERSONNEL FROM SCHOOL/GOVERNMENT AGENCIES

Purpose of the Strategy

1. Improve confidence in official interactions

2. Strengthen school-parent partnerships

3. Reduce anxiety and stress

How to Do It

At Tier 2, this strategy is done with small groups. A peer or a specialist demonstrates how to act in a given situation. The situation is explained in home and community language, when possible, and each step is modeled. Parents may suggest situations with which they want assistance. Parents, students, and community members then practice each stage of the interaction, taking different roles each time until comfortable and successful in appropriate behaviors.

Research Base

Carrigan, 2001; see pages 54–58

What to Watch for With ELL/CLD Students

1. Depending on their particular history, parents and community members from particular cultures may have had very negative relationships with government agencies and representatives in their country or region of origin.

2. Personnel working with diverse families need extensive training in how to be most effective cross-culturally while at the same time sensitive to and responsive to the differences in specific speech communities.

3. Families and parents from diverse communities may need preparation and training in how to interact with government officials and representatives.

4. They may also need assistance in how to ask for help, how to request interpreters, how to access services, and the like.

73. SURVIVAL STRATEGIES FOR PARENTS/FAMILIES

Purpose of the Strategy

1. Build transfer skills

2. Build awareness of appropriate behaviors for school language and rules

3. Develop confidence in school culture interactions

4. Develop personal control of situations

5. Reduce culture shock

How to Do It

At Tier 2, this strategy is done with small groups. A liaison or a specialist identifies basic rules of social and formal interaction that parents will need to know immediately. Parents may identify situations where they have made mistakes or where they would like assistance. The facilitator and parents discuss situations and what is expected in these situations. Parents practice and discuss their responses and strategies in these situations, with opportunity for student input.

Research Base

Carrigan, 2001

C. Collier, 2003

What to Watch for With ELL/CLD Students

1. Particular social groups and cultures have different expectations of adults and children when it comes to being accountable for task completion. This is a learned difference between cultures. The teacher needs to be aware that the expectations in an American school may need to be taught directly to CLD students and should not assume that they are understood.

2. One way to introduce the idea of behavior and strategies specific to your classroom is to ask students about how their parents have them behave at home or how they learned to play games. This can then be expanded to the idea of acting appropriately in a classroom.

3. Demonstrate all of the desired behaviors and strategies. Some role-play may be helpful. Examples of inappropriate behaviors may be used with caution.

74. VIDEOTAPES AND BOOKLETS ABOUT NORTH AMERICAN SCHOOLS, COMMUNITIES, SOCIAL SERVICE PROVIDERS, AND LAWS

Purpose of the Strategy

1. Build awareness of appropriate academic behavior

2. Build transfer skills

3. Reinforce school-parent partnership

4. Reduce culture shock

5. Develop personal control of situations

How to Do It

At Tier 2, this strategy is done with small groups. Groups of students and/or their families view videos developed locally or available from national organizations and others about public schools and about interacting with service personnel. These are best shown in home and community language and with a facilitator. Students are encouraged to discuss with their families what they see and experience in school.

Research Base

Carrigan, 2001; see pages 54–58

Cochran-Smith & Zeichner, 2005

Kamps et al., 2007

Koskinen & Blum, 1984

Prasad, 2005

Wood & Algozzine, 1994

Wood & Harmon, 2001

Zutell & Rasinski, 1991

What to Watch for With ELL/CLD Students

1. Always introduce school expectations and rules to ELL and CLD students by explaining them in their most proficient language.

2. ELL/CLD students who have had prior schooling might be asked what sort of rules and expectations they were familiar with and that could become part of the classroom routine.

3. There are some excellent locally produced materials about school and service options within and for specific communities. The local school district may keep these in the media center. They may also be available through a local college or university.

4. The teacher should be aware of the diversity of reaction to depictions of official or government agencies and laws. These can raise the *affective filter* or emotional response of both students and parents to discussions about services.

5. Always have interpreters available for in-depth discussion of the materials presented.

75. VIDEOTAPES ABOUT INTERACTION PATTERNS IN NORTH AMERICA

Purpose of the Strategy

1. Build awareness of school culture expectations

2. Develop familiarity with school language and rules for academic and social interaction patterns

3. Reduce culture shock

How to Do It

At Tier 2, this strategy is done with small groups. Groups of students and/or their families view videos developed locally or available from Intercultural Press and others about life in North America and about interacting with North Americans. It is best if they are shown in the home and community language and with an experienced facilitator.

Research Base

Cochran-Smith & Zeichner, 2005

Prasad, 2005

What to Watch for With ELL/CLD Students

1. There are many dialects of spoken English and differences of opinion about what is the proper dialect to use as the model for ELL/CLD students.

2. The teacher should be aware of the diversity of reaction to specific dialects of spoken English in North America and be prepared to address expressions of prejudice or value judgments about certain speakers shown on the videotapes.

3. The most practical way to deal with this is to prescreen the videos and select segments that most closely represent the dialects common in your local communities plus a few as examples of the diversity that exists in our country.

76. MODELING

Purpose of the Strategy

1. Reduce code-switching

2. Develop cognitive academic language

3. Build transfer skills

4. Develop content knowledge foundation

How to Do It

At Tier 2, this strategy is done with small groups. The teacher models academic responses and expectations. The situation is explained in home and community language when possible, and each response and expectation is modeled. Students then practice each response and interaction until comfortable and successful.

Research Base

Cole, 1995

Tovani, 2000

What to Watch for With ELL/CLD Students

1. Remember that some ELL and CLD students have had very little experience with school or with being with people outside of their family or culture. They may not know what action you are modeling if it is something they have never experienced or seen.

2. The desired action and response need to be explained in the students' most proficient language.

COMMUNICATION ISSUES AT TIER 2

77. ACADEMIC LANGUAGE INSTRUCTION AND TRANSITION

Purpose of the Strategy

1. Develop cognitive academic language

2. Build transfer skills

3. Reduce code-switching

How to Do It

At Tier 2, this strategy is done with small groups. The teacher working with student peers or an assistant discusses the language of learning and the classroom. Bilingual posters and signs about academic language are posted and referred to regularly. Periodically, the teacher will stop a lesson in various content areas and ask students what is being discussed and how the material is being presented as well as expected academic behaviors.

Research Base

Law & Eckes, 2000

What to Watch for With ELL/CLD Students

1. Proficiency in using and understanding academic language will develop and grow with exposure and practice.

2. Some ELL/CLD students will have limited or no prior experience in classrooms, instructional settings, or school buildings and will need step-by-step guidance in the vocabulary and language of instruction and the classroom environment.

78. BILINGUAL AIDE

Purpose of the Strategy

1. Develop cognitive academic language

2. Build transfer skills

3. Build awareness of appropriate academic behavior

4. Strengthen knowledge of academic content

How to Do It

At Tier 2, this strategy is done with small groups. An instructional assistant or aide is available in the classroom to assist ELL/LEP students in home and community language when possible, regarding content instruction, academic behavior, and communication. The instructional assistant coordinates with the teacher in presenting content area instruction to all students. The aide must be trained in providing bilingual assistance and must plan lessons with the teacher.

Research Base

Cole, 1995

E. E. Garcia, 2005

Kovelman, Baker, & Petitto, 2008

What to Watch for With ELL/CLD Students

1. When this strategy is used for sequential translation (i.e., the teacher speaks and then the aide speaks), ELL/LEP students may become dependent on the bilingual aide and remain unengaged while the teacher speaks in English, waiting for the interpretation and explanation by the bilingual aide.

2. Better use would be for the aide to prepare the ELL/LEP students for the English lesson by reviewing key vocabulary words, explaining what will be occurring, and discussing what the teacher's expectations will be for the students' performance. This would then be followed by the teacher presenting the lesson in English. Students would be given the opportunity to ask for specific clarification only during the lesson.

3. Students could work on their projects subsequent to the English lesson with the assistance of the bilingual aide as needed. Content discussion and clarification should be in the students' most proficient language while they are preparing their task or project for presentation in English with the rest of the class.

79. BILINGUAL PEERS

Purpose of the Strategy

1. Develop cognitive academic language

2. Develop basic interpersonal communication

3. Build transfer skills

4. Develop content knowledge foundation

How to Do It

At Tier 2, this strategy is done with small groups. Home and community language peers who are more proficient in English assist home and community language students in specific content area lessons and activities. The peer assistants are given training in being a tutor, with guidelines about how to facilitate learning without doing another's work, how to translate appropriately, and how to monitor for understanding.

Research Base

E. E. Garcia, 2005

Kovelman et al., 2008

What to Watch for With ELL/CLD Students

1. With specific first-generation refugee, indigenous, migrant, and immigrant groups, teachers must be careful about pairing students based on their perceptions of them coming from similar language backgrounds. There can be cultural and class differences that will make the partners uncomfortable with one another.

2. The teacher must be prepared to deal with prejudice between populations where language is the same but culture, class, or racial issues may impede comfort and communication. American all togetherness may come in time, but the teacher must proceed slowly and not push.

3. Students may interact more as they become more comfortable in the classroom or more trusting that they are accepted and valued.

80. BILINGUAL TEXTS

Purpose of the Strategy

1. Develop cognitive academic language

2. Build language transfer skills

3. Strengthen knowledge of academic content

4. Develop confidence in academic interactions

How to Do It

1. At Tier 2, this strategy is done with small groups. Duplicate or parallel texts are available in English and home and community language of students for all content areas. Reference texts are available in English, bilingual, or home and community language format. Students are shown how and when to access the texts.

2. One source for bilingual materials in Spanish is the Colorín Colorado Web site and organization (http://www .colorincolorado.org).

3. Another source is the CONEVyT. CONEVyT was created in 2002 in Mexico to provide primary and secondary education and training to adults (15 and older) left behind in education in that country as well as migrant populations living in the United States. Through an online portal and a network of Plazas Comunitarias where direct instruction, assessment, and varied materials can be found, both U.S. and Mexican governments make educational support available for anyone willing to learn or to teach. For more information go to www.conevyt.org.mx.

Research Base

Cole, 1995

E. E. Garcia, 2005

Hu & Commeyras, 2008

Kovelman et al., 2008

Ma, 2008

What to Watch for With ELL/CLD Students

1. Not all ELL/CLD students are literate in their home or community language.

2. Picture dictionaries with bilingual words and definitions are usually the most practical reference to use with younger, less educated students.

81. BILINGUAL VIDEOTAPES ABOUT NORTH AMERICAN SPEECH

Purpose of the Strategy

1. Build awareness of appropriate social and academic language

2. Build transfer skills

3. Develop confidence in school language and rules for academic and social interactions

How to Do It

At Tier 2, this strategy is done with small groups. Groups of students and/or their families view videos developed locally or available from Intercultural Press and other publishers about North American idioms, communication structures, and expectations. They are best shown bilingually and with an experienced facilitator.

Research Base

Cole, 1995

C. Collier, 2003

What to Watch for With ELL/CLD Students

1. There are many dialects of spoken English and differences of opinion about what is the proper dialect to use as the model for ELL/CLD students.

2. The teacher should be aware of the diversity of reaction to specific dialects of spoken English in North America and be prepared to address expressions of prejudice or value judgments about certain speakers shown on the videotapes.

3. The most practical way to deal with this is to prescreen the videos and select segments that most closely represent the dialects common in your local communities plus a few as examples of the diversity that exists in our country.

82. ACTIVE PROCESSING

Purpose of the Strategy

1. Build awareness of learning

2. Develop academic language

3. Develop personal control of situations

4. Facilitate access of prior knowledge

5. Reduce low-persistence behaviors

How to Do It

1. At Tier 2, this strategy is done with small groups. Students work through a task aloud, naming each step and asking themselves the appropriate questions for the task. Steps for students to follow in implementing the strategy are the following.

What is my task?
What do I need to do to complete my task?
How will I know my task is done correctly?
How will I monitor the implementation?
How do I know the task is completed correctly?

2. For example, suppose you want your students to complete a new unit in language arts about bears in fact and fiction. Some of your diverse learners are not familiar with the concept of fact versus fiction as used on our society and have no words in their native language for this distinction; also several of them have little or incomplete prior schooling. You could modify your preparation for this unit by integrating the active processing strategy into the lessons. Begin having the students in your class speak with one another in small groups about what they know about bears and other animals following the steps in active processing. Do this within the context of reinforcement and review of prior content the students have

successfully accomplished until the students are familiar with the active processing process itself. Then introduce the concept of fact versus fiction to your class. Have them discuss how these differ using real-life experiences from their homes or communities. Use visual and physical examples of the concept, such as a photograph of a car and a sketch or drawing of a car, a realistic portrait of a child and an abstract painting of a child, a picture of astronauts on the moon and a picture of children playing on the moon, and the like to ensure that students are aware of what is involved. Have students discuss examples from their communities or lives. Discuss how to tell the difference and what is involved in the process (Step 1 of active processing, "What is my task?"). Have the groups discuss what they will need to compare and contrast fact from fiction and what actions are involved. Have those who are more successful describe the process and what it was like for them to learn it. Talk about the importance of learning this skill and discuss the steps involved. Have your students work in groups to develop a set of rules outlining the steps to follow (Step 2 of active processing, "What do I need to do to complete my task?"). Discuss what an acceptable performance might be for various levels of skill and knowledge. Explain some of the strategies that help students be successful at separating fact from fiction. Discuss how to check for the accuracy and the steps involved (Step 3 of active processing, "How will I know my task is done correctly?"). Provide suggestions for relieving stress during the lesson and ideas for self-monitoring their progress through the different steps of the process (Step 4 of active processing, "How will I monitor the implementation?"). Discuss ways to identify when it is time to move to another question or example and what to do when they have finished each set of comparisons (Step 5 of active processing, "How do I know the task is completed?").

Research Base

Cole, 1995

Collier, 2003

Law & Eckes, 2000

Tovani, 2000

What to Watch for With ELL/CLD Students

1. The strategy preparation can be done in the native language or dialect of the students to assure their understanding of your expectations and their task prior to carrying the assignment out in English or other communication mode.

2. Students who are less proficient in English will need guidance in using the steps of active processing; the process can be explained and practiced in the students' most proficient language before going on in English.

3. Active processing can be used in any language of instruction and in any content area or age level.

83. ORAL DISCUSSIONS

Purpose of the Strategy

1. Reduce code-switching

2. Develop cognitive academic language

3. Develop basic interpersonal communication

4. Build transfer skills

5. Develop confidence in school language and rules for academic and social interactions

How to Do It

At Tier 2, this strategy is done with small groups. Target students are given opportunities to discuss all aspects of content lessons and to prepare for assessment situations. They are encouraged to hold discussions in both home and community language and English whenever they need to clarify content or directions. Specific homogeneous and heterogeneous discussion groups may be established and used alternately in varied content-focused activities.

Research Base

C. Collier, 2003; *see pages 281, 358*

Flowerdew & Peacock, 2001

Law & Eckes, 2000; *see pages199–201*

Youb, 2008

What to Watch for With ELL/CLD Students

1. Some teachers are threatened or concerned about students speaking to one another when they do not understand what they are saying. To assure teachers that the students are indeed on task, the teacher can always have these oral discussions focus on specific tasks, with worksheets or other task production involved that they can see is being attended to.

2. The teacher can also have bilingual student monitors report on what was discussed after these activities.

84. CROSS-CULTURAL COMMUNICATION STRATEGIES

Purpose of the Strategy

1. Build transfer skills

2. Build awareness of appropriate communication behaviors for school language and rules

3. Develop confidence in school language and rules for academic and social interactions

How to Do It

At Tier 2, this strategy is done with small groups. The teacher models the cross-cultural communication strategies such as reflection, proxemics, latency, and active listening. Students and the teacher practice using these strategies in a variety of interactions.

Research Base

Croom & Davis, 2006

Gibbons, 2002

Trudeau & Harle, 2006

What to Watch for With ELL/CLD Students

1. All cultures have different mores about how close you can stand or sit next to another person (proxemics), who or what you may touch, how much time should elapse before you speak after another person (latency), and so on. The teacher should become familiar with these differences regarding the students in this classroom.

2. The strategy of reflection can look like mockery and mimicry if not done with sensitivity. The goal is to reflect—not imitate—the mode of the speaker.

85. GUIDED PRACTICE AND PLANNED INTERACTIONS WITH DIFFERENT SPEAKERS

Purpose of the Strategy

1. Build transfer skills

2. Build awareness of appropriate school language and rules for communication behaviors

3. Develop confidence in school language and rules for academic and social interactions

4. Develop cognitive academic language

5. Develop personal control of situations

6. Reduce anxiety in social/academic interactions

7. Reduce response fatigue

How to Do It

At Tier 2, this strategy is done with small groups. A peer or a specialist demonstrates how to act or speak in a given school culture situation. The situation is explained in home and community language when possible, and each part of the situation is modeled. Representatives of school language and rules who are familiar to the learners come into the classroom and act out the situation with the instructor. Students then practice each part of the interaction with these familiar participants until comfortable with the interaction.

Expansion: Students select new interactions they wish to learn.

Research Base

Cole, 1995

Haneda, 2008

Reggy-Mamo, 2008

Ross, 1971

What to Watch for With ELL/CLD Students

1. It is important to have the example speakers be people with whom the students are familiar and comfortable.

2. This can be paired with role-play of school interactions.

86. ROLE-PLAYING IN SOCIAL AND ACADEMIC LANGUAGE DEVELOPMENT

Purpose of the Strategy

1. Build transfer skills

2. Build awareness of appropriate communication behaviors for school language and rules

3. Develop cognitive academic language

4. Develop confidence in school language and rules for academic and social interactions

5. Reduce code-switching

How to Do It

At Tier 2, this strategy is done with small groups. The teacher and assistant model the appropriate and inappropriate ways to use basic interpersonal communication and cognitive academic language in various school settings, both in and out of the classroom. Students take different roles in the interactions and practice with one another and with the teacher. Students may suggest communication situations they want specific assistance with and teacher facilitates role-plays.

Research Base

J. E. Johnson et al., 1999

Kim & Kellogg, 2007

Livingstone, 1983

Magos & Politi, 2008

What to Watch for With ELL/CLD Students

1. Many societies and cultures have specific beliefs and understandings about pretending to be something one is not in reality; there are cultural guidelines for make-believe, play, and assuming the role or character of someone or something.

2. Be clear that in public schools and classrooms, we sometimes are like actors in movies or television stories (although understanding that some people may think those are all real) for the purpose of illustrating or demonstrating something.

3. Be clear that they will not become the character or thing and that it is a temporary action to illustrate or demonstrate a particular interaction you want them to learn.

4. It may be easier with some students to start with puppets or drawings and then work up to individual people doing the actions.

87. PEER TUTORING

Purpose of the Strategy

1. Develop cognitive academic language

2. Develop basic interpersonal communication

3. Build transfer skills

4. Ensure learning gains are experienced by both students

5. Improve retention

6. Develop higher tolerance for ambiguity

7. Utilize prior knowledge

8. Develop thinking/planning skills

9. Develop positive peer relationships

10. Develop content knowledge foundation

How to Do It

1. At Tier 2, this strategy is done with small groups. Home and community language peers who are more proficient in English assist home and community language students in specific content area lessons and activities. The peers are given training in being a tutor, with guidelines about how to facilitate learning without doing another's work, how to translate appropriately, and how to monitor for understanding.

Expansion: Students develop code of ethics and their own guidelines for tutoring.

2. Students assist in the classroom by working with other students. Tutors may receive training about objectives, reinforcement, and so on. A student who has mastered a list of sight words or math facts presents these items on flash cards to another student needing assistance in this area. Students help other learners of similar or different ages in the classroom to complete assignments or other responsibilities. This strategy has been shown to provide learning gains for both the tutor and the tutee, and it allows the teacher to work closely with more students. The teacher should always be clear about the objectives of the tutoring session and hold the students accountable for their work.

3. For example, the tutoring students share their reports with the tutees. In preparation, the tutors identify key concepts and vocabulary used in the report and present these on tag board cards to the tutees. The tutees tell the tutors in their own words what they understood from the report.

4. Home and community language peers who are more proficient in English assist home and community language students in specific content area lessons and activities. The peers are given training in being a tutor, with guidelines about how to facilitate learning without doing another's work, how to translate appropriately, and how to monitor for understanding.

Expansion: Peer helpers develop a code of ethics and their own guidelines for tutoring.

5. As students become more comfortable, they may be paired with more diverse peers and tutors.

Research Base

Carrigan, 2001; see pages 44–45

Cole, 1995

What to Watch for With ELL/CLD Students

1. With specific first-generation refugee, indigenous, migrant, and immigrant groups, teachers must be careful about pairing students based on their perceptions of them coming from similar language backgrounds. There can be cultural and class differences that will make the partners uncomfortable with one another.

2. The teacher must be prepared to deal with prejudice between populations where language is the same but culture, class, or racial issues may impede comfort and communication. American all togetherness may come in time, but the teacher must proceed slowly and not push.

3. Students may interact more as they become more comfortable in the classroom or more trusting that they are accepted and valued.

88. SHELTERED INSTRUCTION

Purpose of the Strategy

1. Reduce distractibility

2. Develop cognitive academic language proficiency

3. Develop content area skills

4. Develop personal control of situations

How to Do It

At Tier 2, this strategy is done with small groups. The teacher always presents lessons with concrete, physical models and demonstrations of both content and expected performance. Language is simplified and content focused.

Expansion: Students are encouraged to discuss lesson in home and community language and work in small groups on content activities.

Research Base

Cole, 1995

Echevarria et al., 2007

Echevarria & Graves, 2006

What to Watch for With ELL/CLD Students

1. Building familiarity is critical for the success of this strategy. Not all ELL/CLD students will know what the objects or models represent.

2. The teacher will need to introduce the models or objects in full-scale representations or use the actual items to build a true understanding. Only after students have actually seen, felt, smelled, and possibly tasted an apple will they respond to a picture of an apple.

89. SHELTERED INTERACTIONS

Purpose of the Strategy

1. Develop higher tolerance

2. Facilitate access to prior knowledge

3. Build transfer skills

4. Develop confidence in school culture interactions

How to Do It

At Tier 2, this strategy is done with small groups. The teacher develops a game or other casual group interaction activity. A teacher or a specialist explains in home and community language when possible what is going to occur and who the students are going to meet. The home and community culture students are introduced to the school culture students, and they engage in the game or activity together.

Research Base

Cloud et al., 2000

Cole, 1995

Echevarria et al., 2007

Echevarria & Graves, 2006

Garber-Miller, 2006

What to Watch for With ELL/CLD Students

1. It is important to have the interaction speakers be people with whom the students are familiar and comfortable.

2. This can be paired with role-play of school interactions.

90. SHELTERED LANGUAGE

Purpose of the Strategy

1. Develop cognitive academic language proficiency

2. Develop content area skills

3. Reduce distractibility

How to Do It

At Tier 2, this strategy is done with small groups. The teacher presents lessons with concrete models and demonstrations of both content and expected performance. Language is simplified and content focused.

Research Base

Cloud et al., 2000

Echevarria, 1995

Echevarria et al., 2007

Gibbons, 2002

Hansen-Thomas, 2008

Short & Echevarria, 2004

What to Watch for With ELL/CLD Students

1. Building familiarity is critical for the success of this strategy. Not all ELL/CLD students will know what the objects or models represent.

2. The teacher will need to introduce the models or objects in full-scale representations or use the actual items to build a true understanding. Only after students have actually seen, felt, smelled, and possibly tasted an apple will they respond to a picture of an apple.

LITERACY ISSUES AT TIER 2

91. BILINGUAL TEXTS

Purpose of the Strategy

1. Develop cognitive academic language

2. Build language transfer skills

3. Strengthen knowledge of academic content

4. Develop confidence in academic interactions

How to Do It

1. At Tier 2, this strategy is done with small groups. Duplicate or parallel texts are available in English and home and community language of students for all content areas. Reference texts are available in English, bilingual, or home and community language format. Students are shown how and when to access the texts.

2. One source for bilingual materials in Spanish is the Colorín Colorado Web site and organization, (http://www.colorincolorado.org).

3.   Another source is the CONEVyT. CONEVyT was created in 2002 in Mexico to provide primary and secondary education and training to adults (15 and older) left behind in education in that country as well as migrant populations living in the United States. Through an online portal and a network of Plazas Comunitarias where direct instruction, assessment, and varied materials can be found, both U.S. and Mexican governments make educational support available for anyone willing to learn or to teach. For more information go to www.conevyt.org.mx.

Research Base

Cole, 1995

 E. E. Garcia, 2005

Hu & Commeyras, 2008

Kovelman et al., 2008

Ma, 2008

What to Watch for With ELL/CLD Students

1.   Not all ELL/CLD students are literate in their home or community language.

2.   Picture dictionaries with bilingual words and definitions are usually the most practical reference to use with younger, less educated students.

92. GUIDED READING AND WRITING IN HOME AND COMMUNITY LANGUAGE

Purpose of the Strategy

1. Improve motivation

2. Minimize behavior problems

3. Build transfer skills

4. Develop confidence in school language and rules for academic and social interactions

5. Reduce code-switching

6. Develop cognitive academic language

How to Do It

At Tier 2, this strategy is done with small groups. The teacher directs advanced-fluency student to lead a guided reading or writing activity in the home and community language. Students can reread parts of a story in pairs after the directed reading activity rather than have one student read while the others all listen. Students then write summaries of what they have read. Writing can be in either home and community language or English. During this time, the students have a chance to help one another. Advanced-fluency students can dramatize and create dialogue to illustrate the action.

Research Base

Cole, 1995; see pages 150–152

Haneda, 2008

Reggy-Mamo, 2008

Ross, 1971

Strickland, Ganske, & Monroe, 2002; see page 217

What to Watch for With ELL/CLD Students

1. Not all ELL/CLD students are literate in their home or community language.

2. Picture dictionaries with bilingual words and definitions are usually the most practical reference to use with younger, less educated students.

93. WRITING STRATEGIES—TOWER

Purpose of the Strategy

1. Build awareness of learning

2. Develop personal control of situations

3. Develop thinking and planning skills

4. Improve access to prior knowledge

5. Reduce off-task behaviors

6. Strengthen language development

How to Do It

1. At Tier 2, this strategy is done with small groups. TOWER provides a structure for completing initial and final drafts of written reports. It may be used effectively with the COPS proofreading strategy structure.

2. The steps in COPS are

    Capitalization
    Overall appearance
    Punctuation
    Spelling

3. To help the students remember the steps in TOWER, the teacher can provide the students with a printed form with the letters T, O, W, E, R down the left side and their meaning next to each letter.

4. The steps in TOWER are

    Think
    Order ideas
    Write
    Edit
    Rewrite

Research Base

Cole, 1995

Ellis & Colvert, 1996

Ellis & Lenz, 1987

Goldsworthy, 2003

What to Watch for With ELL/CLD Students

1. Newcomers will need to have the TOWER steps modeled and explained in their most proficient language before they can proceed independently.

2. Students can be paired with partners who are slightly more bilingual than they are to facilitate their learning of this process.

94. WRITING STRATEGIES—DEFENDS

Purpose of the Strategy

Assist learners to defend a particular position in a written assignment

How to Do It

1. At Tier 2, this strategy is done with small groups. The DEFENDS writing strategy framework provides a structure for competing initial and final drafts of written reports.

2. It may be used effectively with the COPS proofreading strategy structure.

3. The steps in COPS are

Capitalization
Overall appearance
Punctuation
Spelling

4. To help the students remember the steps in DEFENDS, the teacher can provide the students with a printed form with the letters D, E, F, E, N, D, S down the left side and their meaning beside each letter.

5. The steps in DEFENDS are

Decide on a specific position
Examine own reasons for this position
Form list of points explaining each reason
Expose position in first sentence of written task
Note each reason and associated points
Drive home position in last sentence
Search for and correct any errors

Research Base

Ellis & Colvert, 1996

Ellis & Lenz, 1987

Goldsworthy, 2003

What to Watch for With ELL/CLD Students

1. Newcomers will need to have the DEFENDS steps modeled and explained in their most proficient language before they can proceed independently.

2. Students can be paired with partners who are slightly more bilingual than they are to facilitate their learning this process.

95. VISUALIZATION

Purpose of the Strategy

1. Develop higher tolerance

2. Develop thinking and planning skills

3. Improve mnemonic retrieval

4. Improve retention

How to Do It

1. At Tier 2, this strategy is done with small groups. Students put small red stop signs at the end of sentences in an assigned reading. As they read the passage, they stop at each sign and answer questions about the passage. They then make a picture in their mind of what the passage means. This is repeated for each subsequent passage with the mental pictures forming a moving visualization or motion picture of what the passage means. (I usually remind students to think of TV shows.) This visualization strategy can also be used with other content activities, in science and social studies for example. Steps for students to follow in implementing this strategy

> Where do I stop?
> Who is doing what, where, how, and why?
> What do I see in my mind?
> How does this all go together?

2. When applying the visualization strategy, students work through problems or tasks using the sequence of self-monitoring questions.

3. Suppose you are having your students read, *The Story of Ferdinand* by Munro Leaf (2000). You would have students work in pairs or in small mixed-skill groups as they read this story together. They would help put small red Post-it circles at the end of each sentence or at the end of two sentences, depending on their skill level (Step 1 of rehearsal, "Where should I stop to think?"). Suppose one group was reading this passage:

> All the other bulls that had grown up with him in the same pasture would fight each other all day.● They would butt each other and stick each other with their horns.● What they wanted most of all was to be picked to fight at the bullfights in Madrid.● But not Ferdinand—he still liked to sit just quietly under the cork tree and smell the flowers (pp. 10–12).●

4. Students would take turns reading aloud to one another. The first reader would read up to the first red spot and stop. The students would then review the six *W* questions about what had just been read (Step 2 of rehearsal, "Who is doing what, where, when, how, and why?"). Who = the other bulls, what = fight each other, where = in the pasture, when = all day. As this is the first sentence, the readers do not yet know the answers to all the questions (how and why = don't know yet). After answering the questions, the group will next take turns telling the others how they visualize this sentence (Step 3 of rehearsal, "What picture do I see in my mind regarding these?"). The picture in the book shows the bulls gazing up at a poster about the bullfights in Madrid, so they will have to use their imagination about what it might look like to see these young bulls play fighting. They will then go on to read the next sentence and repeat Steps 2 and 3; this time adding Step 4. Who = the bulls, what = fight each other, where = in the pasture, when = all day, how = butt each other and stick each other with their horns, why = still don't know. They can now expand their first imaginative picture of these bulls by adding some action to the movie they are making in their minds (Step 5 of rehearsal, "What do I see when I put the pictures from each stop together?"). The group goes on the next sentence and repeats Steps 2, 3, 4, and 5. Who = the young bulls, what = fighting each other, where = in the pasture, how = butting heads, why = to be picked to fight in Madrid. They expand their visualization to showing the longing of the young bulls while they are fighting. They then read the final sentence and complete to movie in their minds. Who = the young bulls and Ferdinand, what = the young bulls

fighting and Ferdinand sitting, where = fighting in the pasture while Ferdinand is under the cork tree, how = fighting by butting their heads while Ferdinand is smelling flowers, why = the young bulls want to be picked to fight in Madrid but Ferdinand doesn't want to do anything but smell the flowers.

5. The use of the visualization strategy will slow down impulsive learners, reinforce reflective habits, and guide students to a more accurate understanding of what they are reading.

Research Base

Harwell, 2001

Klingner, Vaughn, & Boardman, 2007

Naughton, 2008

B. Tomlinson, 1998

Tovani, 2000

What to Watch for With ELL/CLD Students

1. Students with limited school experience will not know what visualization means and will need to have direct instruction in the vocabulary and actions expected.

2. This can be introduced in the primary language and examples given from literature and art with which the students are more familiar.

96. READING STRATEGIES—RIDER

Purpose of the Strategy

1. Build transfer skills

2. Expand and elaborate on learning foundation

3. Improve access to prior knowledge

4. Improve retention of information

5. Improve reading comprehension

6. Strengthen language development

How to Do It

At Tier 2, this strategy is done with small groups. This visualization strategy cues the learner to form a mental image of what was read and assists the student in making connections with previously learned materials. The steps in RIDER are

Read a sentence
Image (form a mental picture)
Describe how new information differs from previous
Evaluate image to ensure it is comprehensive
Repeat process with subsequent sentences

Research Base

Cole, 1995; see page 80

Klingner et al., 2007

Naughton, 2008

B. Tomlinson, 1998

What to Watch for With ELL/CLD Students

1. Newcomers will need to have the RIDER steps modeled and explained in their most proficient language before they can proceed independently.

2. Students can be paired with partners who are slightly more bilingual than they are to facilitate their learning this process.

97. TEST-TAKING STRATEGY—SCORER

Purpose of the Strategy

Improve test-taking skills

How to Do It

At Tier 2, this strategy is done with small groups. This test-taking strategy provides a structure for completing various tests by assisting the student to carefully and systematically complete test items. The steps in SCORER are

Schedule time effectively
Clue words identified
Omit difficult items until the end
Read carefully
Estimate answers requiring calculations
Review work and responses

Research Base

Elliot & Thurlow, 2005

Ritter & Idol-Maestas, 1986

What to Watch for With ELL/CLD Students

1. Newcomers will need to have the SCORER steps modeled and explained in their most proficient language before they can proceed independently.

2. Students can be paired with partners who are slightly more bilingual than they are to facilitate their learning this process.

98. MATH WORD PROBLEMS STRATEGY—SQRQCQ

Purpose of the Strategy

1. Improve comprehension

2. Improve retention of information

3. Improve problem solving of math word problems

4. Strengthen language development

How to Do It

At Tier 2, this strategy is done with small groups. This strategy provides a systematic structure for identifying the question being asked in a math word problem, computing the response, and ensuring that the question in the problem is answered. The steps in SQRQCQ are

Survey word problems
Question asked is identified
Read more carefully
Question process required to solve problem
Compute the answer
Question self to ensure that the answer solves the problem

Research Base

Cole, 1995

Elliot & Thurlow, 2005

What to Watch for With ELL/CLD Students

1. Newcomers will need to have the SQRQCQ steps modeled and explained in their most proficient language before they can proceed independently.

2. Students can be paired with partners who are slightly more bilingual than they are to facilitate their learning this process.

99. READING COMPREHENSION STRATEGY—SQ3R

Purpose of the Strategy

1. Build transfer skills

2. Expand and elaborate on learning foundations

3. Improve access to prior knowledge

4. Improve comprehension

5. Strengthen language development

How to Do It

At Tier 2, this strategy is done with small groups. This strategy reminds students to go through any passage or lesson carefully and thoughtfully. Students can make cue cards to remember each step. The steps in SQ3R are

Survey
Question
Read
Recite
Review

Research Base

Allington & Cunningham, 2002; see pages 89–116

Artis, 2008

Cole, 1995; *see pages 75–94*

Fisher & Frey, 2004

Irvin & Rose, 1995

Law & Eckes, 2000

Moore, Alvermann, & Hinchman, 2000; *see page 139*

Robinson, 1946

Sakta, 1999

Tovani, 2000

What to Watch for With ELL/CLD Students

1. Newcomers will need to have the SQ3R steps modeled and explained in their most proficient language before they can proceed independently.

2. Students can be paired with partners who are slightly more bilingual than they are to facilitate their learning this process.

100. LISTENING COMPREHENSION STRATEGY—TQLR

Purpose of the Strategy

1. Build awareness of learning

2. Develop personal control of situations

3. Improve access to prior knowledge

4. Strengthen language development

How to Do It

At Tier 2, this strategy is done with small groups. This strategy assists with listening comprehension. Students generate questions and listen for specific statements related to those questions. The steps in TQLR are

Tuning in
Questioning
Listening
Reviewing

Research Base

Artis, 2008

Fisher & Frey, 2004

Irvin & Rose, 1995

Law & Eckes, 2000

Popp, 1997

Robinson, 1946

Sakta, 1999

What to Watch for With ELL/CLD Students

1. Newcomers will need to have the TQLR steps modeled and explained in their most proficient language before they can proceed independently.

2. Students can be paired with partners who are slightly more bilingual than they are to facilitate their learning this process.

101. READING STRATEGY—FIST

Purpose of the Strategy

Assist students to actively pursue responses to questions related directly to materials being read

How to Do It

At Tier 2, this strategy is done with small groups. Students follow steps while reading paragraphs in assigned readings. The steps in FIST are

First sentence is read
Indicate a question based on first sentence
Search for the answer to the question
Tie question and answer together through paraphrasing

Research Base

Allington & Cunningham, 2002

Cole, 1995

Dang, Dang, & Ruiter, 2005

Derwinger, Stigsdotter Neely, & Bäckman, 2005

Ellis & Lenz, 1987

Moore et al., 2000

Odean, 1987

What to Watch for With ELL/CLD Students

1. Newcomers will need to have the FIST steps modeled and explained in their most proficient language before they can proceed independently.

2. Students can be paired with partners who are slightly more bilingual than they are to facilitate their learning this process.

102. GUIDED LECTURE PROCEDURE

Purpose of the Strategy

1. Build listening skills

2. Build study skills

3. Facilitate students taking control of learning

4. Provide students with a structure for taking notes during lectures

How to Do It

1. At Tier 2, this strategy is done with small groups. Group activity is involved to facilitate effective note taking. Students listen to teacher or student presentation. The speaker pauses periodically to allow groups to compare notes and fill in missing information.

2. Teacher monitors note taking and stops frequently to see that students are taking notes and noting key points.

Research Base

Kelly & Holmes, 1979

Kirschner, Sweller, & Clark, 2006

Toole, 2000

What to Watch for With ELL/CLD Students

1. This strategy is especially useful with upper-elementary and secondary students. The teacher may need to physically model how to listen and take notes appropriately.

2. Not all students will have prior educational experiences where they have listened to someone present and are then responsible for taking notes or developing commentary about what was said.

3. This can be paired with general guided practice in test preparation and test taking.

103. RETENTION STRATEGY—PARS

Purpose of the Strategy

1. Build retention of information and learning

2. Reduce distraction

3. Strengthen focus on task

How to Do It

1. At Tier 2, this strategy is done with small groups. This is a strategy for retention of content.

2. PARS is recommended for use with younger students and with those who have limited experiences with study strategies. Students can create cue cards or use posters to remind themselves of the steps. The steps in PARS are

> Preview
> Ask questions
> Read
> Summarize

Research Base

Derwinger et al., 2005

S. W. Lee, 2005

Smith, 2000

What to Watch for With ELL/CLD Students

1. Newcomers will need to have the PARS steps modeled and explained in their most proficient language before they can proceed independently.

2. Students can be paired with partners who are slightly more bilingual than they are to facilitate their learning this process.

104. TEST-TAKING STRATEGY—PIRATES

Purpose of the Strategy

1. Build cognitive academic language

2. Build learning strategies

3. Facilitate test-taking success

4. Reduce distractibility

How to Do It

1. At Tier 2, this strategy is done with small groups. It improves test-taking skills for typical achievement tests.

2. PIRATES may assist learners to complete tests more carefully and successfully. Students can create cue cards of the mnemonic and use them to work through each test and individual test item. The steps in PIRATES are

Prepare to succeed
Inspect instructions carefully
Read entire question, remember strategies, and reduce choices
Answer question or leave until later
Turn back to the abandoned items
Estimate unknown answers by avoiding absolutes and eliminating similar choices
Survey to ensure that all items have a response

Research Base

DeVries Guth & Stephens Pettengill, 2005

Hughes, Deshler, Ruhl, & Schumaker, 1993

Lebzelter & Nowacek, 1999

What to Watch for With ELL/CLD Students

1. Newcomers will need to have the PIRATES steps modeled and explained in their most proficient language before they can proceed independently.

2. Students can be paired with partners who are slightly more bilingual than they are to facilitate their learning this process.

105. READING COMPREHENSION STRATEGY—PQ4R

Purpose of the Strategy

1. Improve reading comprehension

2. Improve access to prior knowledge

3. Expand and elaborate on learning foundation

4. Build transfer skills

How to Do It

At Tier 2, this strategy is done with small groups. PQ4R may assist students to become more-discriminating readers and retain more of what they are reading. The steps in PQ4R are

Preview
Question
Read
Reflect
Recite
Review

Research Base

Anderson, 2000

Hamachek, 1994

Pelow & Colvin, 1983

Sanacore, 1982

What to Watch for With ELL/CLD Students

1. Newcomers will need to have the PQ4R steps modeled and explained in their most proficient language before they can proceed independently.

2. Students can be paired with partners who are slightly more bilingual than they are to facilitate their learning this process.

106. PARAPHRASING—RAP

Purpose of the Strategy

Reading comprehension technique to improve retention of information

How to Do It

At Tier 2, this strategy is done with small groups. This strategy assists students to learn information through paraphrasing. The steps in RAP are

Read paragraph
Ask self the main idea and two supporting details
Put main idea and details into own words

Research Base

Cole, 1995; see page 80

Dang et al., 2005

Ellis & Lenz, 1987

Odean, 1987

What to Watch for With ELL/CLD Students

1. Newcomers will need to have the RAP steps modeled and explained in their most proficient language before they can proceed independently.

2. Students can be paired with partners who are slightly more bilingual than they are to facilitate their learning this process.

107. ADVANCED ORGANIZERS

Purpose of the Strategy

1. Build language transfer skills

2. Build awareness of the appropriate content language in English culture/language

3. Develop confidence in academic interactions

How to Do It

1. The teacher or the assistant previews the lesson content in first language when possible, outlining key issues, rehearsing vocabulary, and reviewing related prior knowledge. The teacher may use analogy strategy described next to teach one or more of the advanced organizer tools (e.g., KWL, W-star, graphic organizer, mind map). Students implement strategy with a specific task or lesson.

2. Steps for teaching advanced organizers

   a. *Inform* the students what advanced organizers are, how they operate, when to use them, and why they are useful. Begin by saying that advanced organizers are a way to help them (the students) plan and remember. They work by previewing or putting information concerning the lesson or assignment they are working on into graphic form. Once they learn how to use advanced organizers, they can use them anytime and with any content or lesson you give them to do.

   b. *Use cues,* metaphors, analogies, or other means of elaborating on a description of advanced organizers combined with visual cues. One way to do this is to have the group look at a blueprint of a house or other building they are familiar with. Have them see how the architect had to plan for everything ahead of time and create a preview or graphic image of what everyone was going to have to do to complete the construction. Explain that almost anyone could help construct the house or building by reading the blueprint and the ability to read and understand these is a special and critical skill that will be useful to them later in life.

   c. *Lead group discussions* about the use of advanced organizers. Have students start by talking about a lesson they have just successfully completed. They can go back through the lesson or book using different advanced organizer tools to see how they work and what is required. Encourage them to ask you anything about the learning process they want clarified.

   d. *Provide guided practice* in applying advanced organizers to particular tasks. Work directly with student groups demonstrating and modeling how to identify elements. Have more-skilled students demonstrate for the class.

   e. *Provide feedback* on monitoring use and success of advance organizers. While students use advanced organizers in small groups, you should move around the room listening and supplying encouragement for consistent use of the tools. As students get more comfortable using these tools, you can have them monitor one another in the use of the strategy.

Research Base

Harwell, 2001; see page 214

Heacox, 2002; see pages 91–98

Moore et al., 2000; see pages 143, 198–205

Opitz, 1998; see pages 115–121

What to Watch for With ELL/CLD Students

1. There are cultural differences in cognitive/learning style and some ELL/CLD students may not respond to the brainstorming construct behind most advanced organizers.

2. By keeping the graphic design of the advanced organizer as close as possible to the illustrations in the text or some aspect of the lesson, the teacher can more tightly connect the concepts being studied with the what/who/where questioning that precedes the lesson.

3. This is another activity that works best with preparation in the students' most proficient language and relevance to their culture before proceeding.

108. ANALOGY

Purpose of the Strategy

1. Develop higher tolerance

2. Facilitate access of prior knowledge

3. Build transfer skills

4. Develop categorization skills

How to Do It

1. At Tier 2, this strategy is done with small groups. Students each share something that is meaningful to them. They go through the steps of analogy in pairs as they share their items with one another. Steps for students to follow in implementing this analogy strategy are the following.

   a. What do I already know about this item or concept?

   b. How does what I already know about this idea or item compare with the new idea or item?

   c. Can the known idea or item be substituted for the new item or idea and still make sense?

   d. How can I elaborate on these comparisons through analogies?

2. A basic description of analogy is that you have students work through a task describing, comparing, and contrasting things that are meaningful to them. They go through the steps of analogy in pairs or groups as they share their items with one another, asking one another four specific questions that guide them through the application of the steps involved in analogy. Eventually, they ask themselves these four self-guiding questions silently as they complete tasks.

3. An example of a content application of analogy that I have used is having students compare an object representing a new subject we are going to study with an object they are familiar with, describing the objects and making analogies between the two items. For example, I brought examples of different dragons (Chinese, Japanese, English, Javanese, and Scandinavian) to share with students after we had read *The Reluctant Dragon* by Kenneth Grahame (1983), and when we were about to move into a unit on Asia, I had them make analogies between and among the various types of dragons, discussing cultural and linguistic manifestations of these different impressions of and perspectives on a mythological figure. I then had them do expansions related to our Asian unit. The students were to all bring something they had that was meaningful to them that was from Asia and share it with others using the analogy strategy. They created Venn diagrams showing the many ways their various objects were similar and different from one another.

4. Steps for teaching analogy

   a. *Inform* the students what analogy is, how it operates, when to use it, and why it is useful. Begin by saying that analogy is a tool for learning and remembering. It works by asking and answering a series of five questions concerning the lesson or assignment they are working on. Once they learn how to use analogy, they can use it anytime and with any content or lesson you give them to do.

b. *Use cues,* metaphors, or other means of elaborating on a description of analogy combined with visual cues. One way to do this is to have the group compare their jackets or shoes or something else everyone in the class has with them. Have them see how although everyone has the same object, there are many ways these are different and many ways they are similar to one another. You can also use favorite stories or activities, anything where a fundamental similarity exists along with distinct differences.

c. *Lead group discussions* about the use of analogy. Have students start by talking about a lesson they have just successfully completed. They can go back through the lesson using the analogy question steps to see how they work and what information is required. Encourage your students to ask you anything about the learning process they want clarified.

d. *Provide guided practice* in applying analogy to particular tasks. Here is an example of guided practice as the teacher leads the students through the use of analogy. Examples of both teacher and student comments are shown.

Teacher: "The first step is to see if you can you recall something from your language or experiences that is similar to this item?"

Student: "What do I know that is like this item? Is there something in my background, language, or experiences that is similar to the item?"

Comparison

Teacher: "Second, examine how these items are similar or different. Do they have similar uses?"

Student: "How are these items similar and different? Are they used in similar ways?"

Teacher: "Third, identify the items or parts of items that might be substituted for these items. Why would this substitution work? Why might it not work?"

Student: "Can I use these similar elements interchangeably? What other items might be substituted for these items?"

Elaboration

Teacher: "Fourth, think about other experiences, words, or actions from your life, language, or culture that are similar to elements of English or your life here in this community. In what ways are they similar and different? How could you use your prior knowledge effectively in new situations?"

Student: "When the teacher asks for examples, I can provide them based on my experiences and do not have to use American examples. I know that aspects of a new situation may be similar to something I know from my previous experiences."

e. *Provide feedback* on monitoring use and success of analogy. While students use analogy in small groups, you should move around the room listening and supplying encouragement for consistent use of the question and answer steps. As students get more comfortable using this strategy, you can have them monitor one another in the use of the strategy, encouraging one another to ask and/or answer the questions.

f. *Provide generalization* activities. Have your students use analogy for a variety of lessons and tasks. You should be sure to identify the strategy by name and point to the poster or visual cues about the strategy whenever you have students use it. Hold enhanced cognitive discussions about the use of analogy in these different lesson settings, and encourage discussion of how useful students found this strategy in particular tasks.

5. For example, students are shown an object that looks familiar, such as a metal rod used to connect two wheels on a toy car. They generate words describing the rod such as "long," "shiny," "manufactured," "connects," and "an axle." They

then are shown another metal rod that is unfamiliar to them. They generate more words describing the new object. Some of the words will be similar, some different. Example words might be "long," "shiny," "threaded ends," "connects something," "pointy," "heavy," and "metallic." They may actually try to substitute the new rod for the toy axle, or they may make guesses about substitution and conclude that it could be done but won't work exactly. They generate sentences such as "The axle is smaller than the new rod'" "The new rod is larger than the axle of the toy car'" "The new rod has threaded ends while the axle does not;" "The axle is to a car as the new rod is to something else;" and "The axle is as shiny as the new rod."

Research Base

Cole, 1995

Tovani, 2000

What to Watch for With ELL/CLD Students

1. Be sure students are matched with peers with whom they can communicate comfortably while they are all learning the strategy and steps in the process.

2. After students learn the process and steps, posters or cards with reminder illustrations and the words of the steps can be put up around the room.

3. Once students can use analogy without prompting, they can be paired up with nonbilingual peers for more applications.

109. EXPERIENCE-BASED WRITING/READING

Purpose of the Strategy

1. Build transfer skills

2. Develop cognitive academic language

3. Develop content knowledge foundation

4. Facilitate analogy strategies

How to Do It

1. At Tier 2, this strategy is done with small groups. In primary grades, the teacher guides students to illustrate specific experiences in which students have participated. Activity may be paired with field trips or other shared experiences; it may also be in reference to prior life experiences of ELL/LEP students.

2. Community members may make presentations about events significant to students' families. The teacher then has students tell what their illustrations depict and writes down verbatim what the students say. Students then read back to the teacher what has been written.

3. In intermediate and secondary grades, the teacher guides students to illustrate and write stories about their experiences. These stories can be put into collections and bound for use by other students. Stories can be kept in the classroom, library, or media center.

Research Base

Echevarria et al., 2007

Gibbons, 2002

Nessel & Nixon, 2008

What to Watch for With ELL/CLD Students

1. Some shared experiences will be very novel for particular cultural members of a group, more than for other members. Be sure to give those who have never seen something before extra preparation time and explanations of what they are going to see or do during the field trip or experience.

2. Be sure students are matched with peers with whom they can communicate comfortably while they are all learning the strategy and steps in the process.

3. Be sensitive to cultural mores about certain experiences and businesses. You may need to spend extra time discussing what is going to be seen and heard or, in some cases, be prepared to have some students participate in a related but separate activity.

110. GUIDED READING AND WRITING IN HOME AND COMMUNITY LANGUAGE

Purpose of the Strategy

1. Improve motivation

2. Minimize behavior problems

3. Build transfer skills

4. Develop confidence in school language and rules for academic and social interactions

5. Reduce code-switching

6. Develop cognitive academic language

How to Do It

Tier 2, this strategy is done with small groups. With guided home and community language (or English) oral reading, each student participates either as an interested listener or reader, while the teacher moves from pair to pair listening. Guided oral reading should be varied, with changing partners. Students can reread parts of a story in pairs after the directed reading activity rather than have one student read while the others all listen. Students then write summaries of what they have read/heard. Writing can be in either home and community language or English. During this time, students have a chance to help one another.

Expansion: Students can create a dialogue and dramatize it to illustrate the action of the story or passage.

Research Base

Cole, 1995; see pages 150–152

Haneda, 2008

Reggy-Mamo, 2008

Ross, 1971

Strickland et al., 2002; see page 217

What to Watch for With ELL/CLD Students

1. Not all ELL/CLD students are literate in their home or community language.

2. Picture dictionaries with bilingual words and definitions are usually the most practical reference to use with younger, less educated students.

111. LANGUAGE GAMES

Purpose of the Strategy

1. Develop cognitive academic language

2. Develop basic interpersonal communication

3. Build transfer skills

4. Develop content knowledge foundation

How to Do It

1. At Tier 2, this strategy is done with small groups. Students play language games that reinforce specific content. The games are structured to reinforce and elaborate on content knowledge while developing home and community language and English language skills including turn taking; asking questions; giving appropriate responses; giving directions; and other game, communication, and interaction skills.

2. These are also useful in illustrating second-language learning strategies. All of the three basic games (sets, pairs, and memory) can be played to reinforce receptive and expressive language, visual and auditory memory, or content literacy.

3. The games can be played periodically during the school year to provide a review of foundation concepts when making a transition to a new topic or subject matter. The cards may also be used individually as flashcards to review the vocabulary words and language content.

4. The games may be used as an alternate assessment process. By watching the students play the card games, especially when a lot of expressive and receptive language is required, the teacher will be able to observe the extent to which individual students have acquired the learning concepts and content or how well they have retained previously presented information.

5. All of the games can be played to reinforce receptive and expressive language, visual and auditory memory, or content literacy. If students are nonverbal, the games can be played through cognitive visual matching. If students do not speak English or are LEP, the games can be played in their native language or bilingually. They can play using as much English as they have acquired, and eventually they will be able to play completely in English.

6. For example, the weather game may be used in versatile ways to supplement content lessons at any grade level. It is best used as a review, reinforcement, or assessment tool. Three basic games can be played with these cards: sets, pairs, and memory. Each of the three basic games can be varied according to specific lesson objectives. The weather cards consist of nine sets of four cards per set, illustrating common weather conditions in English. These are the weather words most often used in calendar activities in the classroom.

Players: Two to six in each group playing.

Object: Collect the most sets of four of a kind.

Deal: Cards are dealt one at a time. Each player receives five cards. The rest of the pack is placed face down in the center of the table to form the draw pile.

Play: Have the students choose the first player by names alphabetically, ages, or other device. Starting with the first player, each player calls another by name and requests cards of a specific type, such as, "David, do you have any sunny days?" The player asking must hold at least one of the type of card requested. The player asked must give up the card requested, saying, "Yes, Kala, I have a sunny day." Another variation of this is to have the player ask for a category first. If Kala successfully identifies the picture, "cloudy day," then she gets the card. The player asked does not have to say if she has more of the same set of cards. The player requesting has to ask for each individual card (e.g., "David, do you have another cloudy day?").

If the player asked does not have any cards of the type requested, then she says, "Draw!" and the asker draws the top card from the draw pile. A player's turn to ask continues so long as she is successful in getting the cards requested. If she is told to draw and happens to draw a card of the type requested, the player may show this card, name it, and continue the turn. As soon as players get a set of all four cards of one type, they must show them and give the names of the cards aloud, placing them on the table in front of them. If played competitively, the player who collects the most sets by the end of the game wins.

Research Base

Ajibade & Ndububa, 2008

Law & Eckes, 2000; see pages 204–206

Padak & Rasinski, 2008

Wright, Betteridge, & Buckby, 2006

What to Watch for With ELL/CLD Students

1. Be sure to establish consistent game-playing rules and phrases that all students are to use when playing the game. At first, these can be as simple as "Do you have a _____?" "Is this a _____?" "Here are _____."

2. The phrases can become more complex and more natural as students become more comfortable playing the games.

112. CONTEXT-EMBEDDED STRATEGIES

Purpose of the Strategy

1. Develop cognitive academic language proficiency

2. Develop content area skills

3. Develop personal control of situations

4. Reduce distractibility

How to Do It

1. At Tier 2, this strategy is done with small groups. The teacher always presents lessons with concrete, physical models and demonstrations of both content and expected performance. Language is simplified and content focused. Students are encouraged to discuss lessons in home and community language and work in small groups on content activities.

Research Base

Cummins, 1984

Cummins, Baker, & Hornberger, 2001

Donaldson, 1978

Roessingh, Kover, & Watt, 2005

What to Watch for With ELL/CLD Students

1. Vocabulary may be previewed with fluent speakers in the students' most proficient language.

2. Some cultures may have strictures against children handling or being too close to certain objects. Always screen items ahead of time with knowledgeable community members.

3. This strategy is consistent with the Sheltered Instruction Observation Protocol (SIOP) model used in many ELL programs.

4. Newcomers who have never attended school may become confused if every lesson and activity occurs in seemingly random patterns. They do not know what is expected of them at various stages of the lesson. They do not know what to attend to and what is less important.

5. This is also going to impact students with undiagnosed attention deficit disorders that they have not yet learned to accommodate.

6. It is better to start out with simple consistent steps and add as students become comfortable and familiar with what is going to happen in the classroom.

113. WRITING STRATEGY—PENS

Purpose of the Strategy

Expand language arts capabilities

How to Do It

At Tier 2, this strategy is done with small groups. PENS is appropriate for developing basic sentence structure and assists students to write different types of sentences following formulas for sentence construction. The steps in PENS are

Pick a formula
Explore different words that fit the formula
Note the words selected
Subject and verb selections follow

Research Base

Derwinger et al., 2005

Eskritt & McLeod, 2008

What to Watch for With ELL/CLD Students

1. Newcomers will need to have the PENS steps modeled and explained in their most proficient language before they can proceed independently.

2. Students can be paired with partners who are slightly more bilingual than they are to facilitate their learning this process.

114. RECIPROCAL QUESTIONING

Purpose of the Strategy

1. Use an inquiry approach

2. Develop thinking and planning skills

3. Improve mnemonic retrieval

4. Improve reading comprehension

5. Improve retention

6. Use a discourse technique

How to Do It

At Tier 2, this strategy is done with small groups. The teacher and the students ask each other questions about a selection. Student modeling of teacher questions and teacher feedback are emphasized as the learner explores the meaning of the reading material.

Research Base

Cole, 1995; see pages 113–114

Moore et al., 2000; see pages 141–142

What to Watch for With ELL/CLD Students

1. Provide initial setup in the student's most proficient language.

2. Students can practice reciprocal questioning with one another in their native language and then proceed with English proficient students.

115. MATH WORD PROBLEMS—SQRQCQ

Purpose of the Strategy

1. Improve comprehension

2. Improve retention of information

3. Improve problem solving of math word problems

4. Strengthen language development

How to Do It

At Tier 2, this strategy is done with small groups. This strategy provides a systematic structure for identifying the question being asked in a math word problem, computing the response, and ensuring that the question in the problem was answered. The steps in SQRQCQ are

Survey word problems
Question asked is identified
Read more carefully
Question process required to solve problem
Compute the answer
Question self to ensure that the answer solves the problem

Research Base

Cole, 1995; see pages 65–66, 127–128, 132

Elliot & Thurlow, 2005

What to Watch for With ELL/CLD Students

1. Newcomers will need to have the SQRQCQ steps modeled and explained in their most proficient language before they can proceed independently.

2. Students can be paired with partners who are slightly more bilingual than they are to facilitate their learning this process.

116. DOUBLE ENTRY

Purpose of the Strategy

1. Build reading comprehension

2. Develop note-taking skills

3. Reduce impulsivity

4. Develop reflection

How to Do It

1. At Tier 2, this strategy is done with small groups. Double entry is a method of taking comprehensive notes as well as reflecting on what is read.

2. Students divide a piece of paper in half, lengthwise. In the left-hand column, they copy sentences or summarize a passage. In the right-hand column, they write down their interpretation, inferences, and critical thinking about the passage. This activity can also be done as a journal in which the pages are divided into the two columns.

Research Base

Strickland et al., 2002; see page 204

Tovani, 2000; see pages 30–32

What to Watch for With ELL/CLD Students

1. This is an easy strategy to assist students who are beginning to do more reading and writing to organize and think about what they are reading.

2. This can be done in any language in which the students are literate.

117. MARKING TEXT

Purpose of the Strategy

1. Build reading comprehension

2. Develop note-taking skills

3. Reduce impulsivity

4. Develop reflection

5. Reduce distraction

6. Focus attention

How to Do It

1. At Tier 2, this strategy is done with small groups. Also called coding text (Davey, 1983), students mark their text as a way to stay engaged in their reading.

2. They use codes to indicate the type of thinking they are to use with particular passages. For example, if you want the students to make connections between their lives and the text, they might mark those passages with "REM" for "remember when." Students can also put "?" marks where they have questions about the text.

Research Base

Tovani, 2000; *see pages 29–30*

What to Watch for With ELL/CLD Students

1. This is an easy strategy to assist students who are beginning to do more reading to organize and think about what they are reading.

2. This can be done in any language in which the students are literate.

118. SCAFFOLDING

Purpose of the Strategy

1. Build a foundation for learning

2. Facilitate steady growth in learning

3. Build confidence in learning process

4. Develop cognitive academic learning skills

5. Support students who are new to schooling

How to Do It

1. At Tier 2, this strategy is done with small groups. Scaffolding is a way to support, elaborate, and expand on students' language as they learn to read (and write).

2. Scaffolds are temporary frameworks that offer students immediate access to meaning.

3. For example, one scaffolding strategy is paired reading. The teacher has students sit in pairs with one copy of the same book between them. All students are to read along during the activity, but only those students who the teacher taps or stands behind are to read aloud. The teacher may move around the room in a random manner, tapping or standing behind different pairs of students. When the teacher taps the new pair, they start reading wherever the previous pair stopped reading. The voices may overlap slightly. The same story may then be read by groups of various sizes in the same manner.

4. Another scaffolding technique is to have various students holding puppets or models representing characters or passages in the reading and when the person or persons reading get to that passage, the puppets or pictures representative of that passage are held up for all to see. Sentence level scaffolds and discourse scaffolds (such as story mapping) are further examples of supporting language and reading.

Research Base

Opitz, 1998; *see pages 150–157*

Vygotsky, 1978

What to Watch for With ELL/CLD Students

1. Teachers will need to lay a foundation for learning and continue to support new learners through the process until they are ready to go on their own.

2. It is important to remember not to continue extensive scaffolding beyond the point of skill acquisition. The learner must become empowered to proceed on his or her own.

3. Vygotsky (1978) discusses this in the context of the zone of proximal development.

119. WORDLESS PICTURE BOOKS

Purpose of the Strategy

1. Improve sequencing skills

2. Facilitate reading process

3. Improve vocabulary

How to Do It

1. At Tier 2, this strategy is done with small groups. Using wordless picture books with emerging readers of all ages is very effective. It builds on learners' oral language skills to develop the reading process. This allows for variations in phonology, syntax, vocabulary, intonation, and the like to be accommodated in an integrated classroom (i.e., all students can participate in the activity regardless of reading level).

2. The teacher selects a wordless picture book of high interest content to the students. Wordless picture books are available at all age/grade levels. The students can "read" the pictures in small groups or individually, telling the "story" as they see it. Students can also make wordless picture books.

Research Base

Opitz, 1998; see pages 130–135

What to Watch for With ELL/CLD Students

1 Teachers may need to model how to go through a book and how to follow the sequence of the story through the pictures.

2. Begin with pictures the students recognize from their experiences. Introduce new and unusual illustrations after the students understand what the process of reading is like in a wordless picture book.

3. Another variation on this is to use modern pop-up books for telling the story. Some of these are quite sophisticated and may be used in math and science lessons as well.

120. PROOF READING—COPS

Purpose of the Strategy

1. Build review skills

2. Facilitate critical thinking

3. Expand writing and reading skills

How to Do It

1. At Tier 2, this strategy is done with small groups. This strategy provides a structure for proofreading written work prior to submitting it to the teacher.

2. The steps in COPS are

Capitalization
Overall appearance
Punctuation
Spelling

Research Base

Cole, 1995; *see pages 108–110*

What to Watch for With ELL/CLD Students

1. Newcomers will need to have the COPS steps modeled and explained in their most proficient language before they can proceed independently.

2. Students can be paired with partners who are slightly more bilingual than they are to facilitate their learning this process.

121. GUIDED LECTURE PROCEDURE

Purpose of the Strategy

1. Build listening skills

2. Build study skills

3. Facilitate students taking control of learning

How to Do It

1. At Tier 2, this strategy is done with small groups. This strategy provides students with a structure for taking notes during lectures.

2. Group activity is involved to facilitate effective note taking. Students listen to the teacher's or another student's presentation. The speaker pauses periodically to allow groups to compare notes and fill in missing information.

Research Base

Kelly & Holmes, 1979

Kirschner et al., 2006

Toole, 2000

What to Watch for With ELL/CLD Students

1. This strategy is especially useful with upper-elementary and secondary students. The teacher may need to model how to listen and take notes appropriately.

2. Not all students will have prior educational experiences where they have listened to someone present and are then responsible for taking notes or developing commentary about what was said.

3. This can be paired with general guided practice in test preparation and test taking.

BEHAVIOR ISSUES AT TIER 2

122. ACCOUNTABILITY

Purpose of the Strategy

1. Strengthen internal locus of control

2. Increase time spent on-task

3. Develop confidence in learning

How to Do It

1. At Tier 2, this strategy is done with small groups. It ensures that students are aware of and responsible for their own actions.

2. This strategy develops awareness of the connection between students' actions and the consequences of these actions.

3. Establish rewards and consequences for completion of work and appropriate behavior, ensuring that these rewards and consequences are consistently implemented. For example, the teacher assists the students in setting up an agenda or plan of a personalized list of tasks that the students must complete in a specified time.

Research Base

C. A. Tomlinson, 1999; see pages 66–68

What to Watch for With ELL/CLD Students

1. Particular social groups and cultures have different expectations of adults and children when it comes to being accountable for task completion. This is a learned difference between cultures. The teacher needs to be aware that the expectations in an American school may need to be taught directly to CLD students and should not assume that they are understood.

2. One way to introduce the idea of your classroom rules is to ask students about any rules their parents have for them at home or rules they have learned about crossing the street or playing games. This can then be expanded to the idea of rules for completing tasks and acting appropriately in a classroom.

123. ALTERNATE RESPONSE METHODS

Purpose of the Strategy

1. Facilitate learning

2. Accommodate diverse learning styles

3. Develop task completion

How to Do It

1. At Tier 2, this strategy is done with small groups. Adapt the mode of response required of students.

2. Students respond to questions in a manner compatible with their needs. Allow students who have difficulty with writing activities to record their answers. Students are allowed to express their understanding of a question or issue in varied ways to meet their individual needs. This ensures that students have the best possible chance to show that they have acquired and retained skills and knowledge.

3. For example, students may record their oral responses to questions given in class. For the geography unit, provide the questions in writing for the student to take home and practice responding. Some names of American states are very difficult to pronounce; provide time for students to work alone or with a peer to write the difficult state names on tag board cards that they can hold up during class discussion rather than say the name aloud.

Research Base

Bailey, 1993

Gardner, 1993a

Gardner, 1993b

Tannenbaum, 1996

What to Watch for With ELL/CLD Students

1. Some CLD students have had previous schooling in situations where students have no choice in how they will respond to questions and tasks and teachers are authority figures who direct every action in the classroom.

2. When the teacher wishes to make learning empowerment an instructional goal, this strategy is an excellent direction to take.

3. Demonstrate how the various responses can be made, including color coding or otherwise graphically illustrating the different choices.

4. Some role-play in the process from initial choice to final task completion may be helpful.

124. CHOICES

Purpose of the Strategy

1. Facilitate learning

2. Accommodate diverse learning styles

3. Develop task completion

4. Alleviate power struggles between teacher and student

5. Reduce fears associated with assignments

How to Do It

1. At Tier 2, this strategy is done with small groups. It provides students the opportunity to select one or more activities developed by the teacher.

2. Teacher provides two different reading selections of interest to the student, both of which address the same desired objective. Allow the student to select one of the selections for the assignment. If the student does not choose either of the selections, introduce a third selection or ask the student to choose a content-appropriate reading selection.

Research Base

Ainley, 2006

Cordova & Lepper, 1996

Flowerday & Schraw, 2003

Flowerday, Schraw, & Stevens, 2004

Kragler & Nolley, 1996

Sanacore, 1999

What to Watch for With ELL/CLD Students

1. Some CLD students have had previous schooling in situations where students have no choice and teachers are authority figures who direct every action in the classroom.

2. When the teacher wishes to make choice and student empowerment an instructional goal, this strategy is an excellent direction to take.

3. Demonstrate how the choices are to be made, including color coding or otherwise graphically illustrating the different choices.

4. Some role-play in the process from initial choice to final task completion may be helpful.

125. CONTENT MODIFICATION

Purpose of the Strategy

1. Improve motivation and response

2. Reduce frustration

3. Facilitate learner empowerment

How to Do It

1. At Tier 2, this strategy is done with small groups. This strategy adapts content to meet individual or unique student needs.

2. The teacher can present the target content objective and then demonstrate various ways for the students to explore and learn this content.

3. For example, the teacher uses subject matter rather than specific linguistic skill exercises to teach English to students with limited proficiency in English.

4. For example, allow students who have difficulty with writing to record their answers or use a transcription program on a computer.

Research Base

Arkoudis, 2005

Brinton, Wesche, & Snow, 2003

Echevarria & Graves, 2006

McIntyre, Kyle, Chen, Kraemer, & Parr, 2009

Weisman & Hansen, 2007

What to Watch for With ELL/CLD Students

1. This can be done in any language and content lesson but will need to be explained the student's most proficient language.

2. Provide lots of practice and modeling.

3. When presenting a topic, the teacher can ask students for what specifically they would like to learn about this topic.

126. CONTRACTING

Purpose of the Strategy

1. Improve motivation

2. Facilitate learner empowerment

3. Reduce distractibility

How to Do It

1. At Tier 2, this strategy is done with small groups. It clarifies responsibilities, assignments, and rewards.

2. Establish a verbal or written mutual agreement between teacher and student.

3. For example, sign a written document stating the agreement that the student will complete 20 math problems with 80% accuracy during the regular math period. The student will receive 10 minutes of extra free time if contract conditions are met.

Research Base

Harwell, 2001; *see pages 124–125*

C. A. Tomlinson, 1999; *see pages 66–68, 87–91*

What to Watch for With ELL/CLD Students

1. Contracts will need to be explained in the students' most proficient language.

2. Examples should be provided from their family or community experience.

127. EXPECTATIONS AWARENESS/REVIEW

Purpose of the Strategy

1. Reduce frustration in students because of unclear expectations

2. Minimize ambiguity in classroom

How to Do It

1. At Tier 2, this strategy is done with small groups. This strategy ensures that each student is familiar with specific academic and behavioral expectations.

2. This strategy modifies or breaks down general classroom rules into specific behavioral expectations, to ensure that each student knows exactly what is meant by acceptable behaviors.

Research Base

Davis, 2005

J. R. Nelson, Martella, & Galand, 1998

Rubenstein, 2006

What to Watch for With ELL/CLD Students

1. Particular social groups and cultures have different expectations of adults and children when it comes to being accountable for task completion. This is a learned difference between cultures. The teacher needs to be aware that the expectations in an American school may need to be taught directly to CLD students and should not assume that they are understood.

2. One way to introduce the idea of your classroom rules is to ask students about any rules their parents have for them at home or rules they have learned about crossing the street or playing games. This can then be expanded to the idea of rules for completing tasks and acting appropriately in a classroom.

3. Demonstrate all of the desired behaviors and rules. Some role-play may be helpful. Examples of inappropriate behaviors may be used with caution.

128. PARTNERS

Purpose of the Strategy

1. Improve motivation

2. Minimize behavior problems

How to Do It

At Tier 2, this strategy is done with small groups. With paired oral reading, each student participates either as an interested listener or as a reader while the teacher moves from pair to pair listening. Reading can be varied by changing partners. Children can reread parts of a story in pairs after the directed reading activity rather than have one student read while the others all listen. During this time, the students have a chance to help one another.

Research Base

Kamps et al., 2007

Koskinen & Blum, 1984

Wood & Algozzine, 1994

Wood & Harmon, 2001

Zutell & Rasinski, 1991

What to Watch for With ELL/CLD Students

1. Partners must be selected carefully with specific objectives in mind. If competence and understanding of the content is the goal, then similar language skills are necessary.

2. If expansion and transition of learning is the goal, then pairing a less proficient with a more proficient bilingual partner will help.

3. If challenging application is the goal, then pairing very differently skilled parties may work.

129. PLANNED IGNORING

Purpose of the Strategy

1. Reduce confrontations over minor misbehaving

2. Eliminate inappropriate behavior after a few moments

How to Do It

1. At Tier 2, this strategy is done with small groups. The teacher purposely ignores certain behaviors exhibited by students.

2. For example, the teacher elects to ignore some whispering between two students during independent work time.

Research Base

Grossman, 2003

Hall & Hall, 1998

Rafferty, 2007

What to Watch for With ELL/CLD Students

1. Some ELL and CLD students may have limited experience with attending schools and not know what the rules are in classrooms.

2. In some cultures, students who understand some task are expected to assist their relatives or friends who may not be doing so well, so some quiet helping should be allowed as long as it appears to be on task.

130. PLANNED MOVEMENT

Purpose of the Strategy

1. Prevent inappropriate moving around the room

2. Minimize behavior problems in the classroom

How to Do It

1. At Tier 2, this strategy is done with small groups. Periodically, the teacher provides students opportunities to move about the classroom for appropriate reasons.

2. For example, the teacher allows students to move to a learning center or study booth for part of their independent work time instead of remaining seated at their desks for the entire period.

Research Base

Evertson & Neal, 2006

Evertson & Weinstein, 2006

Kaufman, 2001

Williams, 2008

What to Watch for With ELL/CLD Students

1. Differences in mobility and movement by children are learned differences among cultures and social groups. In some families, children are expected to get up and move around whenever they want to, in others children are expected to remain seated or in one place unless and until they are given permission to move elsewhere.

2. Some children may have undiagnosed conditions that inhibit their sitting or standing in one place without moving occasionally. Using planned movement and making accommodations for opportunities for students to move facilitates learning for all students.

131. POSITIVE REINFORCEMENT

Purpose of the Strategy

1. Increase the frequency of appropriate responses or behaviors

2. Facilitate students' comfort with learning environment

How to Do It

1. Provide rewards for completing appropriate tasks.

2. For example, the teacher provides students extra free time when their math or reading assignment has been completed.

Research Base

Cole, 1995; *see pages 115–116*

Harwell, 2001; *see pages 126–127*

Opitz, 1998; *see page 61*

What to Watch for With ELL/CLD Students

1. What is rewarding to one person is not necessarily rewarding to another. This is another learned preference.

2. The teacher should use a variety of affirmatives, words, and phrases to denote reinforcement.

3. When using physical rewards, always do some research to identify cultural, developmental, and gender appropriate items.

4. When using extra time or a special activity as a reward, vary these depending on the students' interests.

132. PROXIMITY (PROXEMICS)

Purpose of the Strategy

1. Increase students' time spent on task

2. Reassure frustrated students

How to Do It

1. At Tier 2, this strategy is done with small groups. The teacher and/or other students are strategically positioned to provide support and to prevent or minimize misbehaviors.

2. For example, the teacher circulates throughout the classroom during group or independent activities, spending more time next to particular students.

Research Base

Etscheidt, Stainback, S. B., & Stainback, W. C., 1984

Evertson & Weinstein, 2006

Gunter & Shores, 1995

Marable & Raimondi, 1995

What to Watch for With ELL/CLD Students

1. All cultures have guidelines about how close or how far away to stand or sit next to another person. These are mostly unspoken and learned through being raised in the culture and community where the proximity to another person is seen and remarked on by those around you.

2. These space relations are also affected by whether someone is standing over or sitting under another person. These relative positions convey power and control relationships, which vary from culture to culture.

3. Teachers must familiarize themselves with the proximity rules of the various cultures represented in their classrooms before expecting to use proxemics strategically to promote learning.

133. REDUCED STIMULI

Purpose of the Strategy

1. Enhance ability of students to focus on learning

2. Encourage questioning and exploration of new learning

3. Reduce response fatigue

4. Reduce culture shock

5. Develop personal control of situations

How to Do It

At Tier 2, this strategy is done with small groups. The teacher starts the room with relatively blank walls and empty spaces, also monitoring the use of music and other auditory materials. The teacher does not display or use visual/auditory materials until students have been introduced to the content or have produced the materials themselves. Visual, tactile, and auditory experiences are introduced gradually and with demonstration.

Research Base

P. Nelson, Kohnert, Sabur, & Shaw, 2005

Wortham, 1996

What to Watch for With ELL/CLD Students

1. Newcomers may become overly stimulated by lots of bright, new, unfamiliar, and strange objects, signs, sounds, and miscellany in their new classroom. They do not know what is important to attend to and what is not important. It is all new and exciting.

2. This is also going to impact students with undiagnosed neurological conditions that they have not yet learned to accommodate.

3. It is better to start out with less and add more as students become comfortable and familiar with what is in the classroom

134. REST AND RELAXATION TECHNIQUES

Purpose of the Strategy

1. Enhance ability of students to learn new things

2. Develop self-monitoring skills

3. Reduce anxiety and stress responses

4. Reduce culture shock side effects

How to Do It

At Tier 2, this strategy is done with small groups. Relaxation techniques are shown in video or demonstration form with an explanation in home and community language when possible. Students discuss when they might need to use these techniques.

Research Base

Allen & Klein, 1997

Page & Page, 2003

Thomas, 2006

What to Watch for With ELL/CLD Students

1. Heightened anxiety, distractibility, and response fatigue are all common side effects of the acculturation process and attributes of culture shock.

2. ELL and CLD students need more time to process classroom activities and tasks. Building in rest periods will provide thinking and processing breaks in their day.

135. SELF-REINFORCEMENT

Purpose of the Strategy

1. Build awareness of learning

2. Develop personal control of situations

3. Develop thinking and planning skills

4. Facilitate access of prior knowledge

5. Facilitate language development

6. Improve motivation and response

7. Reduce off-task behaviors

How to Do It

1. At Tier 2, this strategy is done with small groups. Individual students reward themselves for appropriate behavior and performance by using self-developed checklists.

2. As students become familiar with what is desired, they can check off points on their checklists.

3. Individual students reward themselves for appropriate behavior and performance at specific check-in points during the lesson. Eventually, each student uses a self-developed checklist and gives reward to self upon completion of tasks.

Research Base

C. A. Tomlinson, 1999; see pages 66–68

What to Watch for With ELL/CLD Students

1. ELL students who are LEP may need the process explained in their most proficient language.

2. Points are not intrinsically reinforcing. What is rewarding to one person is not necessarily rewarding to another. This is a learned preference.

3. The points may initially be paired with some more directly rewarding action, and then gradually progress to use of only points.

136. SIGNALS

Purpose of the Strategy

1. Facilitate nondirective guidance about student misbehavior

2. Prevent minor inappropriate behaviors from escalating

3. Reduce specific attention to the students misbehaving

How to Do It

1. At Tier 2, this strategy is done with small groups. Use nonverbal cues or signals to control inappropriate behavior.

2. For example, the teacher flicks the classroom lights on and off when the noise level in the class becomes too loud.

Research Base

Marable & Raimondi, 1995

Petrie, Lindauer, Bennett, & Gibson, 1998

Rogers, 2006

What to Watch for With ELL/CLD Students

1. Always introduce signals to ELL and CLD students by explaining them in their most proficient language.

2. ELL/CLD students who have had prior schooling might be asked what sort of signals they were familiar with and that could become part of the classroom routine.

137. SUCCESS

Purpose of the Strategy

1. Improve confidence and self-esteem

2. Facilitate student's view of himself or herself as a successful person

3. Improve retention

4. Utilize prior knowledge

5. Develop thinking and planning skills

How to Do It

1. At Tier 2, this strategy is done with small groups. Ensure that each student successfully completes assigned tasks. The teacher initially reduces the level of difficulty of materials and gradually increases the level of difficulty as easier tasks are met with success. The teacher reduces the complexity level of vocabulary or concepts in written material to help the students complete a reading task. Through this strategy, learners may read material similar to others in the class without requiring an excessive amount of individual attention from the teacher.

2. For example, the teacher places a transparency over a page of written material, (with a fine-point marker) crosses out the more difficult words, and writes simpler equivalents of those words above or in the margin next to the crossed-out words. As students read, they substitute the simpler words for those marked out.

Research Base

Gibbons, 2003

Krumenaker, Many, & Wang, 2008

Leki, 1995

C. A. Tomlinson, 1999

What to Watch for With ELL/CLD Students

1. The teacher needs information or professional development about all of the diverse learning styles, cultures, and languages in the classroom to design accessible learning activities for all students.

2. There is as much diversity in the ELL and CLD population as there is between the non-ELL and ELL population as a whole.

138. SURVIVAL STRATEGIES FOR STUDENTS

Purpose of the Strategy

1. Build awareness of appropriate behaviors for school language and rules

2. Build transfer skills

3. Develop confidence in school culture interactions

4. Develop personal control of situations

5. Reduce response fatigue

How to Do It

At Tier 2, this strategy is done with small groups. The teacher identifies basic rules of social and formal interaction that students will need to know immediately. Students may identify situations where they made mistakes. The teacher, assistant, and peers discuss situations and what interactions are expected. Students may need to practice these interactions.

Research Base

Ashworth & Wakefield, 2004

Felix-Brasdefer, 2008

Jackson, Boostrom, & Hansen, 1998

B. Johnson, Juhasz, Marken, & Ruiz, 1998

What to Watch for With ELL/CLD Students

1. Particular social groups and cultures have different expectations of adults and children when it comes to following rules. This is a learned difference between cultures. The teacher needs to be aware that the expectations in an American school may need to be taught directly to CLD students and not just assume that they are understood.

2. One way to introduce the idea of behavior and strategies specific to your classroom is to ask students about how their parents have them behave at home or the rules they have learned about playing games. This can then be expanded to the idea of acting appropriately in a classroom.

3. Demonstrate all of the desired behaviors and strategies. Some role-play may be helpful. Examples of inappropriate behaviors may be used with caution.

139. TIME-OUT

Purpose of the Strategy

1. Facilitate student regaining control over self

2. Strengthen learner empowerment

How to Do It

1. At Tier 2, this strategy is done with small groups. The strategy promotes student thinking about her behavior and behavioral expectations of the teacher.

2. Students are removed temporarily from the immediate environment to reduce external stimuli.

3. For example, the teacher removes a student to a quiet or time-out area for three to five minutes when student is unable to respond to a situation in a nonaggressive manner.

Research Base

Harwell, 2001; see page 129

What to Watch for With ELL/CLD Students

1. Some ELL and CLD students have limited experience with public schools and the rules expected in the classroom.

2. Time-outs should be explained to the student in their most proficient language before using them or while taking the student out of a situation.

140. TOUCH

Purpose of the Strategy

1. Increase time spent on task

2. Build student's self-awareness of behavior

How to Do It

1. At Tier 2, this strategy is done with small groups. Use touch to minimize misbehaviors and convey messages to learners.

2. For example, if a student is looking around the room during independent work time, the teacher can walk up to the student and gently tap on the student's shoulder as a signal to focus on the assignment.

Research Base

Koenig, 2007

Little & Akin-Little, 2008

Marable & Raimondi, 1995

What to Watch for With ELL/CLD Students

1. All cultures have guidelines about how a person can touch another person. These are mostly unspoken and learned through being raised in the culture and community where touching another person is seen and remarked on by those around you.

2. These touch relations are also affected by whether someone is related to the other person. These relative positions convey power and control relationships, which vary from culture to culture.

3. The teachers must familiarize themselves with the touch rules of the various cultures represented in their classrooms before expecting to use touch strategically to promote learning.

141. COPING

Purpose of the Strategy

1. Build awareness of learning process

2. Develop extended time on task

3. Develop higher tolerance

4. Develop problem-solving skills

5. Lower anxiety levels

6. Develop personal control of situations

How to Do It

1. At Tier 2, this strategy is done with small groups. The teacher directs students to identify specific problem(s) they want to solve as a group. Each group follows the coping steps as the students address their problem, writing down their answers and ideas for each stage.

2. Steps for students to follow in implementing the coping strategy are the following.

    a. What is the problem?

    b. What are possible solutions?

    c. What is my action plan?

    d. Where can I go for help?

    e. When should I start?

    f. How will I deal with setbacks?

    g. What is my outcome?

3. When applying the coping strategy, students work through problems or tasks using the sequence of self-monitoring questions. Let us suppose that you are about to have your students begin a new unit in social studies about your local community services and service people. You tend to enjoy challenges and usually teach these lessons by having students "discover" local resources and people on their own, but you have several students who are new to your community and from a CLD background. You could modify your usual instructional approach by building in an opportunity for your students to examine what your expectations are and identify any problems they may have in meeting your expectations (Step 1 of coping, "What is the problem?"). The student groups then would identify what they will do to successfully complete the lesson (Step 2 of coping, "What are my action steps?"), discussing ahead of time who they might see, where they

might go, and what might happen. This might include identifying vocabulary words and discourse patterns they will need to use and possibly some practice ahead of time in speaking with adults from different speech communities from their own. They identify ahead of time where sources of information and assistance are available to them (Step 3 of coping, "Where can I go for help?") including people at the school, church, or other community groups. During this planning time, they also discuss what might happen to prevent them getting information or achieving parts of your outcomes. They come up with a supportive, group plan for dealing with barriers in accomplishing their tasks (Step 4 of coping, "How will I deal with setbacks?"). Finally, they create a clear idea in their minds of what exactly an acceptable outcome of this activity will be (Step 5 of coping, "What will my outcome be?"). By following these steps and keeping all of this in mind while working on the lesson you have for them, they will greatly reduce their anxiety level about the task and will increase their likelihood of completing the task successfully.

Research Base

McCain, 2005

Reid, Webster-Stratton, & Hammond, 2007

What to Watch for With ELL/CLD Students

The strategy preparation can be done in the native language or dialect of the students to assure their understanding of your expectations and their task prior to carrying the assignment out in English or other communication mode.

142. CROSS-CULTURAL COUNSELING

Purpose of the Strategy

1. Enhance awareness of school adaptation process

2. Reduce anxiety and stress

3. Develop personal control of situations

How to Do It

1. At Tier 2, this strategy is done with small groups. In primary grades, teachers and assistants receive training in cross-cultural stress response patterns and interventions for use in the classroom.

2. In intermediate grades, teachers receive training in cross-cultural stress response patterns and interventions for use in the classroom. Specialist with training in cross-cultural stress responses and culture shock provides counseling and guidance.

3. In secondary grades, a specialist with training in cross-cultural stress responses and culture shock provides counseling and guidance.

Research Base

Burnham, Mantero, & Hooper, 2009

R. Johnson, 1995

Landis, Bennett, & Bennett, 2004

McAllister & Irvine, 2000

What to Watch for With ELL/CLD Students

1. Many cultures have adverse reactions to "official" personnel getting involved with the family and particularly with someone telling them how to raise their children.

2. The specialist facilitating the counseling must not only be trained in cross-cultural techniques but also be familiar with the particular culture and language of the family being assisted.

143. GUIDED PRACTICE AND PLANNED INTERACTIONS WITH DIFFERENT SPEAKERS

Purpose of the Strategy

1. Build transfer skills

2. Build awareness of appropriate school language and rules for communication behaviors

3. Develop confidence in school language and rules for academic and social interactions

4. Develop cognitive academic language

5. Reduce anxiety in social/academic interactions

How to Do It

1. At Tier 2, this strategy is done with small groups. A peer or a specialist demonstrates how to act or speak in a given school culture situation. The situation is explained in home and community language when possible, and each stage is modeled. Representatives of school language and rules who are familiar to the learners come into the classroom and role-play the situation with the instructor. Students then practice each stage of the interaction with these familiar participants until comfortable with the interaction.

Research Base

Cole, 1995

Haneda, 2008

Reggy-Mamo, 2008

Ross, 1971

What to Watch for With ELL/CLD Students

1. It is important to have the example speakers be people with whom the students are familiar and comfortable.

2. This can be paired with role-play of school interactions.

144. GUIDED PRACTICE IN CLASSROOM BEHAVIOR EXPECTATIONS AND SURVIVAL STRATEGIES

Purpose of the Strategy

1. Develop personal control of situations

2. Improve confidence in school interactions

3. Reduce distractibility

4. Reduce acting-out behaviors

How to Do It

1. At Tier 2, this strategy is done with small groups. In primary grades, an intermediate student, a peer, or a specialist demonstrates how to act in a given school or school culture situation. The situation is explained in home and community language when possible, and each stage is modeled. Students then practice each stage of the interaction with familiar participants until comfortable and successful in appropriate behaviors.

2. In intermediate grades, a secondary student, a peer or a specialist demonstrates how to act in a given school or school culture situation. The situation is explained in home and community language when possible, and each stage is modeled. Students then practice each stage of the interaction with familiar participants until comfortable and successful in appropriate behaviors.

3. In secondary grades, an older peer or a specialist demonstrates how to act in a given school or school culture situation. The situation is explained in home and community language when possible, and each stage is modeled. Students then practice each stage of the interaction with familiar participants until comfortable and successful in appropriate behaviors.

Research Base

Buchanan, 1990

Davis, 2005

Hafernik, Messerschmitt, & Vandrick, 2002

J. R. Nelson et al., 1998

Rubenstein, 2006

What to Watch for With ELL/CLD Students

1. Particular social groups and cultures have different expectations of adults and children when it comes to being accountable for task completion. This is a learned difference between cultures. The teacher needs to be aware that the expectations in an American school may need to be taught directly to CLD students and should not assume that they are understood.

2. One way to introduce the idea of behavior and strategies specific to your classroom is to ask students about how their parents have them behave at home or the rules they have learned about playing games. This can then be expanded to the idea of acting appropriately in a classroom.

3. Demonstrate all of the desired behaviors and strategies. Some role-play may be helpful. Examples of inappropriate behaviors may be used with caution.

145. GUIDED PRACTICE IN CROSS-CULTURAL CONFLICT RESOLUTION STRATEGIES

Purpose of the Strategy

1. Develop personal control of situations

2. Enhance ability to resolve conflicts with others

3. Facilitate the school adaptation process

4. Reduce acting-out behaviors

5. Reduce number of conflicts with other students

How to Do It

At Tier 2, this strategy is done with small groups. A peer or a specialist demonstrates conflict-resolution techniques in a given school culture situation. The situation is explained in home and community language when possible, and each step is modeled. Students then practice each step of the resolution with familiar participants until comfortable and successful in appropriate behaviors.

Research Base

Aram & Shlak, 2008

Fitzell, 1997

Hafernik et al., 2002

Ovando & Collier, 1998

What to Watch for With ELL/CLD Students

1. Particular social groups and cultures have different expectations of adults and children when it comes to conflict resolution. This is a learned difference between cultures. The teacher needs to be aware that the expectations in an American school may need to be taught directly to CLD students and not just assume that they are understood.

2. One way to introduce the idea of conflict-resolution behavior and strategies specific to your classroom is to ask students about how their parents have them behave at home when they disagree with their siblings. This can then be expanded to the idea of acting appropriately in a classroom.

3. Demonstrate all of the desired behaviors and strategies. Some role-play may be helpful. Examples of inappropriate behaviors may be used with caution.

146. ROLE-PLAYING

Purpose of the Strategy

1. Build awareness of appropriate behaviors for school language and rules communication

2. Build transfer skills

3. Develop confidence in school language and rules interactions

4. Develop higher tolerance

5. Develop thinking and planning skills

6. Improve retention of content

7. Utilize prior knowledge

How to Do It

1. At Tier 2, this strategy is done with small groups. The teacher assigns students specific roles and creates a situation where roles are acted out based on how the students believe their characters would act. A specific problem, such as

discrimination, is identified and described. Students role-play how they would confront the problem and discuss their roles or behaviors upon completion. Students learn how to confront the reactions of others and ways to deal with situations similar to the role-play.

2.   Students identify a number of uncomfortable or uncertain social or formal interactions. The teacher and assistant model the appropriate and inappropriate ways to handle these interactions. Students take different roles in the interaction and practice with one another and the teacher. Students read a dialogue prepared by the teacher or by other students.

3.   Teachers and assistants model the appropriate and inappropriate ways to use cognitive academic language and cognitive learning strategies. Students take different roles in the interactions and practice these with one another and the teacher. Students practice the cognitive learning strategies in varied academic content areas with the teacher or assistant monitoring.

4.   The teacher and assistant model the appropriate and inappropriate ways to use basic interpersonal communication and cognitive academic language in various school settings, both in and out of the classroom. Students take different roles in the interactions and practice these with one another and with the teacher. Students may suggest communication situations they want specific assistance with and teacher facilitates role-plays. Students create dialogues and interaction situations to enact.

5.   Assign students specific roles and create situations where roles are acted out based on how the students believe their characters would act. A specific problem, such as discrimination, is identified and described. Students role-play how they would confront the problem and discuss their roles or behaviors upon completion. Students learn how to confront the reactions of others and ways to deal with situations similar to the role-play.

Research Base

C. Collier, 2003; see page 183

J. E. Johnson et al., 1999

Kim & Kellogg, 2007

Livingstone, 1983

Magos & Politi, 2008

Rymes, Cahnmann-Taylor, & Souto-Manning, 2008

Webster-Stratton & Reid, 2004

What to Watch for With ELL/CLD Students

1.   Many societies and cultures have specific beliefs and understandings about pretending to be something one is not in reality; there are cultural guidelines for make-believe, play, and assuming the role or character of someone or something.

2.   Be clear that in public schools and classrooms, we sometimes are like actors in movies or television stories (although understanding that some people may think those are all real) for the purpose of illustrating or demonstrating something.

3.   Be clear that they will not become the character or thing and that it is a temporary action to illustrate or demonstrate a particular interaction you want them to learn.

4.   It may be easier with some students to start with puppets or drawings and then work up to individual people doing the actions.

147. SELF-MONITORING TECHNIQUES

Purpose of the Strategy

1. Develop confidence in cognitive academic interactions

2. Develop independence in learning situations

3. Develop personal control of situations

4. Increase time spent on task

5. Facilitate student assuming responsibility for learning

6. Reduce response fatigue

7. Reduce inappropriate behaviors

How to Do It

1. At Tier 2, this strategy is done with small groups. Individual students monitor their learning behaviors using teacher or student-made checklists.

2. For example, students record a checkmark each time they catch themselves being distracted, tapping their pencils on their desks, or each time they complete a specified portion of an assignment.

Research Base

Borba, 2001; see pages 81–118

Strickland et al., 2002; see page 216

C. A. Tomlinson, 1999; see pages 66–68

What to Watch for With ELL/CLD Students

1. All cultures have expectations and rules about the degree to which a child is responsible for his actions. This is related to differences in cultural practices regarding locus of control.

2. Students can learn this strategy and benefit from it, but the teacher has to directly teach this process and not assume that students automatically understand the purpose.

3. Use the students' most proficient language to explain what the process and purpose of the strategy are.

4. Teachers must familiarize themselves with the self-control rules of the various cultures represented in their classrooms before expecting to use self-monitoring strategically to promote learning.

148. SHELTERED INTERACTIONS

Purpose of the Strategy

1. Build transfer skills

2. Develop confidence in school culture interactions

3. Develop higher tolerance

4. Facilitate access of prior knowledge

How to Do It

At Tier 2, this strategy is done with small groups. The teacher develops a game or other casual group interaction activity. The teacher or specialist explains in home and community language, when possible, what is going to occur and who the students are going to meet. The home and community culture students are introduced to the school culture students, and they engage in the game or activity together.

Research Base

Cloud et al., 2000

Cole, 1995; see page 65

Echevarria et al., 2007

Echevarria & Graves, 2006

Garber-Miller, 2006

What to Watch for With ELL/CLD Students

1. It is important to have the example speakers be people with whom the students are familiar and comfortable.

2. This can be paired with role-play of school interactions.

149. SURVIVAL STRATEGIES REGARDING RULES OF INTERACTIONS AND EXPECTATIONS

Purpose of the Strategy

1. Build awareness of appropriate school language and rules for academic and social behaviors

2. Build transfer skills

3. Develop confidence in school culture interactions

4. Develop personal control of situations

5. Reduce response fatigue

How to Do It

At Tier 2, this strategy is done with small groups. The teacher identifies basic rules of social and formal interaction that students will need to know immediately. Students may identify situations where they made mistakes. The teacher, assistant, and peers discuss situations and what interactions are expected. Students may need to practice these interactions.

Research Base

Ashworth & Wakefield, 2004

Felix-Brasdefer, 2008

Jackson et al., 1998

B. Johnson et al., 1998

What to Watch for With ELL/CLD Students

1. Particular social groups and cultures have different expectations of adults and children when it comes to following rules. This is a learned difference between cultures. The teacher needs to be aware that the expectations in an American school may need to be taught directly to CLD students and not just assume that they are understood.

2. One way to introduce the idea of behavior and strategies specific to your classroom is to ask students about how their parents have them behave at home or the rules they have learned about playing games. This can then be expanded to the idea of acting appropriately in a classroom.

3. Demonstrate all of the desired behaviors and strategies. Some role-play may be helpful. Examples of inappropriate behaviors may be used with caution

150. VIDEOTAPES AND BOOKLETS OF SCHOOL PROCEDURES AND EXPECTATIONS

Purpose of the Strategy

1. Build awareness of appropriate academic behavior

2. Build transfer skills

3. Build awareness of appropriate cognitive academic language

4. Develop personal control of situations

5. Reinforce school/parent partnership

How to Do It

At Tier 2, this strategy is done with small groups. Groups of students and/or their families view videos developed locally or available from Intercultural Press and others about public schools and about interacting with school personnel. They are best if shown in the home and community language and with a facilitator. Students are encouraged to discuss with their families what they see and experience in school.

Research Base

Carrigan, 2001; see pages 54–58

Kamps et al., 2007

Koskinen & Blum, 1984

Wood & Algozzine, 1994

Wood & Harmon, 2001

Zutell & Rasinski, 1991

What to Watch for With ELL/CLD Students

1. Always introduce school expectations and rules to ELL and CLD students by explaining them in their most proficient language.

2. ELL/CLD students who have had prior schooling might be asked what sort of rules and expectations they were familiar with and that could become part of the classroom routine.

3. There are some excellent locally produced materials about school and service options in and for specific communities. The local school district may keep these in the media center. They may also be available through a local college or university.

4. The teacher should be aware of the diversity of reaction to depictions of official or government agencies and laws. These can raise the affective filter or emotional response of both students and parents to discussions about services.

5. Always have interpreters available for in-depth discussion of the materials presented.

151. CLASS BUDDIES/PEER HELPERS/PEER TUTORS

Purpose of the Strategy

1. Build transfer skills

2. Develop basic interpersonal communication

3. Develop cognitive academic language

4. Develop content knowledge foundation

5. Develop higher tolerance

6. Develop positive peer relationships

7. Develop thinking and planning skills

8. Improve retention

9. Utilize prior knowledge

How to Do It

1. At Tier 2, this strategy is done with small groups. Home and community language peers who are more proficient in English assist home and community language students in specific content area lessons and activities. The peers are given training in being a tutor, with guidelines about how to facilitate learning without doing another's work, how to translate appropriately, and how to monitor for understanding.

2. Students assist in the classroom by working with other students. Tutors may receive training about objectives, reinforcement, and the like. A student who has mastered a list of sight words or math facts presents these items on flash cards to another student needing assistance in this area. Students help other learners of similar or different ages in the classroom to complete assignments or other responsibilities. This strategy has been shown to provide learning gains for both the tutor and the tutee, and allows the teacher to work closely with more students. The teacher should always be clear about the objectives of the tutoring session and hold the students accountable for their work.

3. For example, the tutoring students share their reports with the tutees. In preparation, the tutors identify key concepts and vocabulary used in the report and present these on tag board cards to the tutees. The tutees tell the tutors, in their own words, what they understood from the report.

4. Home and community language peers who are more proficient in English assist home and community language students in specific content area lessons and activities. The peers are given training in being a tutor, with guidelines about how to facilitate learning without doing another's work, how to translate appropriately, and how to monitor for understanding.

Expansion: Peer helpers develop a code of ethics and their own guidelines for tutoring.

Research Base

Carrigan, 2001; see pages 44–45

What to Watch for With ELL/CLD Students

1. With specific first-generation refugee, indigenous, migrant, and immigrant groups, teachers must be careful about pairing students based on their perceptions of them coming from similar language backgrounds. There can be cultural and class differences that will make the partners uncomfortable with one another.

2. The teacher must be prepared to deal with prejudice between populations where language is the same but culture, class, or racial issues may impede comfort and communication. American all togetherness may come in time, but the teacher must proceed slowly and not push.

3. Students may interact more as they become more comfortable in the classroom or more trusting that they are accepted and valued.

152. VIDEOTAPES OR BOOKLETS ABOUT INTERACTION PATTERNS IN NORTH AMERICA

Purpose of the Strategy

1. Build awareness of school culture expectations

2. Develop familiarity with school language and rules for academic and social interaction patterns

3. Reduce culture shock

How to Do It

Groups of students and/or their families view videos developed locally or available from Intercultural Press and others about life in North America and about interacting with North Americans. It is best if they are shown in the home and community language and with an experienced facilitator.

Research Base

Carrigan, 2001; see pages 54–58

Cochran-Smith & Zeichner, 2005

Prasad, 2005

What to Watch for With ELL/CLD Students

1. There are many dialects of spoken English and differences of opinion about what is the proper dialect to use as the model for ELL/CLD students.

2. The teacher should be aware of the diversity of reaction to specific dialects of spoken English in North America and be prepared to address expressions of prejudice or value judgments about certain speakers shown on the videotapes.

3. The most practical way to deal with this is to prescreen the videos and select segments that most closely represent the dialects common in your local communities plus a few as examples of the diversity that exists in our country.

153. CROSS-CULTURAL COMMUNICATION STRATEGIES

Purpose of the Strategy

1. Build transfer skills

2. Build awareness of appropriate communication behaviors for school language and rules

3. Develop confidence in school language and rules for academic and social interactions

How to Do It

1. At Tier 2, this strategy is done with small groups. The teacher models cross-cultural communication strategies such as reflection, proxemics, latency, and active listening. Reflection is positioning yourself in an almost mirror image to

the posture of the other person, using similar rate of speech. Proxemics is paying attention to how close you are to the other speaker, and latency is the culturally learned length of time between one speaker's turn and the next speaker's turn to speak. Active listening is showing that you are paying attention and responding in culturally appropriate ways to indicate your attention. This may include repeating some portion of what was said.

2. The teacher has the students practice using these strategies in a variety of interactions.

Research Base

Croom & Davis, 2006

Gibbons, 2002

Trudeau & Harle, 2006

What to Watch for With ELL/CLD Students

1. All cultures have different mores about how close you can stand or sit next to another person (proxemics), who or what you may touch, how much time should elapse before you speak after another person (latency), and so on. The teacher should become familiar with these differences regarding the students in this classroom.

2. The strategy of reflection can look like mockery and mimicry if not done with sensitivity. The goal is to reflect—not imitate—the mode of the speaker.

154 BUILDING CONNECTIONS

Purpose of the Strategy

1. Develop self-esteem

2. Encourage pride in home language and culture

3. Strengthen home–school relationship

How to Do It

1. At Tier 2, this strategy is done with small groups. Teachers or assistants establish support groups and give workshops on learning how to cope with a new environment.

2. Teachers or assistants establish and support parent–teen support groups and give workshops on learning how to cope with a new environment.

3. Teachers establish school clubs for specific acculturation issues, holidays, and the like.

Research Base

Brownlie & King, 2000; see pages 21–28

Carrigan, 2001; see page 49

What to Watch for With ELL/CLD Students

1. Learning to survive and thrive in a new environment is challenging for anyone. This can be especially difficult for ELL and CLD learners and their families.

2. Small, social support groups in the school and in the community can provide a safe group within which to ask questions and learn ways to succeed at tasks or in solving problems.

155. GUIDED PRACTICE IN CONSTRUCTIVE QUALITY INTERACTIONS

Purpose of the Strategy

1. Build transfer skills

2. Build awareness of appropriate school language and rules for academic and social behaviors

3. Develop confidence in school language and rules for academic and social interactions

4. Develop personal control of situations

5. Reduce response fatigue

How to Do It

At Tier 2, this strategy is done with small groups. A peer or a specialist demonstrates how to act or speak in a given school culture situation. The situation is explained in home and community language when possible, and each stage is modeled. Representatives of school language and rules who are familiar to the learners come into the classroom and role-play the situation with the instructor. Students then practice each stage of the interaction with these familiar participants until comfortable with the interaction.

Research Base

Carrigan, 2001; see page 49

Cole, 1995; see pages 150–152

What to Watch for With ELL/CLD Students

1. Learning to survive and thrive in a new environment is challenging for anyone. This can be especially difficult for ELL and CLD learners and their families as they learn to interact in a new language and with new social rules and expectations.

2. Bring in people from the community with whom the participants are comfortable first. Gradually expand the interaction circle as folks become more confident.

3. Small, social support groups in the school and in the community can provide a safe group within which to ask questions and learn ways to succeed at tasks or in solving problems.

156. PEER TUTORING

Purpose of the Strategy

1. Develop higher tolerance

2. Develop positive peer relationships

3. Develop thinking and planning skills

4. Ensure learning gains are experienced by both students

5. Improve retention

6. Utilize prior knowledge

How to Do It

1. At Tier 2, this strategy is done with small groups. Students assist in the classroom by working with other students. Tutors may receive training about objectives, reinforcement, and the like. A student who has mastered a list of sight words or

math facts presents these items on flash cards to another student needing assistance in this area. Students help other learners of similar or different ages in the classroom to complete assignments or other responsibilities. This strategy has been shown to provide learning gains for both the tutor and the tutee, and it allows the teacher to work closely with more students. The teacher should always be clear about the objectives of the tutoring session and hold the students accountable for their work.

2. For example, the tutoring students share their report with the tutees. In preparation, the tutors identify key concepts and vocabulary used in the report and present these on tag board cards to the tutees. The tutees tell the tutor in their own words what they understood from the report.

Research Base

Carrigan, 2001; see pages 44–45

Cole, 1995; see page 66

What to Watch for With ELL/CLD Students

1. With specific first-generation refugee, indigenous, migrant, and immigrant groups, teachers must be careful about pairing students based on their perceptions of them coming from similar language backgrounds. There can be cultural and class differences that will make the partners uncomfortable with one another.

2. The teacher must be prepared to deal with prejudice between populations where language is the same but culture, class, or racial issues may impede comfort and communication. American all togetherness may come in time, but the teacher must proceed slowly and not push.

3. Students may interact more as they become more comfortable in the classroom or more trusting that they are accepted and valued.

157. ROLE-PLAYING IN SOCIAL AND ACADEMIC LANGUAGE DEVELOPMENT

Purpose of the Strategy

1. Build transfer skills

2. Build awareness of appropriate communication behaviors for school language and rules

3. Develop confidence in school language and rules for academic and social interactions

4. Develop cognitive academic language

5. Reduce code-switching

How to Do It

1. At Tier 2, this strategy is done with small groups. The teacher and assistant model the appropriate and inappropriate ways to use basic interpersonal communication and cognitive academic language in various school settings, both in and out of the classroom. Students take different roles in the interactions and practice with one another and with the teacher. Students may suggest communication situations they want specific assistance with and teacher facilitates role-plays. Students create dialogues and interaction situations to enact.

2. Assign students specific roles and create situations where roles are acted out based on how the students believe their characters would act. A specific problem, such as discrimination, is identified and described. Students role-play how they would confront the problem and discuss their roles or behaviors upon completion. Students learn how to confront the reactions of others and ways to deal with situations similar to the role-play.

Research Base

J. E. Johnson et al., 1999

Kim & Kellogg, 2007

Livingstone, 1983

Magos & Politi, 2008

What to Watch for With ELL/CLD Students

1. Many societies and cultures have specific beliefs and understandings about pretending to be something one is not in reality; there are cultural guidelines for make-believe, play, and assuming the role or character of someone or something.

2. Be clear that in public schools and classrooms, we sometimes are like actors in movies or television stories (although understanding that some people may think those are all real) for the purpose of illustrating or demonstrating something.

3. Be clear that they will not become the character or thing and that it is a temporary action to illustrate or demonstrate a particular interaction you want them to learn.

4. It may be easier with some students to start with puppets or drawings and then work up to individual people doing the actions.

158. USE OF FIRST LANGUAGE

Purpose of the Strategy

1. Build transfer skills

2. Develop confidence in school language and rules for academic and social interactions

3. Develop cognitive academic language

4. Improve motivation

5. Minimize behavior problems

6. Reduce code-switching

How to Do It

At Tier 2, this strategy is done with small groups. The teacher directs an advanced-fluency student to lead a guided activity in the home and/or community language. Students can retell parts of a story in pairs after the directed activity rather than have one student speak while the others all listen. Students then write summaries of what they have heard. Writing can be in either home or community language or English. During this time, the students have a chance to help one another. Advanced-fluency students can dramatize and create a dialogue to illustrate the action.

Research Base

Carrigan, 2001; see page 191

What to Watch for With ELL/CLD Students

1. The language helper can prepare the ELL/LEP students for an English lesson by reviewing key vocabulary words, explaining what will be occurring, and discussing what the teacher's expectations will be for the students' performances.

This would then be followed by the teacher presenting the lesson in English. Students would be given the opportunity to ask for specific clarification in their first language.

2. Students could work on their projects subsequent to the English lesson with the assistance of the bilingual helper as needed. Content discussion and clarification should be in the students' most proficient language while they are preparing their task or project for presentation in English with the rest of the class.

159. RETENTION STRATEGY—CAN DO

Purpose of the Strategy

1. Develop higher tolerance

2. Develop thinking and planning skills

3. Improve mnemonic retrieval

4. Improve retention

5. Utilize prior knowledge

How to Do It

At Tier 2, this strategy is done with small groups. This visualization technique may assist with memorization of lists of items. The steps in CAN-DO are

Create list of items to learn
Ask self if list is complete
Note details and main ideas
Describe components and their relationships
Over-learn main items followed by learning details

Research Base

Derwinger et al., 2005

Eskritt & McLeod, 2008

Jutras, 2008

S. W. Lee, 2005

What to Watch for With ELL/CLD Students

1. Newcomers will need to have the CAN-DO steps modeled and explained in their most proficient language before they can proceed independently.

2. Students can be paired with partners who are slightly more bilingual than they are to facilitate their learning this process.

160. CONSISTENT SEQUENCE

Purpose of the Strategy

1. Build academic transfer skills

2. Build awareness of appropriate academic behaviors

How to Do It

At Tier 2, this strategy is done with small groups. The teacher presents all content lessons with the same instructional language and direction sequence to the extent possible.

Expansion: Students can role-play giving the directions themselves.

Research Base

Mathes et al., 2007

Vaughn & Linan-Thompson, 2007

What to Watch for With ELL/CLD Students

1. This strategy is consistent with the Sheltered Instruction Observation Protocol (SIOP) model used in many ELL programs.

2. Newcomers who have never attended school may become confused if every lesson and activity occurs in seemingly random patterns. They do not know what is expected of them at various stages of the lesson. They do not know what to attend to and what is less important.

3. This is also going to impact students with undiagnosed attention deficit disorders that they have not yet learned to accommodate.

4. It is better to start out with simple consistent steps and add to them as students become comfortable and familiar with what is going to happen in the classroom

161. DEMONSTRATION

Purpose of the Strategy

1. Improve confidence in academic interactions

2. Reduce distractibility

3. Build academic transfer skills

4. Develop content knowledge foundation

How to Do It

At Tier 2, this strategy is done with small groups. The teacher, an assistant, or a peer demonstrates the content of the lesson. The content is explained in home and community language when possible, and each aspect of the lesson is demonstrated. Students demonstrate their understanding of the lesson and content. Activities and assessment are designed to facilitate demonstration of understanding.

Research Base

Echevarria et al., 2007

Gibbons, 2006

What to Watch for With ELL/CLD Students

1. This strategy is consistent with both Sheltered Instruction Observation Protocol (SIOP) and the Guided Language Acquisition Design (GLAD) process used in many ELL programs.

2. Students who have never been schooled before will not know what is expected and will benefit from concrete direct demonstrations of content elements and activity expectations.

162. RETENTION STRATEGY—STAR

Purpose of the Strategy

1. Build awareness of learning

2. Develop personal control of situations

3. Improve access to prior knowledge

4. Reduce off-task behaviors

5. Strengthen language development

How to Do It

At Tier 2, this strategy is done with small groups. This strategy can be used for all content areas and for behavior modification. Students can make cue cards for each step. The steps in STAR are

Stop
Think
Act
Review

Research Base

Agran, King-Sears, Wehmeyer, & Copeland, 2003

Carpenter, 2001

S.-H. Lee et al., 2006

What to Watch for With ELL/CLD Students

1. Newcomers will need to have the STAR steps modeled and explained in their most proficient language before they can proceed independently.

2. Students can be paired with partners who are slightly more bilingual than they are to facilitate their learning this process.

COGNITIVE ISSUES AT TIER 2

163. ADVANCED ORGANIZERS

Purpose of the Strategy

1. Build language transfer skills

2. Build awareness of appropriate content language for school language and rules

How to Do It

1. At Tier 2, this strategy is done with small groups. The teacher has the target student preview the lesson for less-advanced students, outlining key issues, rehearsing vocabulary, and reviewing related prior knowledge. Advanced-fluency students help less-advanced students understand how to organize their reading and writing materials.

2. These are anticipatory cognitive activities that set the stage for what is to come as well as previewing the content and your expectations for what the students are to do in the lesson. You can use one or a combination of these in sequence prior to a lesson and continue as long as needed to ensure comprehension and readiness of your students.

3. These can be a combination visualization and vocabulary preview. Ask your students to imagine someone or something that illustrates the concept or main ideas that you are about to have them delve into. Some examples in subject areas are listed here.

   a. Language arts: "Think about a person who turned out to be something other than what your first impression led you to believe." (Such as in *Paper Bag Princess*, *The Tawny Scrawny Lion*, or *Othello*)

   b. Science: "Think about how you know it will rain." (Lessons about temperature, weather, clouds)

   c. Math: "Think about buying four things at the store when you have $11.75 in your pocket." (Lessons on subtraction, addition, fractions)

   d. Social Studies: "Think about something your family does together that may be different from other families' activities." (Lessons about holidays, diversity, community)

4. KWL charts have students tell what they already know about the upcoming content and list it on the chart under *know*. Have students say what they want to know related to the upcoming lesson and list it on the chart under *want* (to learn). Have the students discuss the various ways that they might learn the answers to their questions and how you as the teacher might teach them about the topic. You will come back to the chart after the lesson is over to review what students *learned* and how they learned it.

5. W-stars give the students the topic you are about to teach, show the students the cover of the book you are about to read or pictures in the story, and then ask them the five questions on each point of the star (who, what, where, when, and why). Students' guesses are recorded on the points. You will then come back to the star for review after the lesson.

6. Graphic organizers are cognitive tools for illustrating how ideas, content, and elements in a story or lesson relate to one another. They can be used as preview and review tools as well as assist in embedding the lesson elements cognitively for the diverse learner. There are several other ways to shape and use these, including Venn diagrams, charting, and growth spirals, but we will discuss one specific example in this book. This a model of a graphic organizer for literature that is also useful when comparing and contrasting story elements and content across many pieces of literature and from many cultural traditions. Students can assist in filling in the graphic organizer in groups or through a jigsaw activity (each small group of students is assigned to fill in one or two of the boxes).

Research Base

Collier, 2003

Harwell, 2001

Heacox, 2002

Moore et al., 2000

Opitz, 1998

What to Watch for With ELL/CLD Students

1. There are cultural differences in cognitive/learning style and some ELL/CLD students may not respond to the brainstorming construct behind most advanced organizers.

2. By keeping the graphic design of the advanced organizer as close as possible to the illustrations in the text or some aspect of the lesson, the teacher can more tightly connect the concepts being studied with the W questioning that precedes the lesson.

3. This is another activity that works best with preparation in the students' most proficient language and relevance to their culture before proceeding.

164. EVALUATION

Purpose of the Strategy

1. Build awareness of learning process

2. Develop categorization skills

3. Develop extended time spent on task

4. Develop personal control of situations

How to Do It

1. At Tier 2, this strategy is done with small groups. Students use evaluation cards to cue themselves for each step. They select a specific problem or task and use the cards as mnemonics as they proceed through the assignment. Steps for students to follow in implementing the strategy are listed here.

   a. How will I evaluate the problem?

   b. What are the important elements of this problem?

   c. How will I get feedback?

   d. How can I generalize the information?

2. Steps for teaching evaluation

   a. *Inform* the students what evaluation is, how it operates, when to use it, and why it is useful. Begin by saying that evaluation is a way to help them analyze and monitor their learning. It works by asking and answering the series of five questions concerning a lesson they are working on. Once they learn how to use evaluation, they can use it anytime and with any content or lesson you give them to do.

   b. *Use cues*, metaphors, analogies, or other means of elaborating on a description of evaluation combined with visual cues. One way to do this is to have the group watch a panel discussion or other presentation on television where a group is analyzing a problem or evaluating a proposal to do something. Another is to show a video of scientists working in a laboratory to evaluate whether a substance works effectively. Show how everyone can analyze, monitor, and control learning when they go step by step.

   c. *Lead group discussions* about the use of evaluation. Have students start with talking about a science or math lesson they have just successfully solved. They can go back through the lesson or interaction stopping to show how each step of the lesson can be analyzed and monitored using the evaluation steps to see how they work and what is required. Encourage them to ask you anything about the learning process they want clarified.

   d. *Provide guided practice* in applying evaluation to particular tasks. Here is an example of guided practice as the teacher leads the students through the use of evaluation. Examples of both teacher and student comments are shown here.

Teacher: "First, you must analyze the task to determine what it requires. This includes items such as materials, time, space, or types of actions. What is the expected outcome of the task? What steps must you follow to complete the task? Review other completed assignments to determine possible steps you might take to complete this task."

Student: "What do I need to do to complete this task, and do I have all necessary materials and resources? What should the expected outcome look like? What steps must I follow to effectively achieve the expected outcome?"

Teacher: "Second, after you have analyzed the task, you must identify possible strategies that might be used to accomplish the task. Think about strategies you have used in the past to complete similar tasks. One or more of these may be necessary to complete this task."

Student: "What strategies do I know that might be appropriate for this particular task? Why might these be useful in this particular situation?"

Strategy Implementation

Teacher: "Third, prior to using a selected strategy, review the steps in that strategy. Remember that one strategy may be used in several different situations and different situations may require the use of more than one strategy."

Student: "I've selected these strategies for this task. I'll review the process associated with each strategy prior to implementation. I'll use these strategies while I complete this task."

Feedback

Teacher: "Fourth, you must become aware of how useful it is to use the strategies you have selected. They assist you to complete the task accurately and efficiently. Periodically, reflect upon how you are doing and how effective the strategy is for completing the task at hand."

Student: "How useful is this strategy for this particular task? Is this strategy helping me to accurately and efficiently confront the assigned task? Do I need to use a different strategy?"

Teacher: "Finally, think of other previously completed tasks where use of one or more of these strategies would have been beneficial to confronting the tasks. Could you have completed those tasks more efficiently had you used these strategies? Think of other types of tasks or future tasks where you might appropriately use one or more of these strategies."

Student: "Why were these strategies useful to this particular task? In what other types of situations would the use of these strategies be beneficial?"

e. *Provide feedback* on monitoring use and success of evaluation. While students use evaluation in small groups, you should move around the room listening and supplying encouragement for consistent use of the question and answer steps. As students get more comfortable using this strategy, you can have them monitor one another in the use of the strategy, encouraging one another to ask and/or answer the questions.

f. *Provide generalization* activities. Have your students use evaluation for a variety of lessons and tasks. You should be sure to identify the strategy by name and point to the poster or visual cues about the strategy whenever you have students use it. Hold enhanced cognitive discussions about the use of evaluation in these different lesson settings, and encourage discussion of how useful or not useful students found this strategy in particular tasks.

Research Base

Brown & Palincsar, 1989

Cole, 1995; see pages 115–116

Opitz, 1998; see page 61

Pressley, Borkowski, & O'Sullivan, 1984

What to Watch for With ELL/CLD Students

1.   Because these students may be limited in English proficiency, the monolingual, English-speaking teacher must increase the amount of demonstration and visual cues and rely less on verbal descriptions and cues. If available, bilingual assistance from peers or other education personnel may be useful in translating what is discussed in the classroom. This is especially important to provide explicit information to students concerning the rationale and value of the strategy. In addition, analogy elaboration of the evaluation strategy may be drawn from the students' cultural and linguistic backgrounds. This reinforces the validity of the students' previous successful learning and increases the ability of the students to make associations that will strengthen their cognitive development.

2.   Students who have never been in school before will not know what is expected of them and what measuring, analyzing, and evaluating look like.

3.   Some translation and discussion in the ELL students' more proficient language may be necessary to clarify what is to be done and why.

165. TEST-TAKING STRATEGY—PIRATES

Purpose of the Strategy

1.   Build cognitive academic language

2.   Build learning strategies

3.   Facilitate test-taking success

4.   Reduce distractibility

How to Do It

At Tier 2, this strategy is done with small groups. PIRATES may assist learners to complete tests more carefully and successfully. Students can create cue cards of the mnemonic and use them to work through each test and test item. The steps in PIRATES are

Prepare to succeed
Inspect instructions carefully
Read entire question, remember strategies, and reduce choices
Answer question or leave until later
Turn back to the abandoned items
Estimate unknown answers by avoiding absolutes and eliminating similar choices
Survey to ensure that all items have a response

Research Base

DeVries Guth & Stephens Pettengill, 2005

Hughes et al., 1993

Lebzelter & Nowacek, 1999

What to Watch for With ELL/CLD Students

1.   Newcomers will need to have the PIRATES steps modeled and explained in their most proficient language before they can proceed independently.

2.   Students can be paired with partners who are slightly more bilingual than they are to facilitate their learning this process.

166. REALITY-BASED LEARNING APPROACHES

Purpose of the Strategy

1. Build awareness of learning

2. Reduce confusion in locus of control

3. Reduce off-task behaviors

4. Improve motivation

How to Do It

At Tier 2, this strategy is done with small groups. Teachers provide students with real purposes and real audiences for reading, writing, speaking, and presenting mathematical and scientific hypotheses or calculations. When students write about and speak to intended purposes and audiences, they are more likely to be motivated and to obtain valuable feedback on their efforts.

Research Base

Cole, 1995; see pages 25–26

What to Watch for With ELL/CLD Students

1. In some societies and cultures, children are actively discouraged from speculation and make-believe and are encouraged to stay focused on real life and real objects and real interactions.

2. It is not always apparent when your students come from homes where make-believe and fantasy are not supported. Always introducing new content by giving real examples and real applications will assist students in accessing and comprehending the content of the lesson.

3. The teacher can begin introducing make-believe examples and applications as students become comfortable with the general learning process. Teachers should always make it clear when something is nonfiction and when something is fiction.

167. INTERDISCIPLINARY UNIT

Purpose of the Strategy

1. Build transfer skills

2. Develop thinking and planning skills

3. Facilitate connections between known and new

4. Improve access to prior knowledge

5. Strengthen language development

How to Do It

1. At Tier 2, this strategy is done with small groups. The teacher uses thematic, interdisciplinary teaching to help students connect what they learn from one subject to another to discover relationships.

2. In primary grades, students plan a trip to the grocery store. They set up a schedule, timing, measuring, counting, reading, identifying, describing, comparing, assessing, and budgeting activities in relation to their trip.

3. In intermediate grades, the same trip to the grocery store is planned, but they add spatial orientation, nutrition, and considerations of the quality of life.

4. In secondary grades, students study the social impact of a given scientific or technological development at the same time that they are becoming acquainted with the science or technology itself.

5. Bondi (1988) recommends the following steps in designing interdisciplinary units.

   a. *Select a theme together.* Brainstorm together possible themes. Look for themes that relate to district/school goals and that interest students. Expand or narrow your theme as appropriate to reflect the teaching situation in which you are involved. Appoint a team leader for the duration of the development of the unit.

   b. *Work independently.* Identify topics, objectives, and skills from within your subject area that could be developed in this unit.

   c. *Meet together to define objectives for the unit.* Share all topics, objectives, and skills and combine them into a manageable package.

   d. *Meet together or select activities.* Match these activities to your goals in individual subjects. Stretch a little, if need be. Look for activities that provide student options and exploratory activities.

   e. *Brainstorm resources.* Consider here both material resources and people resources.

   f. *Develop your activities* (individually and collectively). Divide the responsibility among the team to order, collect, and contact.

   g. *Schedule your unit.* This includes setting the dates for not only when to teach it but also scheduling the use of rooms, speakers, and the like.

   h. *Advertise your unit.* Do whatever you can to excite students and parents about the unit. Advertise in the school newsletter. Put up a "Coming Attraction" bulletin board. Wear slogans on your lapel.

   i. *Implement your unit.* Have fun and don't expect everything to be perfect.

Research Base

Bondi, 1988

Cole, 1995; see pages 26–27, 68, 147–148

What to Watch for With ELL/CLD Students

1. This is an excellent strategy for making content relevant to the lives of diverse learners. Be sure to include real activities related to the specific communities that your students come from.

2. For newcomers and beginning-level ELL students, the teacher should assign a bilingual peer helper or partner as the unit is explained.

168. LEARNING CENTERS OR STATIONS

Purpose of the Strategy

Create areas or locations in the classroom where students work on various tasks simultaneously

How to Do It

At Tier 2, this strategy is done with small groups. These areas can be formal or informal and can be distinguished by signs, symbols, or colors. Centers differ from stations in that centers are distinct content locations while stations work in concert with one another. For example, there may be a science center, math center, writing center, and reading center in the classroom; each has its special furniture, equipment, materials, and so on. Assignments or tasks specific to each center or station activity are either handed out ahead of time or available at each location.

Research Base

Ashworth & Wakefield, 2004

Movitz & Holmes, 2007

C. A. Tomlinson, 1999; see pages 62–65, 75–81

What to Watch for With ELL/CLD Students

1. ELL/CLD students should not go to separate learning centers for primary instruction in a content lesson or task. They need direct instruction in the content or task including key vocabulary and guided practice in what is expected of them at each learning center.

2. After the ELL/CLD students have been prepared for the learning centers and shown how to use the materials or equipment at each center, they can join in the activities at each center just as the rest of the class does.

3. Learning centers are a good way to reinforce content knowledge and allow students to become engaged in applications of this new knowledge.

169. ACTIVE PROCESSING

Purpose of the Strategy

1. Build awareness of learning

2. Develop academic language

3. Develop personal control of situations

4. Facilitate access of prior knowledge

5. Reduce off-task behaviors

How to Do It

1. At Tier 2, this strategy is done with small groups. Students work through a task aloud, naming each step and asking themselves the appropriate questions for the task. Steps for students to follow in implementing this strategy are listed here.

    a. What is my task?

    b. What do I need to do to complete my task?

    c. How will I know my task is done correctly?

    d. How will I monitor the implementation?

    e. How do I know the task is correctly completed?

2. When applying the active processing strategy, students work through problems or tasks using the sequence of self-monitoring questions. For example, your students must prepare for the state-administered achievement tests required at this grade level, but several of your diverse learners have never taken such tests before and are unfamiliar with this type of evaluation. They have heard stories of something scary that happens to schoolchildren every year and are bracing themselves to endure this external event. You could modify your preparation for this event by integrating the active processing strategy into the lessons before the testing period. Start by having the students in your class speak aloud with one another in small groups

about the content and process of lessons they are learning following the steps in active processing. Do this in every content area until the students are familiar with the process itself. Then a few weeks before the state assessments, introduce the concept of standardized achievement tests to your class. Have your students discuss how group and norm measures differ from individual and curriculum-based assessments and the implications of this for each participant (Step 1 of active processing, "What is my task?"). Have the groups discuss what they will need to have with them and what the setting is like. Have those students who have taken tests like this describe the process and what it was like for them. Talk about the expectations of test administrators regarding notes, whispering, looking at others, pencils, calculators, and so on (Step 2 of active processing, "What do I need to do to complete my task?"). Discuss what an acceptable performance might be for various levels of completion and knowledge. Explain some of the test strategies that help successful test takers even when they are unsure of the answer. Clarify the expectations of parents, teachers, and others about the test activity (Step 3 of active processing, "How will I know my task is done correctly?"). Provide suggestions for relieving stress during the test and ideas for self-monitoring their progress through the different sections of the test (Step 4 of active processing, "How will I monitor the implementation?"). Discuss how timekeepers work and what the timelines will be on this test. Discuss ways to identify when it is time to move to another section and what to do when they are finished with the test (Step 5 of active processing, "How do I know the task is completed?").

Research Base

Cole, 1995

Collier, 2003; see pages 124–130

Law & Eckes, 2000

Tovani, 2000; see pages 26–29

What to Watch for With ELL/CLD Students

1. The strategy preparation can be done in the native language or dialect of the students to assure their understanding of your expectations and their task prior to carrying the assignment out in English or other communication mode.

2. Students who are less proficient in English will need guidance in using the steps of active processing; the process can be explained and practiced in the students' most proficient language before going on in English.

3. Active processing can be used in any language of instruction and in any content area or age level.

170. ANALOGY

Purpose of the Strategy

1. Build transfer skills

2. Develop categorization skills

3. Develop higher tolerance

4. Facilitate access of prior knowledge

How to Do It

1. At Tier 2, this strategy is done with small groups. Students each share something that is meaningful to them. They go through the steps of analogy in pairs as they share their items with one another. Steps for students to follow in implementing the strategy are listed here.

   a. What do I know about this thing already?

   b. How does what I know compare to this new item?

    c. Can the new and the previous be substituted for each other?

    d. How can I elaborate on the known and unknown?

2. When applying the analogy strategy, students work through problems or tasks using the sequence of self-monitoring questions. Let us suppose that you are about to have your students begin a new unit in social studies about immigration nationally, in your state, and in your local community. You have several students who are newcomers to your community from a different part of the world and from a culturally and linguistically diverse background. You could modify your usual instructional approach by building in an opportunity for your students to compare and contrast their personal experiences with current immigration and refugee policies and procedures with those from their experience. You would have them first discuss the difference between immigrant, colonist, settler, emigrant, and refugee using examples from current news stories on television. You could also have them see videotapes or actually visit an INS office or a center where particular groups of newcomers to America receive services. You then have them share what they know about these terms and services from their personal, current experience (Step 1 of analogy, "What do I know about things like this?"). They could then share how these experiences are similar to others they are familiar with or others in the classroom (Step 2 of analogy, "How is what I know similar to this new thing?"). Then they would discuss the differences between their personal or familiar experiences and what is new to them about the policies, procedures, services, and experiences (Step 3 of analogy, "How is this new thing different from what I know?"). The students could explore how different people's experiences might change if certain elements of their circumstances were substituted for another (Step 4 of analogy, "Can I substitute what I know for this new thing?"). Now the students would be ready to expand this knowledge to identifying ways to improve current models of service and how they might help other newcomers to the community (Step 5 of analogy, "How can I elaborate on this?"). Discussions will naturally rise out of these lessons about comparing and contrasting based on high- versus low-tolerance characteristics.

Research Base

Cole, 1995

Collier, 2002

Tovani, 2000

What to Watch for With ELL/CLD Students

1. Be sure students are matched with peers with whom they can communicate comfortably while they are all learning the strategy and steps in the process.

2. After students learn the process and steps, posters or cards with reminder illustrations and the words of the steps can be put up around the room.

3. Once students can use analogy without prompting, they can be paired up with nonbilingual peers for more applications.

171. PROBLEM SOLVING/COPING

Purpose of the Strategy

1. Build awareness of learning process

2. Develop extended time spent on task

3. Develop higher tolerance

4. Develop personal control of situations

5. Develop problem-solving skills

6. Lower anxiety levels

How to Do It

1. At Tier 2, this strategy is done with small groups. Have students identify a specific problem(s) they want to solve as a group. Each group follows the coping steps as they address their problem, writing down their answers and ideas for each stage of the problem solving.

2. Steps for students to follow in implementing this strategy

   a. What is the problem?

   b. What are possible solutions?

   c. What is my action plan?

   d. Where can I go for help?

   e. When should I start?

   f. How will I deal with setbacks?

   g. What is my outcome?

3. Steps for teaching coping

   a. *Inform* the students what coping is, how it operates, when to use it, and why it is useful. Begin by saying that coping is a way to help them solve problems they may have, either in school or outside of school. It works by asking and answering a series of five questions concerning a problem they are working on. Once they learn how to use coping, they can use it anytime and with any content or lesson you give them to do or with personal problems they may have.

   b. *Use cues*, metaphors, analogies, or other means of elaborating on a description of coping combined with visual cues. One way to do this is to have the group go through an example problem they are all familiar with in one of their favorite stories, for example, *Murmel Murmel Murmel* by Munsch and Martchenko (1982). Have them find out how Robin found a home for the baby by going through specific steps. Compare this process to the steps they follow to solve some mathematics process that they all know well. Show how everyone can solve a problem by going step by step.

   c. *Lead group discussions* about the use of coping. Have students start by talking about a problem they have just successfully solved, either in a lesson or during interpersonal interactions. They can go back through the lesson or interaction using the coping question steps to see how they work and what is required. Encourage them to ask you anything about the learning process they want clarified.

   d. *Provide guided practice* in applying coping to particular tasks. Here is an example of guided practice as the teacher leads the students through the use of coping. Examples of both teacher and student comments are shown here.

Teacher: "First, what are the essential elements of the problem? Have you controlled your feelings about the problem or consequences to the problem?"

Student: "Can I break the problem into several parts? What can I say about this problem? Have I controlled my feelings about the problem?"

Teacher: "Second, break the problem into parts and prioritize them in the order that each should be addressed. Develop a plan for addressing the problem in a step-by-step manner. Imagine what the solution or answer might be. How will you know that you have resolved the problem?"

Student:	"What are the elements of this problem that must be addressed? In what order should I address the elements? What might possible solutions look like? How will I know that I have resolved the problem?"
Teacher:	"Third, study the elements of the problem. Do you need assistance with any of them? Where might you go to find necessary assistance? Everyone needs assistance from time to time. You must recognize when you need assistance and know how to go about finding necessary help."
Student:	"Do I need assistance with any parts of this problem? I know that it is okay to ask for help. Do I know someone who can help me? Do I know how to get necessary help?"
Teacher:	"Fourth, after you have analyzed your problem and come up with a plan for taking action, you must implement that plan. Knowing that you are initiating your plan is important for coping with problems and situations. You may use a gesture or word to signal that you have begun your plan."
Student:	"When I am ready to begin addressing my problem, I will snap my fingers or nod my head. I will know that I am ready to begin when I have my action plan ready and have identified potential sources of assistance."
Teacher:	"Fifth, there are usually several ways to achieve something or solve a problem. Some ways may be more effective than others in different circumstances. Do not stop trying if you have difficulty or meet resistance to solving the problem. Sometimes, you must try another approach to achieve a solution. Think of other times when you had difficulty reaching a solution and what you did to resolve that problem."
Student:	"I will not stop if I meet difficulty or resistance. I will attempt different solutions to the problem until the problem has been resolved."
Teacher:	"Sixth, part of coping with problems is to recognize that a solution has been reached and that the problem has been resolved. Recall what it was you were attempting to accomplish and what you imagined the solution to be like. When you reach this accomplishment and have a solution that addresses the problem, then you can say to yourself that you have resolved this problem. Congratulate yourself for coping with and solving your own problem."
Student:	"I've addressed my problem, developed and implemented a plan of action, modified the plan as necessary, asked for necessary assistance, and generated an appropriate solution. I was able to resolve my problem because I am able to ask for assistance when I need it. The solution that I have reached resolves my problem. I congratulate myself for solving my own problem."

e. *Provide feedback* on monitoring use and success of coping. While students use coping in small groups, you should move around the room listening and supplying encouragement for consistent use of the question and answer steps. As students get more comfortable using this strategy, you can have them monitor one another in the use of the strategy, encouraging each other to ask and/or answer the questions.

f. *Provide generalization* activities. Have your students use coping for a variety of lessons and tasks. You should be sure to identify the strategy by name and point to the poster or visual cues about the strategy whenever you have students use it. Hold enhanced cognitive discussions about the use of coping in these different lesson settings, and encourage discussion of how useful or not useful students found this strategy in particular tasks.

Research Base

McCain, 2005

Reid et al., 2007

What to Watch for With ELL/CLD Students

The strategy preparation can be done in the native language or dialect of the students to assure their understanding of your expectations and their task prior to carrying the assignment out in English or other communication mode.

172. INFORMATION ORGANIZATION (EASY)

Purpose of the Strategy

Organize and prioritize information by focusing on questions designed to identify important content

How to Do It

At Tier 2, this strategy is done with small groups. Students can create cue cards to remember each step. Students follow steps while reading passages or thematic elements. The steps in EASY are

Elicit questions (who, what, where, when, why)
Ask self which information is least difficult
Study easy content initially, followed by difficult
Yes! Provide self-reinforcement through rewards or points for self

Research Base

Lapp, Flood, Brock, & Fisher, 2007

Moore et al., 2000

What to Watch for With ELL/CLD Students

1. Much like the other mnemonics provided in these strategy lists, ELL/CLD students need bilingual explanations of the teacher's expectations and guided practice in implementing the steps in the strategy.

2. Newcomers will need to have the EASY steps modeled and explained in their most proficient language before they can proceed independently.

3. Students can be paired with partners who are slightly more bilingual than they are to facilitate their learning this process.

173. ORGANIZATION

Purpose of the Strategy

1. Develop analytical skills

2. Develop association skills

3. Develop categorization skills

4. Develop field independent skills

5. Improve mnemonic retrieval

How to Do It

1. At Tier 2, this strategy is done with small groups. The teacher directs students to empty out their backpacks and work in small groups. Each small group goes through their steps, sorting all the items in their piles together. They make lists of their groups of items to share with the class. Steps for students to follow in implementing this strategy are listed here.

   a. What elements go together and why?

   b. What do I call these groups?

   c. Can I remember the elements by the group?

   d. How can I generalize this information?

2. When applying the organization strategy, students work through problems or tasks using the sequence of self-monitoring questions. For example, you are going to have a new unit about rocks and minerals (i.e., igneous, sedimentary, conglomerate). Many of your students are unfamiliar with these ways of grouping natural materials that they consider generically as rocks. One group of students comes from a culture where rocks are grouped by hard versus soft; another student comes from a culture that groups rocks by whether they can be used to produce something in the home. You might introduce your class to the lesson by having actual examples of the rocks to be studied present to handle or take the class on a field trip to the museum or a local mine or industrial area to observe them. You could also show pictures or videos of chemists interacting with the materials. Have the students look for patterns in appearance, use, environment, chemical reactions, and the like. They could chart the attributes and characteristics of the rocks and minerals on a graph or in Venn diagrams (Step 1 of organization, "What elements go together?"). Now they should look for distinctive patterns of commonality between rocks and minerals that shows whether they go together (Step 2 of organization, "What attribute of these am I using to group them?"). Ask the students what they would name the group of rocks and minerals based on the major attributes. Now introduce them to the common English name of the group (Step 3 of organization, "What name do I give to each group?"). Discuss how the materials in each group share certain common characteristics, and then discuss the characteristics that all rocks and minerals share in common as rocks and minerals (Step 4 of organization, "How are the groups similar to one another?"). Discuss how the rocks in each group might differ from one another, how each group of rocks and minerals differ from the other groups, and how rocks differ from nonrocks (Step 5 of organization, "How are the groups different from one another?"). Finish the unit with a discussion of how to find patterns in anything you are studying (Step 6 of organization, "What organization patterns do I see?").

3. You might now step back from the lesson and discuss the enhanced cognitive learning that you have provided students, the learning to learn lesson that is represented by the strategy you had them use. At this point, you would discuss how everything in the world is composed of various elements that need to be identified to understand the whole thing being studied (field independence) and that when all the parts are put together, the meaning of the whole thing results (field sensitive).

Research Base

Ferris & Hedgcock, 2005

Iachini, Borghi, & Senese, 2008

What to Watch for With ELL/CLD Students

1. The strategy preparation can be done in the native language or dialect of the students to assure their understanding of your expectations and their task prior to carrying the assignment out in English or other communication mode.

2. Understand that all cultures have different ways of thinking of common attributes of a group of similar objects. What constitutes the criteria to pay attention will vary based on cultural values and learning practices. Although it seems obvious to one group that the predominant surface color of a set of objects is what links them together as a set of objects, to another group it might be that surface texture or size is more important as an attribute for sorting out similarity and difference.

174. RECIPROCAL QUESTIONING

Purpose of the Strategy

1. Improve reading comprehension.

2. Use discourse techniques

3. Use an inquiry approach

4. Improve mnemonic retrieval

5. Improve retention

6. Develop thinking and planning skills

How to Do It

At Tier 2, this strategy is done with small groups. The teacher and student ask each other questions about a selection. Student modeling of teacher questions and teacher feedback are emphasized as the learner explores the meaning of the reading material.

Research Base

Cole, 1995; see pages 113–114

Moore et al., 2000; see pages 141–142

What to Watch for With ELL/CLD Students

1. Provide initial setup in the student's most proficient language.

2. Students can practice reciprocal questioning with one another in their native language and then proceed with English-proficient students.

175. COGNITIVE STRATEGIES IN HOME AND COMMUNITY LANGUAGE

Purpose of the Strategy

1. Improve motivation

2. Minimize behavior problems

3. Build transfer skills

4. Develop cognitive academic language

5. Reduce code-switching

How to Do It

At Tier 2, this strategy is done with small groups. The teacher or the assistant working with student peers discusses the academic language of learning and of the classroom in both English and in the home and community language when possible. Bilingual posters and signs about cognitive academic language proficiency are posted and referred to regularly.

Expansion: Periodically, the teacher will stop a lesson in various content areas and ask students to discuss what is being presented and how and what academic behaviors are expected.

Research Base

Collins Block & Mangieri, 2003

Roessingh et al., 2005

Strickland et al., 2002

Walter, 2004

What to Watch for With ELL/CLD Students

1. Not all ELL/CLD students are academically fluent in their home or community language.

2. Graphics and illustrations representing the cognitive strategies may be used on posters or individual cue card sets for the students. These can be bilingual.

176. EXPERIENCE-BASED LEARNING

Purpose of the Strategy

1. Build transfer skills

2. Develop cognitive academic language

3. Develop content knowledge foundation

4. Facilitate analogy strategies

How to Do It

1. At Tier 2, this strategy is done with small groups.

2. In primary grades, the teacher presents lessons with concrete reference to specific experiences in which students have participated. These activities may be paired with field trips or other shared experiences; they may also be in reference to prior life experiences of ELL/LEP students. Community members may make presentations about events significant to students' families. The teacher then has students tell what their illustrations depict and writes down verbatim what the students say. Students then read back to the teacher what has been written.

3. In intermediate and secondary grades, the teacher guides students to illustrate and write stories about their experiences. These stories can be put into collections and bound for use by other students. Stories can be kept in the classroom, library, or media center.

Research Base

Beckett, 2002

Beckett & Miller, 2006

Beckett & Slater, 2005

Coelho & Rivers, 2003

What to Watch for With ELL/CLD Students

1. Some shared experiences will be very novel for particular cultural members of a group, more than for other members. Be sure to give those who have never seen something before extra preparation time and explanations of what they are going to see or do during the field trip or experience.

2. Be sure students are matched with peers with whom they can communicate comfortably while they are all learning the strategy and steps in the process.

3. Be sensitive to cultural mores about certain experiences and businesses. You may need to spend extra time discussing what is going to be seen and heard or, in some cases, be prepared to have some students participate in a related but separate activity.

177. ALTERNATE RESPONSE METHODS

Purpose of the Strategy

1. Facilitate learning

2. Accommodate diverse learning styles

3. Develop task completion

How to Do It

1. At Tier 2, this strategy is done with small groups. This strategy adapts the mode of response required of students.

2. Students respond to questions in a manner compatible with their needs. Allow students who have difficulty with writing activities to record their answers. Students are allowed to express their understanding of a question or issue in varied ways to meet their individual needs. This practice ensures that students have the best possible chance to show that they have acquired and retained skills and knowledge.

3. For example, students may record their oral responses to questions given in class. For the geography unit, provide the questions in writing for the student to take home and practice responding. Some names of American states are very difficult to pronounce; provide time for the students to work alone or with a peer to write the difficult state names on tag board cards that they can hold up during class discussion rather than say the names aloud.

4. Keep in mind Howard Gardner's (1993a; 1993b) work on multiple intelligences. What other forms might be available to the students to express their understanding? If the topic is westward expansion, the student could find musical examples illustrating the various cultures that came in contact with one another and could make a mixed sound recording to demonstrate the culture clashes and consequences of expansion. The students could draw a map or other illustration supporting the musical representation and their understanding of the geographic concept of the movement of populations from one location to another.

Research Base

Bailey, 1993

Cole, 1995; see pages 34–35

Gardner, 1993a

Gardner, 1993b

Tannenbaum, 1996

What to Watch for With ELL/CLD Students

1. Some CLD students have had previous schooling in situations where students have no choice in their responses and teachers are authority figures who direct every action in the classroom.

2. When the teacher wishes to make student empowerment an instructional goal, this strategy is an excellent direction to take.

3. Demonstrate how the various responses can be made, including color, modeling, illustrating, and the like.

4. Some role-play in the process from initial choice to final task completion may be helpful.

178. SUCCESS

Purpose of the Strategy

1. Develop personal control of situations

2. Facilitate student self-concept as a successful person

3. Improve confidence and self-esteem

4. Improve retention

5. Utilize prior knowledge

How to Do It

1. At Tier 2, this strategy is done with small groups. The teacher ensures that each student successfully completes assigned tasks by initially reducing the level of difficulty of materials and gradually increasing the level of difficulty as easier tasks are met with success. The teacher also reduces the complexity level of vocabulary or concepts in written material to help the students complete a reading task. Through this strategy, learners may read material similar to others in the class without requiring an excessive amount of individual attention from the teacher.

2. For example, the teacher places a transparency over a page of written material, (with a fine-point marker) crosses out the more difficult words, and writes simpler equivalents of those words above or in the margin next to the crossed-out words. As students read, they substitute the simpler words for those marked out.

Research Base

Gibbons, 2003

Krumenaker et al., 2008

Leki, 1995

C. A. Tomlinson, 1999

What to Watch for With ELL/CLD Students

1. The teacher needs information or professional development about all of the diverse learning styles, cultures, and languages in the classroom to design accessible learning activities for all students.

2. There is as much diversity within the ELL and CLD population as there is between the non-ELL and ELL population as a whole.

Tier 3 Interventions

3

INTRODUCTION TO TIER 3 INSTRUCTIONAL FOCUS

Bender and Shores (2007) state that Tier 3 involves highly intensive, specifically targeted individual instruction with even more frequent progress monitoring that may include placement in special education. However, not all three-tier models are alike; in fact, there are differences in models at every tier. Tier 3 also has major differences from program to program and from state to state. In some programs, Tier 3 interventions continue to be provided in small groups, whereas in other programs, Tier 3 interventions are individualized. Yet other programs allow Tier 3 interventions to be provided in small groups or individually.

According to Reschly (2005), "The dual purposes of Tier 3 problem solving are to resolve learning and behavior problems, thus preventing the need for special education, or depending on outcomes, determine eligibility for special education" (p. 514). However, Tier 3 is the most varied tier model. It is especially unclear when the special education process begins and what special education services consist of for students for whom general education is the least restrictive environment (Berkeley, Bender, Peaster, & Saunders, 2009).

PROGRESS MONITORING AT TIER 3

Generally, state requirements include frequent progress monitoring at all tiers and continuous or even more frequent progress monitoring at Tier 3. Specific minimum requirements for progress monitoring are similar across programs. For example, most require biannual or triannual universal screening and at least weekly monitoring of targeted interventions occurring at Tier 3. At Tier 3, the progress monitoring is designed specific to the presenting problems and selected interventions to measure the student's response to intervention (RTI).

Continuing the example from Tier 1 and Tier 2, with students of concern identified as having an unusually high level of distractibility and failure with task completion, the teachers working with them suspect there may be an attention deficit disorder. Before moving the student into a Tier 3 intervention, various interventions at Tier 1 and Tier 2 have been implemented in large and small group settings. None of the interventions have been successful in addressing the attention issue in a sustainable manner. By moving the student into Tier 3 of the RTI/RTII process, the team of instructional personnel is able to focus the intervention strategy in individualized intensive instructional sessions specific to separate elements of the general presenting problem. First, the team identifies a target level of attention and task completion and then establishes how far off the student's current performance varies from this goal. They then select one of the intervention strategies that in their judgment will best show them the following

- If the student responds appropriately given this intervention
- Whether the student has the capacity to modify her attention to task

This latter question to be resolved is an important element of the RTI/RTII process and provides the team with evidence that the student may need special education services and an individualized education plan (IEP) if the student demonstrates an inability to sustain attention and task completion regardless of support and intervention strategies provided.

The targeted intervention is previewed with the ELL/CLD student, and one of the teachers working with the student begins the intervention in a one-to-one setting. These are usually 30- to 40-minute individualized instructional interactions and may occur in varied settings depending on space available and noise level in the immediate vicinity. The interventions are conducted daily at the beginning of the Tier 3. If the intervention selected is effective and the students improve their response by showing measurable increase in attention to task and in task completion, the team would then gradually broaden the application to monitoring the students in all instructional settings and not just the focus session. If the intervention was a success (i.e., the students improve their attention and task completion to the target goal), then the team may cease the individualized Tier 3 sessions and move the student back into small group, Tier 2 assistance, or even a general classroom, Tier 1 setting while retaining an occasional application of the strategies that have been found to be successful for the student to learn.

Table 3.1 shows that the strategy of having the L1 tutor sit next to the student, pointing to each step in the vocabulary task is tried for an entire week. As the student achieves the vocabulary goal only 20% of the time with this intervention, the strategy is modified by having the L1 tutor tell the student what to do and reviewed with the student. In the example, this results in the student being able to achieve the goal 50% of the time; therefore, the strategy is modified again by having the L1 tutor review, assist, and tell the student what to do and touch the student's shoulder to redirect attention. In the example, this results in the student being able to complete vocabulary tasks 90% of the time, and thus only a slight modification is needed (i.e., having tutor touch the student lightly on the knee to redirect attention when needed). In the example, the student is now responding to tasks appropriately and is successful in completing tasks with gradually reduced assistance from the L1 tutor.

If the intervention was not a success (i.e., the student only achieved task completion when the tutor held onto the student's knee for an extended time and immediately reverted to inattention to task or left his or her seat when the tutor's hand was removed), then the intervention team might need to consider more in-depth evaluation and assessment of the presenting problems. Specific strategies (e.g., the intensive redirection strategy by an instructional assistant or teacher within a one-on-one instructional setting) should be tried for at least five sessions before a change of strategy should be made. As stated previously, it is not beneficial to either the learning environment or the challenging student to continue something that is ineffective. Most RTI/RTII models set specific lengths of time to try specific strategies before moving on to either another strategy or another Tier of intervention. However, if the Tier 3 strategies are not effective, do not result in the student being successful or able to sustain achievement, then something more is involved in the student's presenting problem. This could mean that a formal referral to a full evaluation and review of medical records may be needed. This may include a physical and psychological evaluation and assistance, medical intervention, or placing the student on an individualized instructional plan or an IEP at Tier 4.

Table 3.1 Progress Monitoring of Diverse Concerns at Tier 3

Setting: One on One	Week 1	Week 2	Week 3	Week 4	Week 5	Week 6	Week 7
Stepped proxemics one on one with first language (L1)	L1 tutor seated next to student, pointing to task steps	L1 tutor speaking in L1 and sitting next to student	L1 tutor speaking in L1 and touching student's shoulder	L1 tutor speaking in L1 and touching student's knee	L1 tutor speaking in L1 and sitting next to student	L1 tutor seated next to student, pointing to task steps	L1 tutor in room ready to come to student
Response	Task completed 20% of the time	Task completed 50% of the time	Task completed 90% of the time	Task completed 100% of the time	Task completed 100% of the time	Task completed 100% of the time	Task completed 100% of the time
Content goal: Correctly use and spell new English words	Student listens and reads 5 new words	Student correctly uses, copies, and reads 5 words	Student uses, reads, and spells 10 words; adds 5 new words	Student uses, reads, and spells 15 words; adds 5 new words	Student uses, reads, and spells 10 new words	Student uses, reads, and spells 15 new words	Student uses, reads, and spells 15 new words

SO WHAT DO I DO WITH AN ELL STUDENT AT TIER 3?

EXAMPLE FROM CLASSROOM PRACTICE

Tommy and Mary did very well with the combination of the general classroom strategy of *proximity*, and they responded well with differentiation for *oral discussion* and *home language* in the general curriculum lessons. These were accompanied by focused language development lessons in English vocabulary and spelling in small groups to reinforce and support the language lessons done in the larger classroom. I modeled and used *role-play* for their vocabulary words as part of my general instructional practice at Tier 1. Tommy and Mary responded to Tier 1 strategy implementation, but Mary's comprehension and content achievement improved considerably when she was placed in a more focused Tier 2 setting for content instruction. Justin, Clarence, and Irving did not respond satisfactorily to Tier 1 interventions but did a little better with completing tasks when I had them work in Tier 2, small groups of four or five students at a time, especially when given tasks that involved physical activity of some sort. The Tier 2 strategies that worked well for Mary and Justin, and somewhat for Clarence and Irving, were small groups with teacher guidance and attention plus *extended oral discussion*, more use of *home language*, peer *modeling*, as well as focused lessons with *guided practice* with vocabulary and task completion. After this extensive Tier 2 intervention, Justin's academic performance and behavior were much better, especially when I could give him responsibilities as group leader or room monitor. But Irving and Clarence remained easily distracted from their tasks and would frequently be found wandering around the room watching what the other students were doing.

There were bilingual high school students available as part-time tutors for our students, so I asked for assistance with Irving and Clarence, setting up individualized sessions with a tutor in their home language, first with a *bilingual aide,* then *bilingual peers,* (Strategies 179 and 180). Although their English language learner (ELL) and culturally and linguistically diverse (CLD) peers had steadily made gains in English acquisition and bilingual content achievement, neither of these boys had spoken in English or seemed able to complete academic tasks without someone directly guiding them through each step.

Clarence was between seven and eight years old (no medical records were available) when he first enrolled in my class and responded when I spoke him to in his home language though he rarely spoke much in this language. After six months in my class, he responded to my simple English directions but only when accompanied by gestures and movements to reinforce the meaning and intent of the message. After a school year during which I implemented the Tier 1 and Tier 2 strategies previously mentioned, Clarence could write anything that he could copy from a page or that had been written on the chalkboard. However, he printed everything in capital letters including lowercase letters in word and sentence models. He learned to write a version of his name without copying, although he frequently confused the ending of his name and usually wrote it "CLARNC." He liked to draw pictures to accompany group activities and would sit with his small work group while they worked on various projects. During the first part of his second year in my class (students stayed in beginners until they achieved specific exit criteria in English skills and could participate with other ELL/CLD peers at grade level), a bilingual aide worked with him individually for half of the day, and he worked with bilingual peers the other half of the day (Tier 3) in all content areas. We used Reading Rockets units, Visual Math, and leveled readers for science, social science, and other content materials that accommodate individualized lessons for diverse learners. He was able to independently read or write very simple English words and phrases but only when asked to. During independent reading time, he liked to look at picture books, and during independent journal time, he drew pictures in his writing book but would add written labels when assisted.

Irving did not start school at the beginning of the school year but was brought to school by a family member in November. He was small for his age, which was estimated to be about eight years old. He rarely responded when I spoke to him in either English or his home language. He never spoke in either language, but after four months in my class, he would hum along while we sang songs during daily class start-up activities. If I called his name firmly and pointed to a seat or a work area, he would come and sit down, but usually he just played with a piece of paper or work materials. As soon as I left his vicinity, he would start watching what the other students were doing and frequently got up and wandered around the room. After half a year of implementing the Tier 1 strategies previously mentioned and two months of the Tier 2 strategies mentioned, Irving still did not speak in either language, did not recognize any letters or words, never completed any lessons, and only stayed in a seat or work area if an aide or peer sat next to him and kept assisting him. At this point, I got the bilingual tutor mentioned previously and had him work individually with Irving everyday (Tier 3) in every content lesson. By the end of the school year, Irving could reproduce the rhythm of any pattern we modeled for him and had learned to sing the ABCs to the tune of "Twinkle, Twinkle Little Star." He was able to make simple line drawings, and his self-representation had gone from a sort of squiggle with a bump on the end to a narrow shape with appendages and a more head-like shape at the top. He could point at pictures of target spoken words about 50% of the time. He could approximate repeating the sounds and words we made for him but still rarely independently produced words in either language. By the end of the school year, he would take his seat at the beginning of class with the rest of the students but rarely stayed in his seat or work area much longer than five minutes without his tutor or peer partner resting a hand on his knee or shoulder.

COMMUNICATION ISSUES AT TIER 3

179. BILINGUAL AIDE

Purpose of the Strategy

1. Develop cognitive academic language

2. Build transfer skills

3. Build awareness of appropriate academic behavior

4. Strengthen knowledge of academic content

How to Do It

At Tier 3, this strategy is done in individualized, focused, and intensive periods. An instructional assistant or aide is available in the classroom to assist ELL/LEP students in home and community language when possible, regarding content instruction, academic behavior, and communication. The instructional assistant coordinates with the teacher in presenting content area instruction to all students. The aide must be trained in providing bilingual assistance and must plan lessons with the teacher.

Research Base

Cole, 1995; see pages 59–63

C. Collier, 2003

E. E. Garcia, 2005

Kovelman, Baker, & Petitto, 2008

What to Watch for With ELL/CLD Students

1. When this strategy is used for sequential translation (i.e., the teacher speaks and then the aide speaks), ELL/LEP students may become dependent on the bilingual aide and remain unengaged while the teacher speaks in English, waiting for the interpretation and explanation by the bilingual aide.

2. Better use would be for the aide to prepare the ELL/LEP students for the English lesson by reviewing key vocabulary words, explaining what will be occurring, and discussing what the teacher's expectations will be for the students' performance. This would then be followed by the teacher presenting the lesson in English. Students would be given the opportunity to ask for specific clarification only during the lesson.

3. Students could work on their projects subsequent to the English lesson with the assistance of the bilingual aide as needed. Content discussion and clarification should be in the students' most proficient language while they are preparing their task or project for presentation in English with the rest of the class.

180. BILINGUAL PEERS

Purpose of the Strategy

1. Develop cognitive academic language

2. Develop basic interpersonal communication

3. Build transfer skills

4. Develop content knowledge foundation

How to Do It

1.   At Tier 3, this strategy is done in individualized, focused, and intensive periods. Home and community language peers who are more proficient in English assist home and community language students in specific content area lessons and activities. The peer assistants are given training in being a tutor, with guidelines about how to facilitate learning without doing another's work, how to translate appropriately, and how to monitor for understanding.

2.   This can be part of a general classroom buddy system where students are matched up with partners of differing skills for specific activities.

Research Base

Cole, 1995; see pages 59–63

E. E. Garcia, 2005

Kovelman et al., 2008

What to Watch for With ELL/CLD Students

1.   With specific first-generation refugee, indigenous, migrant, and immigrant groups, teachers must be careful about pairing students based on their perceptions of them coming from similar language backgrounds. There can be cultural and class differences that will make the partners uncomfortable with one another.

2.   The teacher must be prepared to deal with prejudice between populations where language is the same but culture, class, or racial issues may impede comfort and communication. American all togetherness may come in time, but the teacher must proceed slowly and not push.

3.   Students may interact more as they become more comfortable in the classroom or more trusting that they are accepted and valued.

181. BILINGUAL TEXTS

Purpose of the Strategy

1.   Develop cognitive academic language

2.   Build language transfer skills

3.   Strengthen knowledge of academic content

4.   Develop confidence in academic interactions

How to Do It

1.   At Tier 3, this strategy is done in individualized, focused, and intensive periods. Duplicate or parallel texts are available in English and home and community language of students for all content areas. Reference texts are available in English, bilingual, or home and community language format. Students are shown how and when to access the texts.

2.   One source for bilingual materials in Spanish is the Colorín Colorado Web site and organization (http://www .colorincolorado.org).

3.   Another source is the National Council for Lifelong Learning and Work Skills (CONEVyT). CONEVyT was created in 2002 in Mexico to provide primary and secondary education and training to adults (15 and older) left behind in education in that country as well as migrant populations living in the United States. Through an online portal and a network of Plazas Comunitarias where direct instruction, assessment, and varied materials can be found, both U.S. and Mexican governments make educational support available for anyone willing to learn or to teach. For more information go to www.conevyt.org.mx.

Research Base

Cole, 1995

E. E. Garcia, 2005

Hu & Commeyras, 2008

Kovelman et al., 2008

Ma, 2008

What to Watch for With ELL/CLD Students

1   Not all ELL/CLD students are literate in their home or community language.

2.   Picture dictionaries with bilingual words and definitions are usually the most practical reference to use with younger, less educated students.

182. ACTIVE PROCESSING

Purpose of the Strategy

1.   Build awareness of learning

2.   Develop academic language

3.   Develop personal control of situations

4.   Facilitate access to prior knowledge

5.   Reduce low-persistence behaviors

6.   Reduce off-task behaviors

7.   Reduce impulsivity

How to Do It

1.   At Tier 3, this strategy is done in individualized, focused, and intensive periods. Students work through a task aloud, naming each step and asking themselves the appropriate questions for the task. Steps for students to follow in implementing the strategy are listed here

    a.   What is my task?

    b.   What do I need to do to complete my task?

    c.   How will I know my task is done correctly?

    d.   How will I monitor the implementation?

    e.   How do I know the task is completed correctly?

2.   When applying the active processing strategy, students work through problems or tasks using the sequence of self-monitoring questions given here. For example, your students must prepare for the state-administered achievement tests required at this grade level, but several of your diverse learners have never taken such tests before and are unfamiliar with this type of evaluation. They have heard stories of something scary that happens to schoolchildren every year and are bracing themselves to endure this external event. You could modify your preparation for this event by integrating the active processing strategy into the lessons before the testing period. Start by having the students in your class speak aloud with one another in small groups about the content and process of lessons they are learning following the steps in active processing. Do this in every content area until the students are familiar with the process itself. Then a few weeks before the

state assessments, introduce the concept of standardized achievement tests to your class. Have your students discuss how group and norm measures differ from individual and curriculum-based assessments and the implications of this for each participant (Step 1 of active processing, "What is my task?"). Have the groups discuss what they will need to have with them and what the setting is like. Have those students who have taken tests like this describe the process and what it was like for them. Talk about the expectations of test administrators regarding notes, whispering, looking at others, pencils, calculators, and the like. (Step 2 of active processing, "What do I need to do to complete my task?"). Discuss what an acceptable performance might be for various levels of completion and knowledge. Explain some of the test strategies that help successful test takers even when they are unsure of the answer. Clarify the expectations of parents, teachers, and others about the test activity (Step 3 of active processing, "How will I know my task is done correctly?"). Provide suggestions for relieving stress during the test and ideas for self-monitoring their progress through the different sections of the test (Step 4 of active processing, "How will I monitor the implementation?"). Discuss how timekeepers work and what the timelines will be on this test. Discuss ways to identify when it is time to move to another section and what to do when they are finished with the test (Step 5 of active processing, "How do I know the task is completed?").

3. For example, suppose you want your students to complete a new unit in language arts about bears in fact and fiction. Some of your diverse learners are not familiar with the concept of fact versus fiction as used on our society and have no words in their native language for this distinction; also several of them have little or incomplete prior schooling. You could modify your preparation for this unit by integrating the active processing strategy into the lessons. Begin having the students in your class speak aloud with one another in small groups about what they know about bears and other animals, following the steps in active processing. Do this within the context of reinforcement and review of prior content the students have successfully accomplished until the students are familiar with active processing itself. Then introduce the concept of fact versus fiction to your class. Have them discuss how these differ, using real-life experiences from their homes or communities. Use visual and physical examples of the concept, such as a photograph of a car and a sketch or drawing of a car, a realistic portrait of a child and an abstract painting of a child, a picture of astronauts on the moon and a picture of children playing on the moon, and the like to ensure that students are aware of what is involved. Have students discuss examples from their communities or lives. Discuss how to tell the difference and what is involved in the process (Step 1 of active processing, "What is my task?"). Have the groups discuss what they will need to compare and contrast fact from fiction and what actions are involved. Have those that are more successful describe the process and what it was like for them to learn it. Talk about the importance of learning this skill and discuss the steps involved. Have your students work in groups to develop a set of rules outlining the steps to follow (Step 2 of active processing, "What do I need to do to complete my task?"). Discuss what an acceptable performance might be for various levels of skill and knowledge. Explain some of the strategies that help students be successful at separating fact from fiction. Discuss how to check for the accuracy and the steps involved (Step 3 of active processing, "How will I know my task is done correctly?"). Provide suggestions for relieving stress during the lesson and ideas for self-monitoring their progress through the different steps of the process (Step 4 of active processing, "How will I monitor the implementation?"). Discuss ways to identify when it is time to move to another question or example and what to do when they have finished each set of comparisons (Step 5 of active processing, "How do I know the task is completed?").

4. Using active processing reduces impulsive tendencies and naturally illustrates how a student can use reflection in answering questions and completing tasks.

Research Base

Cole, 1995

Collier, 2003 see pages 124–130

Law & Eckes, 2000

Tovani, 2000; see pages 26–29

What to Watch for With ELL/CLD Students

1. The strategy preparation can be done in the native language or dialect of the students to assure their understanding of your expectations and their task prior to carrying the assignment out in English or other communication mode.

2. Students who are less proficient in English will need guidance in using the steps of active processing; the process can be explained and practiced in the students' most proficient language before going on in English.

3. Active processing can be used in any language of instruction and in any content area or age level.

183. ASSESSMENT

Purpose of the Strategy

1. Measure performance and set goals and objectives

2. Establish baseline performance levels

3. Establish target goals

How to Do It

1. At Tier 3, this strategy is done in individualized, focused, and intensive periods. Assess the needs and strengths of the student in the content being studied, consistently taking into consideration questions of language development.

2. For example, for a geography lesson on the United States, determine the individual student's general knowledge of the North American continent, countries bordering the United States, the difference between states and countries, how these boundaries are demarcated, and so on. What do the students know about the geography of their country of origin, or city or state? Determine key vocabulary and sentence structures the students need to master for the lesson, building on structures and vocabulary that the students have already mastered.

Research Base

Shores & Chester, 2009

Walker, Carta, Greenwood, & Buzhardt, 2008

What to Watch for With ELL/CLD Students

1. Non-English-speaking or very limited English proficient (LEP) students will need interpreters and lots of modeling and demonstration of how to take a test and how to respond in assessment activities.

2. Explanations and example products should be given in the students' most proficient language before moving into English-only assessment situations. If this is not done, all assessments will become essentially measures of language proficiency and not assessment of content achievement.

184. ORAL DISCUSSIONS

Purpose of the Strategy

1. Reduce code-switching

2. Develop cognitive academic language

3. Develop basic interpersonal communication

4. Build transfer skills

5. Develop confidence in school language and rules for academic and social interactions

How to Do It

At Tier 3, this strategy is done in individualized, focused, intensive and periods. Target students are given opportunities to discuss all aspects of content lessons and to prepare for assessment situations. They are encouraged to hold discussions in both home and community language and English whenever they need to clarify content or directions. Specific homogeneous and heterogeneous discussion groups may be established and used alternately in varied content-focused activities.

Research Base

C. Collier, 2003; see pages 281, 358

Flowerdew & Peacock, 2001

Law & Eckes, 2000; see pages 199–201

Youb, 2008

What to Watch for With ELL/CLD Students

1. Some teachers are threatened on concerned about students speaking to one another when they do not understand what they are saying. To assure teachers that the students are indeed on task, the teacher can always have these oral discussions focus on specific tasks, with worksheets or other task production involved so teachers can see what is being attended to.

2. The teacher can also have bilingual student monitors report on what was discussed after these activities.

185. CROSS-CULTURAL COMMUNICATION STRATEGIES

Purpose of the Strategy

1. Build transfer skills

2. Build awareness of appropriate communication behaviors for school language and rules

3. Develop confidence in school language and rules for academic and social interactions

How to Do It

1. At Tier 3, this strategy is done in individualized, focused, and intensive periods. Students and the teacher practice using these strategies in a variety of interactions.

2. The teacher models cross-cultural communication strategies such as reflection, proxemics, latency, and active listening. Reflection is positioning yourself in an almost mirror image to the posture of the other person, using similar rate of speech. Proxemics is paying attention to how close you are to the other speaker, and latency is the culturally learned length of time between one speaker's turn and the next speaker's turn to speak. Active listening is showing that you are paying attention and responding in culturally appropriate ways to indicate your attention. This may include repeating some portion of what was said.

Research Base

Croom & Davis, 2006

Gibbons, 2002

Trudeau & Harle, 2006

What to Watch for With ELL/CLD Students

1. All cultures have different mores about how close you can stand or sit next to another person (proxemics), who or what you may touch, how much time should elapse before you speak after another person (latency), and the like. The teacher should become familiar with these differences regarding the students in this classroom.

2. The strategy of reflection can look like mockery and mimicry if not done with sensitivity. The goal is to reflect—not imitate—the mode of the speaker.

186. GUIDED PRACTICE AND PLANNED INTERACTIONS WITH DIFFERENT SPEAKERS

Purpose of the Strategy

1. Build transfer skills

2. Build awareness of appropriate school language and rules for communication behaviors

3. Develop confidence in school language and rules for academic and social interactions

4. Develop cognitive academic language

5. Develop personal control of situations

6. Reduce anxiety in social/academic interactions

7. Reduce response fatigue

How to Do It

At Tier 3, this strategy is done in individualized, focused, and intensive periods. Peer or teacher demonstrates how to act or speak in a given school culture situation. The situation is explained in home and community language when possible, and each part of the situation is modeled. Representatives of school language and rules who are familiar to the learners come into the classroom and act out the situation with the instructor. The students then practice each part of the interaction with these familiar participants until comfortable with the interaction.

Expansion: Students select new interactions they wish to learn.

Research Base

Cole, 1995

Haneda, 2008

Reggy-Mamo, 2008

Ross, 1971

What to Watch for With ELL/CLD Students

1. It is important to have the example speakers be people with whom the students are familiar and comfortable.

2. This can be paired with role-play of school interactions.

187. ROLE-PLAYING IN SOCIAL AND ACADEMIC LANGUAGE DEVELOPMENT

Purpose of the Strategy

1. Build transfer skills

2. Build awareness of appropriate communication behaviors for school language and rules

3. Develop cognitive academic language

4. Develop confidence in school language and rules for academic and social interactions

5. Reduce code-switching

How to Do It

1. Teacher and assistant model the appropriate and inappropriate ways to use basic interpersonal communication and cognitive academic language in various school settings, both in and out of the classroom. The students take different roles in the interactions and practice these with the teacher. The students may suggest communication situations they want specific assistance with and the teacher facilitates role-plays. Students create dialogues and interaction situations to enact.

2. Assign the student specific roles and create situations where roles are acted out based on how the student believes their characters would act. A specific problem, such as discrimination, is identified and described. The students role-play how they would confront the problem and discuss their roles or behaviors upon completion. Students learn how to confront the reactions of others and ways to deal with situations similar to the role-play.

Research Base

J. E. Johnson, Christie, & Yawkey, 1999

Kim & Kellogg, 2007

Livingstone, 1983

Magos & Politi, 2008

Rymes, Cahnmann-Taylor, & Souto-Manning, 2008

Webster-Stratton & Reid, 2004

What to Watch for With ELL/CLD Students

1. Many societies and cultures have specific beliefs and understandings about pretending to be something one is not in reality; there are cultural guidelines for make-believe, play, and assuming the role or character of someone or something.

2. Be clear that in public schools and classrooms, we sometimes are like actors in movies or television stories (although understanding that some people may think those are all real) for the purpose of illustrating or demonstrating something.

3. Be clear that they will not become the character or thing and that it is a temporary action to illustrate or demonstrate a particular interaction you want them to learn.

4. It may be easier with some students to start with puppets or drawings and then work up to individual people doing the actions.

188. PEER TUTORING

Purpose of the Strategy

1. Develop cognitive academic language

2. Develop basic interpersonal communication

3. Build transfer skills

4. Ensure learning gains are experienced by both students

5. Improve retention

6. Develop higher tolerance for ambiguity

7. Utilize prior knowledge

8. Develop thinking and planning skills

9. Develop positive peer relationships

10. Develop content knowledge foundation

How to Do It

1. At Tier 3, this strategy is done in individualized, focused, and intensive periods. Home and community language peers who are more proficient in English assist the student in specific content area lessons and activities. The peers are given training in being a tutor, with guidelines about how to facilitate learning without doing the work of the target student, how to translate appropriately, and how to monitor for understanding.

Expansion: Students develop code of ethics and guidelines for tutoring.

2. Student assists in the classroom by working with other students. Tutors may receive training about objectives, reinforcement, and the like. For example, a student who has mastered a list of sight words or math facts presents these items on flash cards to another student needing assistance in this area.

Research Base

Carrigan, 2001; see pages 44–45

Cole, 1995

What to Watch for With ELL/CLD Students

1. Students may wish to discuss their struggles only in the home language and with peers from similar backgrounds. With specific first-generation refugee, indigenous, migrant, and immigrant groups, teachers must be careful about pairing students based on their perceptions of them coming from similar language backgrounds. There can be cultural and class differences that will make the partners uncomfortable with one another.

2. The teacher must be prepared to deal with prejudice between populations where language is the same but culture, class, or racial issues may impede comfort and communication. American all togetherness may come in time, but the teacher must proceed slowly and not push.

3. Students may interact more as they become more comfortable in the classroom or more trusting that they are accepted and valued.

189. ROLE-PLAYING: IN PROBLEM SOLVING

Purpose of the Strategy

1. Improve retention of content

2. Develop higher tolerance

3. Utilize prior knowledge

4. Develop thinking and planning skills

How to Do It

At Tier 3, this strategy is done in individualized, focused, and intensive periods. Teacher assigns the student specific roles and creates situations where roles are acted out based on how the students believe their characters would act. A specific problem, such as discrimination, is identified and described. The students role-play how they would confront the problem and discuss their roles or behaviors upon completion. Student learns how to confront the reactions of others and ways to deal with situations similar to the role-play.

Research Base

C. Collier, 2003; see page 183

J. E. Johnson et al., 1999

Kim & Kellogg, 2007

Livingstone, 1983

Magos & Politi, 2008

Rymes et al., 2008

Webster-Stratton & Reid, 2004

What to Watch for With ELL/CLD Students

1. Many societies and cultures have specific beliefs and understandings about pretending to be something one is not in reality; there are cultural guidelines for make-believe, play, and assuming the role or character of someone or something.

2. Be clear that in public schools and classrooms, we sometimes are like actors in movies or television stories (although understanding that some people may think those are all real) for the purpose of illustrating or demonstrating something.

3. Be clear that they will not become the character or thing and that it is a temporary action to illustrate or demonstrate a particular interaction you want them to learn.

4. It may be easier with some students to start with puppets or drawings and then work up to individual people doing the actions.

190. ROLE-PLAYING: IN COGNITIVE ACADEMIC INTERACTION STRATEGIES

Purpose of the Strategy

1. Build transfer skills

2. Build awareness of appropriate cognitive academic language

3. Develop personal control of situations

4. Reduce response fatigue

5. Reduce distractibility

How to Do It

At Tier 3, this strategy is done in individualized, focused, and intensive periods. Teachers and assistants model the appropriate and inappropriate ways to use cognitive academic language and cognitive learning strategies. The students take different roles in the interactions and practice these with one another and the teachers. Students practice the cognitive learning strategies in varied academic content areas with the teacher or assistant monitoring.

Research Base

J. E. Johnson et al., 1999

Kim & Kellogg, 2007

Livingstone, 1983

Riley, 2006

What to Watch for With ELL/CLD Students

1. Many societies and cultures have specific beliefs and understandings about pretending to be something one is not in reality; there are cultural guidelines for make-believe, play, and assuming the role or character of someone or something.

2. Be clear that in public schools and classrooms, we sometimes are like actors in movies or television stories (although understanding that some people may think those are all real) for the purpose of illustrating or demonstrating something.

3. Be clear that they will not become the character or thing and that it is a temporary action to illustrate or demonstrate a particular interaction you want them to learn.

4. It may be easier with some students to start with puppets or drawings and then work up to individual people doing the actions.

191. SHELTERED INSTRUCTION

Purpose of the Strategy

1. Reduce distractibility

2. Develop cognitive academic language proficiency

3. Develop content area skills

4. Develop personal control of situations

How to Do It

At Tier 3, this strategy is done in individualized, focused, and intensive periods. The teacher always presents lessons with concrete, physical models and demonstrations of both content and expected performance. Language is simplified and content focused.

Expansion: Student is encouraged to discuss lesson in home and community language and work in small groups on content activities.

Research Base

Cole, 1995

Echevarria & Graves, 2006

Echevarria, Vogt, & Short, 2007

What to Watch for With ELL/CLD Students

1. Building familiarity is critical for the success of this strategy. Not all ELL/CLD students will know what the objects or models represent.

2. The teacher will need to introduce the models or objects in full-scale representations or use the actual items to build a true understanding. Only after students have actually seen, felt, smelled, and, possibly, tasted an apple will they respond to a picture of an apple.

192. SHELTERED INTERACTIONS

Purpose of the Strategy

1. Develop higher tolerance

2. Facilitate access to prior knowledge

3. Build transfer skills

4. Develop confidence in school culture interactions

How to Do It

At Tier 3, this strategy is done in individualized, focused, and intensive periods. The teacher develops a game or other casual interaction activity. The teacher or a specialist explains in home and community language, when possible, what is going to occur and who the student is going to meet. The student is introduced to the school culture students and they engage in the game or activity together.

Research Base

Cloud, Genesee, & Hamayan, 2000

Cole, 1995

Echevarria et al., 2007

Echevarria & Graves, 2006

Garber-Miller, 2006

What to Watch for With ELL/CLD Students

1. It is important to have the example speakers be people with whom the students are familiar and comfortable.

2. This can be paired with role-play of school interactions.

193. TOTAL PHYSICAL RESPONSE

Purpose of the Strategy

1. Reduce stress for newcomers

2. Reduce code-switching

3. Develop cognitive academic language

4. Build transfer skills

5. Build awareness of appropriate communication behaviors for school language and rules

How to Do It

1. At Tier 3, this strategy is done in individualized, focused, and intensive periods. The teacher or an assistant models words and phrases in action in various school settings, both in and out of the classroom. This actively involves the student and focuses on understanding the language rather than speaking it. The total physical response (TPR) method asks the student to demonstrate that they understand the new language by responding to a command with an action. At first, the teacher gives the commands and does the actions along with the student. As the student understands the vocabulary, the teacher stops doing the action and has the student do the action alone. Later, the student can give commands to other students or to the teacher.

2. The teacher or an assistant models words and phrases in action in various school settings, both in and out of the classroom. For example, teaching the response to a question such as, "What is this?" or "What can you do with this?" by saying and acting out the phrases "This is a pencil," and "This pencil is used for writing on paper."

3. Total physical response begins with simple directions creating associations between words and actions such as "I am walking," "She is standing," and "Bill is shutting the door."

4. The students take different roles in the interactions and practice these with one another and with the teacher.

Expansion: Student may suggest communication situations in which they would like specific assistance.

Research Base

Asher, 1980

C. Collier, 2003; *see page 351*

Law & Eckes, 2000; *see pages 202–203*

What to Watch for With ELL/CLD Students

1. Although this is a common beginner or newcomer strategy for use with ELL students, the teacher must still be cautious about making assumptions about CLD students' understanding of the actions required in the classroom.

2. The teacher must clearly model and act out every action required before asking students to repeat the action.

LITERACY ISSUES AT TIER 3

194. BILINGUAL TEXTS

Purpose of the Strategy

1. Develop cognitive academic language

2. Build language transfer skills

3. Strengthen knowledge of academic content

4. Develop confidence in academic interactions

How to Do It

At Tier 3, this strategy is done in individualized, focused, and intensive periods. Duplicate or parallel texts are available in English and the home and community language of the student for all content areas. Reference texts are available in English, bilingual, or home and community language format. Students are shown how and when to access the texts.

Research Base

Cole, 1995

E. E. Garcia, 2005

Hu & Commeyras, 2008

Kovelman et al., 2008

Ma, 2008

What to Watch for With ELL/CLD Students

1. Not all ELL/CLD students are literate in their home or community language.

2. Picture dictionaries with bilingual words and definitions are usually the most practical reference to use with younger, less educated students.

195. GUIDED READING AND WRITING IN HOME AND COMMUNITY LANGUAGE

Purpose of the Strategy

1. Improve motivation

2. Minimize behavior problems

3. Build transfer skills

4. Develop confidence in school language and rules for academic and social interactions

5. Reduce code-switching

6. Develop cognitive academic language

How to Do It

At Tier 3, this strategy is done in individualized, focused, and intensive periods. The teacher directs an advanced-fluency student to lead a guided reading or writing activity in the home and community language. Students can reread parts of a story after the directed reading activity. Students then write summaries of what they have read. Writing can be in either home and community language or English. During this time, students have a chance to ask for help. Advanced-fluency students can dramatize and create dialogue to illustrate the action.

Research Base

Cole, 1995; see pages 150–152

Haneda, 2008

Reggy-Mamo, 2008

Ross, 1971

Strickland, Ganske, & Monroe, 2002; see page 217

What to Watch for With ELL/CLD Students

1. Not all ELL/CLD students are literate in their home or community language.

2. Picture dictionaries with bilingual words and definitions are usually the most practical reference to use with younger, less educated students.

196. WRITING STRATEGY—TOWER

Purpose of the Strategy

1. Build awareness of learning

2. Develop personal control of situations

3. Develop thinking and planning skills

4. Improve access to prior knowledge

5. Reduce off-task behaviors

6. Strengthen language development

How to Do It

1. At Tier 3, this strategy is done in individualized, focused, and intensive periods. TOWER provides a structure for competing initial and final drafts of written reports.

2. It may be used effectively with the COPS proofreading strategy structure.

3. To help the student remember the steps in TOWER, the teacher can provide the student with a printed form with the letters T, O, W, E, R down the left side and their meaning next to each letter.

4. The steps in TOWER are

Think
Order ideas
Write
Edit
Rewrite

Research Base

Cole, 1995; see pages 102–104

Ellis & Colvert, 1996

Ellis & Lenz, 1987

Goldsworthy, 2003

What to Watch for With ELL/CLD Students

1. Newcomers will need to have the TOWER steps modeled and explained in their most proficient language before they can proceed independently.

2. Students can be paired with partners who are slightly more bilingual than they are to facilitate their learning this process.

197. WRITING STRATEGIES—DEFENDS

Purpose of the Strategy

Assists learners to defend a particular position in a written assignment

How to Do It

1. At Tier 3, this strategy is done in individualized, focused, and intensive periods.

2. The DEFENDS writing strategy framework provides a structure for completing initial and final drafts of written reports.

3. It may be used effectively with the COPS proofreading strategy structure.

4. To help the student remember the steps in DEFENDS, the teacher can provide the students with a printed form with the letters D, E, F, E, N, D, S down the left side and the meaning next to each letter.

5. The steps in DEFENDS are

Decide on a specific position
Examine own reasons for this position
Form list of points explaining each reason
Expose position in first sentence of written task

Note each reason and associated points

Drive home position in last sentence

Search for and correct any errors

Research Base

Ellis & Colvert, 1996

Ellis & Lenz, 1987

Goldsworthy, 2003

What to Watch for With ELL/CLD Students

1. Newcomers will need to have the DEFENDS steps modeled and explained in their most proficient language before they can proceed independently.

2. Students can be paired with partners who are slightly more bilingual than they are to facilitate their learning this process.

198. VISUALIZATION

Purpose of the Strategy

1. Develop higher tolerance

2. Develop thinking and planning skills

3. Improve mnemonic retrieval

4. Improve retention

How to Do It

1. At Tier 3, the students put small red stop signs at the end of sentences in an assigned reading. As they read the passage, they stop at each sign and answer questions about the passage. They then make a picture in their minds of what the passage means. This is repeated for each subsequent passage with the mental pictures forming a moving visualization or motion picture of what the passage means. (I usually remind students to think of TV shows.) This visualization strategy can also be used with other content activities, in science and social studies for example. Steps for the student to follow in implementing this strategy are listed here.

   a. Where do I stop?

   b. Who is doing what, where, how, and why?

   c. What do I see in my mind?

   d. How does this all go together?

2. When applying the visualization strategy, students work through problems or tasks using the sequence of self-monitoring questions.

3. Suppose you are having your students read *The Story of Ferdinand* by Munro Leaf (2000). You would have students read this story aloud and then silently. They would help put small red Post-it circles at the end of each sentence or at the end of two sentences, depending on their skill level (Step 1 of rehearsal, "Where should I stop to think?"). Suppose a student was reading this passage, for example:

All the other bulls that had grown up with him in the same pasture would fight each other all day.● They would butt each other and stick each other with their horns.● What they wanted most of all was to be picked to fight at the bull-fights in Madrid.● But not Ferdinand—he still liked just to sit quietly under the cork tree and smell the flowers.●

4. Students would read aloud to the teacher or the assistant. The reader would read up to the first red spot and stop. The teacher would then review the six *W* questions about what had just been read (Step 2 of rehearsal, "Who is doing what, where, when, how, and why?"). Who = the other bulls, what = fight each other, where = in the pasture, when = all day. As this is the first sentence, the reader does not yet know the answers to all the questions (how and why = don't know yet). After answering the questions, the students will tell how they visualize this sentence (Step 3 of rehearsal, "What picture do I see in my mind regarding these?"). The picture at the book shows the bulls gazing up at a poster about the bullfights in Madrid, so students will have to use their imaginations about what it might look like to see these young bulls play fighting. They will then go on to read the next sentence and repeat steps 2 and 3, adding Step 4. Who = the bulls, what = fight each other, where = in the pasture, when = all day, how = butt each other and stick one another with their horns, why = still don't know. They can now expand their first imaginative pictures of these bulls by adding some action to the movie they are making in their minds (Step 5 of rehearsal, "What do I see when I put the pictures from each stop together?"). They go on to the next sentence and repeat Steps 2, 3, 4 and 5. Who = the young bulls, what = fighting, where = in the pasture, how = butting heads, why = to be picked to fight in Madrid. They expand their visualization to showing the longing of the young bulls while they are fighting. They then read the final sentence and complete the movie in their minds. Who = the young bulls and Ferdinand, what = the young bulls fighting and Ferdinand sitting, where = fighting in the pasture while Ferdinand is under the cork tree, how = fighting by butting their heads while Ferdinand is smelling flowers, why = the young bulls want to be picked to fight in Madrid but Ferdinand doesn't want to do anything but smell the flowers.

5. The use of the visualization strategy will slow down impulsive learners, reinforce reflective habits, and guide students to a more accurate understanding of what they are reading.

Research Base

Harwell, 2001; see pages 215–217

Klingner, Vaughn, & Boardman, 2007

Naughton, 2008

B. Tomlinson, 1998

Tovani, 2000; see pages 33–34

What to Watch for With ELL/CLD Students

1. Students with limited school experience will not know what visualization means and will need to have direct instruction in the vocabulary and actions expected.

2. This can be introduced in the primary language and examples given from literature and art with which the students are more familiar.

199. VISUALIZATION—RIDER

Purpose of the Strategy

1. Build transfer skills

2. Expand and elaborate on learning foundation

3. Improve access to prior knowledge

4. Improve retention of information

5. Improve reading comprehension

6. Strengthen language development.

How to Do It

At Tier 3, this strategy is done in individualized, focused, and intensive periods. This visualization strategy cues the learner to form a mental image of what was read and assists the student in making connections with previously learned materials. The steps in RIDER are

> Read a sentence
> Image (form a mental picture)
> Describe how new information differs from previous
> Evaluate image to ensure it is comprehensive
> Repeat process with subsequent sentences

Research Base

> Cole, 1995; see page 80
>
> Klingner et al., 2007
>
> Naughton, 2008
>
> B. Tomlinson, 1998

What to Watch for With ELL/CLD Students

1. Students with limited school experience will not know what visualization means and will need to have direct instruction in the vocabulary and actions expected.

2. This can be introduced in the primary language and examples given from literature and art with which the students are more familiar.

3. Newcomers will need to have the RIDER steps modeled and explained in their most proficient language before they can proceed independently.

4. Students can be paired with partners who are slightly more bilingual than they are to facilitate their learning this process.

200. TEST-TAKING—SCORER

Purpose of the Strategy

> Improve test-taking skills

How to Do It

At Tier 3, this strategy is done in individualized, focused, and intensive periods. This test-taking strategy provides a structure for completing various tests by assisting the student to carefully and systematically complete test items. The steps in SCORER are

> Schedule time effectively
> Clue words identified
> Omit difficult items until the end
> Read carefully
> Estimate answers requiring calculations
> Review work and responses

Research Base

> Elliot & Thurlow, 2005
>
> Ritter & Idol-Maestas, 1986

What to Watch for With ELL/CLD Students

1. Newcomers will need to have the SCORER steps modeled and explained in their most proficient language before they can proceed independently.

2. Students can be paired with partners who are slightly more bilingual than they are to facilitate their learning this process.

201. MATH WORD PROBLEMS—SQRQCQ

Purpose of the Strategy

1. Improve comprehension

2. Improve retention of information

3. Improve problem solving of math word problems

4. Strengthen language development

How to Do It

At Tier 3, this strategy is done in individualized, focused, and intensive periods. This strategy provides a systematic structure for identifying the question being asked in a math word problem, computing the response, and ensuring that the question in the problem is answered. The steps in SQRQCQ are

Survey word problems
Question asked is identified
Read more carefully
Question process required to solve problem
Compute the answer
Question self to ensure that the answer solves the problem

Research Base

Cole, 1995; see pages 65–66, 127–128, 132

Elliot & Thurlow, 2005

What to Watch for With ELL/CLD Students

1. Newcomers will need to have the SQRQCQ steps modeled and explained in their most proficient language before they can proceed independently.

2. Students can be paired with partners who are slightly more bilingual than they are to facilitate their learning this process.

202. READING COMPREHENSION—SQ3R

Purpose of the Strategy

1. Build transfer skills

2. Expand and elaborate on learning foundations

3. Improve access to prior knowledge

4. Improve comprehension

5. Strengthen language development

How to Do It

At Tier 3, this strategy is done in individualized, focused, and intensive periods. This strategy reminds the students to go through any passage or lesson carefully and thoughtfully. Students can make cue cards to remember each step. The steps in SQ3R are

Survey
Question
Read
Recite
Review

Research Base

Allington & Cunningham, 2002; see pages 89–116

Artis, 2008

Cole, 1995; see pages 75–94

Fisher & Frey, 2004

Harwell, 2001

Irvin & Rose, 1995

Law & Eckes, 2000

Moore, Alvermann, & Hinchman, 2000; see page 139

Robinson, 1946

Sakta, 1999

Tovani, 2000

What to Watch for With ELL/CLD Students

1. Newcomers will need to have the SQ3R steps modeled and explained in their most proficient language before they can proceed independently.

2. Students can be paired with partners who are slightly more bilingual than they are to facilitate their learning this process.

203. LISTENING COMPREHENSION—TQLR

Purpose of the Strategy

1. Build awareness of learning

2. Develop personal control of situations

3. Improve access to prior knowledge

4. Strengthen language development

How to Do It

At Tier 3, this strategy is done in individualized, focused, and intensive periods. This strategy assists with listening comprehension. Students generate questions and listen for specific statements related to those questions. The steps in TQLR are

Tuning in
Questioning
Listening
Reviewing

Research Base

Artis, 2008

Fisher & Frey, 2004

Irvin & Rose, 1995

Law & Eckes, 2000

Popp, 1997

Robinson, 1946

Sakta, 1999

What to Watch for With ELL/CLD Students

1. Newcomers will need to have the TQLR steps modeled and explained in their most proficient language before they can proceed independently.

2. Students can be paired with partners who are slightly more bilingual than they are to facilitate their learning this process.

204. ANALYZING READING MATERIAL—FIST

Purpose of the Strategy

Assist students to actively pursue responses to questions related directly to materials being read

How to Do It

At Tier 3, this strategy is done in individualized, focused, and intensive periods. Students follow steps while reading paragraphs in assigned readings. The steps in FIST are

First sentence is read
Indicate a question based on first sentence
Search for the answer to the question
Tie question and answer together through paraphrasing

Research Base

Allington & Cunningham, 2002

Cole, 1995

Dang, Dang, & Ruiter, 2005

Derwinger, Stigsdotter Neely, & Bäckman, 2005

Ellis & Lenz, 1987

Moore et al., 2000

Odean, 1987

What to Watch for With ELL/CLD Students

1. Newcomers will need to have the FIST steps modeled and explained in their most proficient language before they can proceed independently.

2. Students can be paired with partners who are slightly more bilingual than they are to facilitate their learning this process.

205. GUIDED LECTURE PROCEDURE

Purpose of the Strategy

1. Build listening skills

2. Build study skills

3. Facilitate students taking control of learning

How to Do It

1. At Tier 3, this strategy is done in individualized, focused, and intensive periods. This strategy provides the student with a structure for taking notes during lectures

2. Group activity is involved to facilitate effective note taking. Students listen to the teacher or the student presentation. Speakers pause periodically to allow groups to compare notes and fill in missing information.

Research Base

Kelly & Holmes, 1979

Kirschner, Sweller, & Clark, 2006

Toole, 2000

What to Watch for With ELL/CLD Students

1. This strategy is especially useful with upper-elementary and secondary students. The teacher may need to model how to listen and take notes appropriately.

2. Not all students will have prior educational experiences where they have listened to someone present and are then responsible for taking notes or developing commentary about what was said.

3. This can be paired with general guided practice in test preparation and test taking.

206. TEST-TAKING—PIRATES

Purpose of the Strategy

1. Build cognitive academic language

2. Build learning strategies

3. Facilitate test-taking success

4. Reduce distractibility

How to Do It

1. At Tier 3, this strategy is done in individualized, focused, and intensive periods. This strategy improves test-taking skills for typical achievement tests.

2. PIRATES may assist the learner to complete tests more carefully and successfully. Student can create cue cards of the mnemonic and use them to work through each test and individual test item. The steps in PIRATES are

Prepare to succeed
Inspect instructions carefully
Read entire question, remember strategies, and reduce choices
Answer question or leave until later
Turn back to the abandoned items
Estimate unknown answers by avoiding absolutes and eliminating similar choices
Survey to ensure that all items have a response

Research Base

DeVries Guth & Stephens Pettengill, 2005

Hughes, Deshler, Ruhl, & Schumaker, 1993

Lebzelter & Nowacek, 1999

What to Watch for With ELL/CLD Students

1. Newcomers will need to have the PIRATES steps modeled and explained in their most proficient language before they can proceed independently.

2. Students can be paired with partners who are slightly more bilingual than they are to facilitate their learning this process.

207. READING COMPREHENSION—PQ4R

Purpose of the Strategy

1. Improve reading comprehension

2. Improve access to prior knowledge

3. Expand and elaborate on learning foundation

4. Build transfer skills

How to Do It

At Tier 3, this strategy is done in individualized, focused, and intensive periods. PQ4R may assist the students to become more-discriminating readers and retain more of what they are reading. The steps in PQ4R are

Preview
Question
Read
Reflect
Recite
Review

Research Base

Anderson, 2000

Hamachek, 1994

Pelow & Colvin, 1983

Sanacore, 1982

What to Watch for With ELL/CLD Students

1. Newcomers will need to have the PQ4R steps modeled and explained in their most proficient language before they can proceed independently.

2. Students can be paired with partners who are slightly more bilingual than they are to facilitate their learning this process.

208. PARAPHRASING—RAP

Purpose of the Strategy

Improve retention of information

How to Do It

At Tier 3, this strategy is done in individualized, focused, and intensive periods. This strategy assists the student to learn information through paraphrasing. The steps in RAP are

Read paragraph
Ask self the main idea and two supporting details
Put main idea and details into own words

Research Base

Cole, 1995; see page 80

Dang et al., 2005

Ellis & Lenz, 1987

Odean, 1987

What to Watch for With ELL/CLD Students

1. Newcomers will need to have the RAP steps modeled and explained in their most proficient language before they can proceed independently.

2. Students can be paired with partners who are slightly more bilingual than they are to facilitate their learning this process.

209. READING COMPREHENSION—SQ3R

Purpose of the Strategy

1. Build transfer skills

2. Expand and elaborate on learning foundations

3. Improve access to prior knowledge

4. Improve comprehension

5. Strengthen language development

How to Do It

At Tier 3, this strategy is done in individualized, focused, and intensive periods. This strategy reminds the student to read any passage or lesson carefully and thoughtfully. Student can make cue cards to remember each step. The steps in SQ3R are

Survey
Question
Read
Recite
Review

Research Base

Allington & Cunningham, 2002; see pages 89–116

Artis, 2008

Cole, 1995; see pages 75–94

Fisher & Frey, 2004

Irvin & Rose, 1995

Law & Eckes, 2000; see pages 83–108.

Moore et al., 2000; see page 139

Robinson, 1946

Sakta, 1999, see pages 265–269

Tovani, 2000

What to Watch for With ELL/CLD Students

1. A high level of literacy is essential to achievement in our schools. Language and literacy strategies address specific language acquisition and transition issues, such as code-switching, to increase the rate of English/second-language acquisition, development of social and academic verbal abilities in both languages, comprehensible input, and other language needs. Law and Eckes (2000) provide an excellent discussion of literacy issues on page 83 through 108 of their book.

2. Newcomers will need to have the SQ3R steps modeled and explained in their most proficient language before they can proceed independently.

3. Students can be paired with partners who are slightly more bilingual than they are to facilitate their learning this process.

210. SOUND CLUES—SSCD

Purpose of the Strategy

1. Build awareness of learning

2. Build transfer skills

3. Develop personal control of situations

4. Develop thinking and planning skills

5. Improve access to prior knowledge

6. Reduce off-task behaviors

7. Strengthen language development

How to Do It

At Tier 3, this strategy is done in individualized, focused, and intensive periods. SSCD encourages the student to remember to use sound, structure, and context clues to address unfamiliar vocabulary. This is followed by dictionary usage if necessary. The steps in SSCD are

Sound clues used
Structure clues used
Context clues used
Dictionary used

Research Base

Opitz, 1998; see pages 82–83

What to Watch for With ELL/CLD Students

1. Newcomers will need to have the SSCD steps modeled and explained in their most proficient language before they can proceed independently.

2. Students can be paired with partners who are slightly more bilingual than they are to facilitate their learning this process.

211. RETENTION STRATEGY—PARS

Purpose of the Strategy

1. Build retention of information and learning

2. Reduce distraction

3. Strengthen focus on task

How to Do It

1. At Tier 3, this strategy is done in individualized, focused, and intensive period.

2. PARS is recommended for use with a younger student and with those who have limited experiences with study strategies. Students can create cue cards or use posters to remind themselves of the steps. The steps in PARS are

Preview
Ask questions
Read
Summarize

Research Base

Derwinger et al., 2005

S. W. Lee, 2005

Smith, 2000

What to Watch for With ELL/CLD Students

1. Newcomers will need to have the PARS steps modeled and explained in their most proficient language before they can proceed independently.

2. Students can be paired with partners who are slightly more bilingual than they are to facilitate their learning this process.

212. ADVANCED ORGANIZERS

Purpose of the Strategy

1. Build language transfer skills

2. Build awareness of the appropriate content language in English culture/language

3. Develop confidence in academic interactions

How to Do It

1. At Tier 3, this strategy is done in individualized, focused, and intensive periods. The teacher has the target student preview the lesson for less-advanced students, outlining key issues, rehearsing vocabulary, and reviewing related prior knowledge. Advanced-fluency students help less-advanced students understand how to organize their reading and writing materials.

2. You may use the analogy strategy described here to teach one or more of the advanced organizer tools (e.g., KWL+, W-star, graphic organizer, mind map). Students implement strategy with a specific task or lesson.

3. KWL+ is done by asking students to discuss the following questions before beginning the lesson: What do you already know about this content? What do you want to know about this content? What will we learn about this? Why should we learn this? And how will we learn this content? This may be done on a chart and student answers posted on the chart.

4. W-star is done by asking the student to brainstorm before beginning a reading: Who do you think this story/event is about? Where do you think the story/event is located? When do you think the story/event occurs? How do you think the story/event turns out? The answers are written onto the points of a star diagram, each point of which represents one of the W questions.

5. Mind mapping has various forms, but the basic idea is to put the central concept or vocabulary word related to what will be in the lesson in a circle on the board or on a piece of paper. Students then generate other words or concepts related to that main idea and connect them to the center like spokes on a wheel. For each of these ideas or words, another set of connections may be made outward from the center concept.

6. When applying the advanced organizer strategy, students work through problems or tasks using a sequence of ordering, sequencing, and connecting techniques. Suppose you want your students to write a short personal reflection about the story *Everybody Cooks Rice* by Norah Dooley (1991), which the class has just finished reading together. You would show a copy of a graphic organizer form outline (Strategy 163) on the overhead projector or drawn on the whiteboard. After reading the story through the first time, the students complete the large or projected graphic organizer. Now, you ask students how this main problem (finding Anthony) was resolved, what were the barriers to resolution that Carrie faced, and what were things in the story that helped Carrie solve her problem. The students can discuss the final resolution (everyone is home for dinner) and what the moral of the story might be in their perspective. You can expand this activity by comparing and contrasting the story with others like it or with happenings in the students' lives.

Research Base

C. Collier, 2003; *see pages* 130–142

Harwell, 2001; *see page* 214

Heacox, 2002; *see pages* 91–98

Moore et al., 2000; *see pages* 143, 198–205

Opitz, 1998; *see pages* 115–121

What to Watch for With ELL/CLD Students

1. There are cultural differences in cognitive/learning style and some ELL/CLD students may not respond to the brainstorming construct behind most advanced organizers.

2. By keeping the graphic design of the advanced organizer as close as possible to the illustrations in the text or some aspect of the lesson, the teacher can more tightly connect the concepts being studied with the W questioning that precedes the lesson.

3. This is another activity that works best with preparation in the students' most proficient language and relevance to their culture before proceeding.

213. ANALOGY

Purpose of the Strategy

1. Develop higher tolerance

2. Facilitate access of prior knowledge

3. Build transfer skills

4. Develop categorization skills

How to Do It

1. At Tier 3, this strategy is done in individualized, focused, and intensive periods.

2. Students share something they already know about the lesson topic, something that is meaningful to them. They go through the steps of analogy in pairs as they share their items/ideas. Steps for the student to follow in implementing this analogy strategy are listed here.

    a. What do I already know about this item or concept?

    b. How does what I already know about this idea or item compare with the new idea or item?

    c. Can the known idea or item be substituted for the new item or idea and still make sense?

    d. How can I elaborate on these comparisons through analogies?

3. A basic description of analogy is that you have the students work through a task describing, comparing, and contrasting things that are meaningful to them. They go through the steps of analogy asking the five specific questions that guide them through the application of the steps involved in analogy. Eventually, the students ask themselves these five self-guiding questions silently as they complete tasks.

4. An example of a content application of analogy that I have used is having students compare an object representing a new subject we are going to study with an object they are familiar with, describing the objects, and making analogies between the two items. For example, I brought examples of different dragons (Chinese, Japanese, English,

Javanese, and Scandinavian) to share with a student after we had read *The Reluctant Dragon* by Kenneth Grahame (1983) and when we were about to move into a unit on Asia. I had the students make analogies between and among the various types of dragons, discussing cultural and linguistic manifestations of these different impressions of and perspectives on a mythological figure. I then had the students do expansions related to our Asian unit. The students were asked to bring something they had that was meaningful to them that was from Asia and share it in class using the analogy strategy. The students created Venn diagrams showing the many ways the various objects were similar and different from one another.

Research Base

Cole, 1995; see page 126

C. Collier, 2003; see pages 143–147

Tovani, 2000; see pages 63–78

What to Watch for With ELL/CLD Students

1. Be sure students are matched with peers with whom they can communicate comfortably while they are all learning the strategy and steps in the process.

2. After students learn the process and steps, posters or cards with reminder illustrations and the words of the steps can be put up around the room.

3. Once students can use analogy without prompting, they can be paired up with nonbilingual peers for more applications.

214. DEMONSTRATION

Purpose of the Strategy

1. Improve confidence in academic interactions

2. Reduce distractibility

3. Build academic transfer skills

4. Develop content knowledge foundation

How to Do It

At Tier 3, this strategy is done in individualized, focused, and intensive periods. Students demonstrate understanding of the lesson and content. Activities and assessment are designed to facilitate demonstration of understanding.

Research Base

Echevarria et al., 2007

Gibbons, 2006

What to Watch for With ELL/CLD Students

1. This strategy is consistent with both Sheltered Instruction Observation Protocol (SIOP) and the Guided Language Acquisition Design (GLAD) process used in many ELL programs.

2. Students who have never been schooled before will not know what is expected and will benefit from concrete, direct demonstrations of content elements and activity expectations.

215. INFORMATION ORGANIZATION—EASY

Purpose of the Strategy

Organize and prioritize information

How to Do It

At Tier 3, this strategy is done in individualized, focused, and intensive periods. Students can create cue cards to remember each step. Students follow steps while reading passages or thematic elements. The steps in EASY are

Elicit questions (who, what, where, when, why)
Ask self which information is least difficult
Study easy content initially, followed by difficult
Yes! Provide self-reinforcement

Research Base

Lapp, Flood, Brock, & Fisher, 2007

Moore et al., 2000

What to Watch for With ELL/CLD Students

1. Much like the other mnemonics provided in these strategy lists, ELL/CLD students need bilingual explanations of the teacher's expectations and guided practice in implementing the steps in the strategy.

2. Newcomers will need to have the EASY steps modeled and explained in their most proficient language before they can proceed independently.

3. Students can be paired with partners who are slightly more bilingual than they are to facilitate their learning this process.

216. EXPERIENCE-BASED WRITING/READING

Purpose of the Strategy

1. Build transfer skills

2. Develop cognitive academic language

3. Develop content knowledge foundation

4. Facilitate analogy strategies

How to Do It

1. At Tier 3, this strategy is done in individualized, focused, and intensive periods. In primary grades, the teacher guides the students to illustrate specific experiences in which they have participated. Activity may be paired with field trips or other shared experiences; they may also be in reference to prior life experiences of ELL/LEP students. Community members may make presentations about events significant to the student's family. The teacher then has students tell what the illustrations depict and writes down verbatim what the students say. Students then read back to the teacher what has been written.

2. In intermediate and secondary grades, the teacher guides students to illustrate and write stories about experiences. These stories can be put into collections and bound for use by other students. Stories can be kept in the classroom, library, or media center.

Research Base

Beckett, 2002

Beckett & Miller, 2006

Beckett & Slater, 2005

Coelho & Rivers, 2003

Cole, 1995; *see page 126*

Echevarria et al., 2007

Gibbons, 2002

Nessel & Nixon, 2008

Wasik, 2004

What to Watch for With ELL/CLD Students

1. Some shared experiences will be very novel for particular cultural members of a group, more than for other members. Be sure to give those who have never seen something before extra preparation time and explanations of what they are going to see or do during the field trip or experience.

2. Be sure students are matched with peers with whom they can communicate comfortably while they are all learning the strategy and steps in the process.

3. Be sensitive to cultural mores about certain experiences and businesses. You may need to spend extra time discussing what is going to be seen and heard or, in some cases, be prepared to have some students participate in a related but separate activity.

217. HOME ACTIVITIES

Purpose of the Strategy

1. Develop cognitive academic language

2. Build transfer skills

3. Improve school-parent partnership

4. Develop content knowledge foundation

How to Do It

1. At Tier 3, this strategy is done in individualized, focused, and intensive periods. The teacher sends home specific content support activities for parents and the student to do together.

2. At the beginning, the students are to teach their parents what has been learned in school by telling them about it in the home language, even when the lesson was in English. As the parents become more familiar with what is being covered in the classroom content, they may be given materials to support this learning at home in the home language.

3. When parents are bilingual, they are asked to read/work through the activities in both home and community language and English with the student.

Research Base

Cole, 1995; *see pages 150–152*

C. Collier, 2003; *see pages 180, 280*

What to Watch for With ELL/CLD Students

1. Not all parents will be literate in their home language, so you cannot just send materials home.

2. Parents will need to have the process and what is expected explained to them in the home language.

3. Some programs provide training to parents about how to read to their children and provide books in the home language to facilitate this process.

218. LEARNING CENTERS

Purpose of the Strategy

1. Facilitate individualization

2. Reinforce specific skills while students work at their own pace

3. Strengthen independent task completion

How to Do It

1. At Tier 3, this strategy is done in individualized, focused, and intensive periods. Designate an area in the classroom where instructional materials are available for use by the students. Design learning centers that allow the students to reinforce specific skills or knowledge at their own pace.

2. For example, create a literacy center where different activities exist for practicing commonly used sight words, reading vocabulary words, and spelling words.

3. An additional example for a geography unit is to designate a learning center where materials and activities are available for individuals. Different activities could include a map of the United States with tracing paper and colored pencils, as well as a map, a puzzle, and, if possible, a computer game that supports the content (such as *Oregon Trail*).

Research Base

Ashworth & Wakefield, 2004

Movitz & Holmes, 2007

C. A. Tomlinson, 1999

What to Watch for With ELL/CLD Students

1. ELL/CLD students should not go to separate learning centers for primary instruction in a content lesson or task. They need direct instruction in the content or task including key vocabulary and guided practice in what is expected of them at each learning center.

2. After the ELL/CLD students have been prepared for the learning centers and shown how to use the materials or equipment at each center, they can join in the activities at each center just as the rest of the class does.

3. Learning centers are a good way to reinforce content knowledge and allow students to become engaged in applications of this new knowledge.

219. WRITING STRATEGY—TOWER

Purpose of the Strategy

1. Build awareness of learning

2. Develop personal control of situations

3. Develop thinking and planning skills

4. Improve access to prior knowledge

5. Reduce off-task behaviors

6. Strengthen language development

How to Do It

1. At Tier 3, this strategy is done in individualized, focused, and intensive periods. TOWER provides a structure for competing initial and final drafts of written reports.

2. It may be used effectively with the COPS proofreading strategy structure.

3. To help the student remember the steps in TOWER, the teacher can provide the students with a printed form with the letters T, O, W, E, R down the left side and their meaning next to each letter.

4. The steps the student follows in TOWER are

Think
Order ideas
Write
Edit
Rewrite

Research Base

Cole, 1995; see pages 102–104

Ellis & Colvert, 1996

Ellis & Lenz, 1987

Goldsworthy, 2003

What to Watch for With ELL/CLD Students

1. Newcomers will need to have the TOWER steps modeled and explained in their most proficient language before they can proceed independently.

2. Students can be paired with partners who are slightly more bilingual than they are to facilitate their learning this process.

220. LISTENING COMPREHENSION—TQLR

Purpose of the Strategy

1. Build awareness of learning

2. Develop personal control of situations

3. Improve access to prior knowledge

4. Strengthen language development

How to Do It

At Tier 3, this strategy is done in individualized, focused, and intensive periods. This strategy assists with listening comprehension. Students generate questions and listen for specific statements related to those questions. The steps in TQLR are

Tuning in
Questioning

Listening

Reviewing

Research Base

Artis, 2008

Fisher & Frey, 2004

Irvin & Rose, 1995

Law & Eckes, 2000

Popp, 1997

Robinson, 1946

Sakta, 1999

What to Watch for With ELL/CLD Students

1. Newcomers will need to have the TQLR steps modeled and explained in their most proficient language before they can proceed independently.

2. Students can be paired with partners who are slightly more bilingual than they are to facilitate their learning this process.

221. CONTEXT-EMBEDDED INSTRUCTION

Purpose of the Strategy

1. Develop cognitive academic language proficiency

2. Develop content area skills

3. Develop personal control of situations

4. Reduce distractibility

How to Do It

At Tier 3, this strategy is done in individualized, focused, and intensive periods. The teacher always presents lessons with concrete, physical models and demonstrations of both content and expected performance. Language is simplified and content focused. The student is encouraged to discuss lessons in home and community language and work in small groups on content activities.

Research Base

Cole, 1995

Cummins, 1984

Cummins, Baker, & Hornberger, 2001

Donaldson, 1978

Echevarria et al., 2007

Echevarria & Graves, 2006

Roessingh, Kover, & Watt, 2005

What to Watch for With ELL/CLD Students

1. Vocabulary may be previewed with fluent speakers in the students' most proficient language.

2. Some cultures may have strictures against children handling or being too close to certain objects. Always screen items ahead of time with knowledgeable community members.

3. This strategy is consistent with the Sheltered Instruction Observation Protocol (SIOP) model used in many ELL programs.

4. Newcomers who have never attended school may become confused if every lesson and activity occurs in seemingly random patterns. They do not know what is expected of them at various stages of the lesson. They do not know what to attend to and what is less important.

5. This is also going to impact students with undiagnosed attention deficit disorders that they have not yet learned to accommodate.

6. It is better to start out with simple consistent steps and add to them as students become comfortable and familiar with what is going to happen in the classroom.

222. WRITING STRATEGIES—DEFENDS

Purpose of the Strategy

Assist learners to defend a particular position in a written assignment

How to Do It

1. At Tier 3, this strategy is done in individualized, focused, and intensive periods. The DEFENDS writing strategy framework provides a structure for completing initial and final drafts of written reports.

2. It may be used effectively with the COPS proofreading strategy structure.

3. To help the student remember the steps in DEFENDS, the teacher can provide the student with a printed form with the letters D, E, F, E, N, D, S down the left side and their meaning next to each letter.

4. The steps in DEFENDS are

Decide on a specific position
Examine own reasons for this position
Form list of points explaining each reason
Expose position in first sentence of written task
Note each reason and associated points
Drive home position in last sentence
Search for and correct any errors

Research Base

Ellis & Colvert, 1996

Ellis & Lenz, 1987

Goldsworthy, 2003

What to Watch for With ELL/CLD Students

1. Newcomers will need to have the DEFENDS steps modeled and explained in their most proficient language before they can proceed independently.

2. Students can be paired with partners who are slightly more bilingual than they are to facilitate their learning this process.

223. WRITING STRATEGY—PENS

Purpose of the Strategy

Expand language arts capabilities

How to Do It

At Tier 3, this strategy is done in individualized, focused, and intensive periods. PENS is appropriate for developing basic sentence structure and assists the student to write different types of sentences following formulas for sentence construction. The steps in PENS are

Pick a formula
Explore different words that fit the formula
Note the words selected
Subject and verb selections follow

Research Base

Derwinger et al., 2005

Eskritt & McLeod, 2008

What to Watch for With ELL/CLD Students

1. Newcomers will need to have the PENS steps modeled and explained in their most proficient language before they can proceed independently.

2. Students can be paired with partners who are slightly more bilingual than they are to facilitate their learning this process.

224. TEST-TAKING STRATEGY—PIRATES

Purpose of the Strategy

1. Build cognitive academic language

2. Build learning strategies

3. Facilitate test-taking success

4. Reduce distractibility

How to Do It

1. At Tier 3, this strategy is done in individualized, focused, and intensive periods . This strategy improves test-taking skills for typical achievement tests.

2. PIRATES may assist learners to complete tests more carefully and successfully. The students can create mnemonic cue cards for each step and then use the cue cards to work through each test and test item. The steps in PIRATES are

Prepare to succeed
Inspect instructions carefully
Read entire question, remember strategies, and reduce choices
Answer question or leave until later
Turn back to the unanswered items
Estimate unknown answers by avoiding absolutes and eliminating similar choices
Survey to ensure that all items have a response

Research Base

DeVries Guth & Stephens Pettengill, 2005

Hughes et al., 1993

Lebzelter & Nowacek, 1999

What to Watch for With ELL/CLD Students

1. Newcomers will need to have the PIRATES steps modeled and explained in their most proficient language before they can proceed independently.

2. Students can be paired with partners who are slightly more bilingual than they are to facilitate their learning this process.

225. READING COMPREHENSION—PQ4R

Purpose of the Strategy

1. Build transfer skills

2. Expand and elaborate on learning foundation

3. Improve access to prior knowledge

4. Improve reading comprehension

How to Do It

1. At Tier 3, this strategy is done in individualized, focused, and intensive periods. PQ4R may assist students to become more-discriminating readers and retain more of what they are reading.

2. The steps in PQ4R are

Preview
Question
Read
Reflect
Recite
Review

Research Base

Anderson, 2000

Hamachek, 1994

Pelow & Colvin, 1983

Sanacore, 1982

What to Watch for With ELL/CLD Students

1. Newcomers will need to have the PQ4R steps modeled and explained in their most proficient language before they can proceed independently.

2. Students can be paired with partners who are slightly more bilingual than they are to facilitate their learning this process.

226. PARAPHRASING—RAP

Purpose of the Strategy

1. Improve retention of information

2. Assist student to learn information through paraphrasing

How to Do It

At Tier 3, this strategy is done in individualized, focused, and intensive periods. The steps in RAP are

Read paragraph
Ask self the main idea and two supporting details
Put main idea and details into own words

Research Base

Cole, 1995; see page 80

Dang et al., 2005

Ellis & Lenz, 1987

Odean, 1987

What to Watch for With ELL/CLD Students

1. Newcomers will need to have the RAP steps modeled and explained in their most proficient language before they can proceed independently.

2. Students can be paired with partners who are slightly more bilingual than they are to facilitate their learning this process.

227. RECIPROCAL QUESTIONING

Purpose of the Strategy

1. Use as an inquiry approach

2. Develop thinking and planning skills

3. Improve mnemonic retrieval

4. Improve reading comprehension

5. Improve retention

6. Use discourse technique

How to Do It

At Tier 3, this strategy is done in individualized, focused, and intensive periods. The teacher and students ask one another questions about a selection. The students modeling of the teacher's questions and teacher feedback are emphasized as the learner explores the meaning of the reading material.

Research Base

Cole, 1995; see pages 113–114

Moore et al., 2000; see pages 141–142

What to Watch for With ELL/CLD Students

1. Provide initial setup in the student's most proficient language.

2. Students can practice reciprocal questioning with one another in their native language and then proceed with English-proficient students.

228. VISUALIZATION—RIDER

Purpose of the Strategy

1. Build transfer skills

2. Expand and elaborate on learning foundation

3. Improve access to prior knowledge

4. Improve reading comprehension

5. Improve retention of information

6. Strengthen language development

How to Do It

At Tier 3, this strategy is done in individualized, focused, and intensive periods. This visualization strategy cues the learner to form a mental image of what was read and assists the student in making connections with previously learned materials. The steps in RIDER are

Read a sentence
Image (form a mental picture)
Describe how new information differs from previous
Evaluate image to ensure it is comprehensive
Repeat process with subsequent sentences

Research Base

Klingner et al., 2007

Naughton, 2008

B. Tomlinson, 1998

What to Watch for With ELL/CLD Students

1. Students with limited school experience will not know what visualization means and will need to have direct instruction in the vocabulary and actions expected.

2. This can be introduced in the primary language and examples given from literature and art with which the students are more familiar.

3. Newcomers will need to have the RIDER steps modeled and explained in their most proficient language before they can proceed independently.

4. Students can be paired with partners who are slightly more bilingual than they are to facilitate their learning this process.

229. TEST-TAKING STRATEGY—SCORER

Purpose of the Strategy

Improve test-taking skills

How to Do It

At Tier 3, this strategy is done in individualized, focused, and intensive periods. This test-taking strategy provides a structure for completing various tests by assisting the student to carefully and systematically complete test items. The steps in SCORER are

Schedule time effectively
Clue words identified
Omit difficult items until the end
Read carefully
Estimate answers requiring calculations
Review work and responses

Research Base

Elliot & Thurlow, 2005

Ritter & Idol-Maestas, 1986

What to Watch for With ELL/CLD Students

1. Newcomers will need to have the SCORER steps modeled and explained in their most proficient language before they can proceed independently.

2. Students can be paired with partners who are slightly more bilingual than they are to facilitate their learning this process.

230. READING COMPREHENSION STRATEGY—SQ3R

Purpose of the Strategy

1. Build transfer skills

2. Expand and elaborate on learning foundations

3. Improve access to prior knowledge

4. Improve comprehension

5. Strengthen language development

How to Do It

At Tier 3, this strategy is done in individualized, focused, and intensive periods. This strategy reminds the student to go through any passage or lesson carefully and thoughtfully. The student can make cue cards to remember each step. The steps in SQ3R are

Survey
Question
Read
Recite
Review

Research Base

Allington & Cunningham, 2002; *see pages 89–116*

Artis, 2008

Cole, 1995; *see pages 75–94*

Fisher & Frey, 2004

Irvin & Rose, 1995

Law & Eckes, 2000

Moore et al., 2000; *see page 139*

Robinson, 1946

Sakta, 1999

Tovani, 2000

What to Watch for With ELL/CLD Students

1. Newcomers will need to have the SQ3R steps modeled and explained in their most proficient language before they can proceed independently.

2. Students can be paired with partners who are slightly more bilingual than they are to facilitate their learning this process.

231. MATH WORD PROBLEM STRATEGY—SQRQCQ

Purpose of the Strategy

1. Improve comprehension

2. Improve retention of information

3. Improve problem solving of math word problems

4. Strengthen language development

How to Do It

At Tier 3, this strategy is done in individualized, focused, and intensive periods. This strategy provides a systematic structure for identifying the question being asked in a math word problem, computing the response, and ensuring that the question in the problem was answered. The steps in SQRQCQ are

Survey word problems
Question asked is identified
Read more carefully
Question process required to solve problem
Compute the answer
Question self to ensure that the answer solves the problem

Research Base

Cole, 1995; *see pages 65–66, 127–128, 132*

Elliot & Thurlow, 2005

What to Watch for With ELL/CLD Students

1. Newcomers will need to have the SQRQCQ steps modeled and explained in their most proficient language before they can proceed independently.

2. Students can be paired with partners who are slightly more bilingual than they are to facilitate their learning this process.

232. SOUND CLUES—SSCD

Purpose of the Strategy

1. Build awareness of learning

2. Build transfer skills

3. Develop personal control of situations

4. Develop thinking and planning skills

5. Improve access to prior knowledge

6. Reduce off-task behaviors

7. Strengthen language development

How to Do It

At Tier 3, this strategy is done in individualized, focused, and intensive periods. SSCD encourages the student to remember to use sound, structure, and context clues to address unfamiliar vocabulary. This strategy is followed by dictionary usage if necessary. The steps in SSCD are

Sound clues used
Structure clues used
Context clues used
Dictionary used

Research Base

Opitz, 1998; see pages 82–83

What to Watch for With ELL/CLD Students

1. Newcomers will need to have the SSCD steps modeled and explained in their most proficient language before they can proceed independently.

2. Students can be paired with partners who are slightly more bilingual than they are to facilitate their learning this process.

233. ACTIVE PROCESSING

Purpose of the Strategy

1. Build awareness of learning

2. Develop academic language

3. Develop personal control of situations

4. Facilitate access to prior knowledge

5. Reduce low-persistence behaviors

6. Reduce off-task behaviors

7. Reduce impulsivity

How to Do It

1. At Tier 3, this strategy is done in individualized, focused, and intensive periods. The students work through a reading task aloud, reading passages and asking themselves the appropriate questions related to the passage.

2. Steps for student to follow in implementing this strategy are listed here.

   a. What is my task?

   b. What do I need to do to complete my task?

   c. How will I know my task is done correctly?

   d. How will I monitor the implementation?

   e. How do I know the task is correctly completed?

3. When applying the active processing strategy, the students work through problems or tasks using the sequence of self-monitoring questions given here. For example, your students must prepare for the state-administered achievement tests required at this grade level, but your diverse learners have never taken such tests before and are unfamiliar with this type of evaluation. They have heard stories of something scary that happens to schoolchildren every year and are bracing to endure this external event. You could modify your preparation for this event by integrating the active processing strategy into the lessons before the testing period. Start by having the student speak aloud about the content and process of lessons following the steps in active processing. Do this in every content area until the student is familiar with the process itself. Then a few weeks before the state assessments, introduce the concept of standardized achievement tests to your students. Have your students discuss how group and norm measures differ from individual and curriculum-based assessments and the implications (Step 1 of active processing, "What is my task?"). Have the students discuss what they will need to have and what the setting is like. Talk about the expectations of test administrators regarding notes, whispering, looking at others, pencils, calculators, and the like (Step 2 of active processing, "What do I need to do to complete my task?"). Discuss what an acceptable performance might be for various levels of completion and knowledge. Explain some of the test strategies that help successful test takers even when they are unsure of the answer. Clarify the expectations of parents, teachers, and others about the test activity (Step 3 of active processing, "How will I know my task is done correctly?"). Provide suggestions for relieving stress during the test and ideas for self-monitoring their progress through the different sections of the test (Step 4 of active processing, "How will I monitor the implementation?"). Discuss how timekeepers work and what the timelines will be on this test. Discuss ways to identify when it is time to move to another section and what to do when they are finished with the test (Step 5 of active processing, "How do I know the task is completed?").

4. For example, suppose you want your student to complete a new unit in language arts about bears in fact and fiction. Your diverse learners may not be familiar with the concept of fact versus fiction as used in our society and have no words in their native language for this distinction. You could modify your preparation for this unit by integrating the active processing strategy into the lessons. Begin having the students speak about what they know about bears and other animals following the steps in active processing. Do this in the context of reinforcement and review of prior content the students have successfully accomplished until the student is familiar with active processing itself. Then introduce the concept of fact versus fiction. Have students discuss how these differ using real-life experiences from home or community. Use visual and physical examples of the concept, such as a photograph of a car and a sketch or drawing of a car, a realistic portrait of a child and an abstract painting of a child, a picture of astronauts on the moon and a picture of children playing on the moon, and the like to ensure that the students are aware of what is involved. Have students describe examples from their communities or lives. Discuss how to tell the difference and what is involved in the process (Step 1 of active processing, "What is my task?").

Have students discuss what is needed to compare and contrast fact from fiction and what actions are involved. Talk about the importance of learning this skill and discuss the steps involved. Have your students develop a set of rules outlining the steps to follow (Step 2 of active processing, "What do I need to do to complete my task?"). Discuss what an acceptable performance might be for various levels of skill and knowledge. Explain some of the strategies that help to be successful at separating fact from fiction. Discuss how to check for the accuracy and the steps involved (Step 3 of active processing, "How will I know my task is done correctly?"). Provide suggestions for relieving stress during the lesson and ideas for self-monitoring progress through the different steps of the process (Step 4 of active processing, "How will I monitor the implementation?"). Discuss ways to identify when it is time to move to another question or example and what to do when they have finished each set of comparisons (Step 5 of active processing, "How do I know the task is completed?").

5. Using active processing reduces impulsive tendencies and naturally illustrates how a student can use reflection in answering questions and completing tasks.

Research Base

Cole, 1995

C. Collier, 2003; see pages 124–130

Law & Eckes, 2000

Tovani, 2000; see pages 26–29

What to Watch for With ELL/CLD Students

1. The strategy preparation can be done in the native language or dialect of the students to assure their understanding of your expectations and their task prior to carrying the assignment out in English or other communication mode.

2. Students who are less proficient in English will need guidance in using the steps of active processing; the process can be explained and practiced in the students' most proficient language before going on in English.

3. Active processing can be used in any language of instruction and in any content area or age level.

234. DOUBLE ENTRY

Purpose of the Strategy

1. Build reading comprehension

2. Develop note-taking skills

3. Reduce impulsivity

4. Develop reflection

How to Do It

1. At Tier 3, this strategy is done in individualized, focused, and intensive periods. Double entry is a method of taking comprehensive notes as well as reflecting on what is read.

2. Students divide a piece of paper in half, lengthwise. In the left-hand column, they copy sentences or summarize a passage. In the right-hand column, they write the interpretation, inferences, and critical thinking about the passage. This activity can also be done as a journal in which the pages are divided into the two columns.

Research Base

Strickland et al., 2002; see page 204

Tovani, 2000; see pages 30–32

What to Watch for With ELL/CLD Students

1. This is an easy strategy to assist students who are beginning to do more reading and writing to organize and think about what they are reading.

2. This can be done in any language in which the students are literate.

235. READING STRATEGY—FIST

Purpose of the Strategy

Assist students to actively pursue responses to questions related directly to materials being read

How to Do It

1. At Tier 3, this strategy is done in individualized, focused, and intensive periods. The students follow steps while reading paragraphs in assigned readings. To help the students remember the steps, the teacher can provide a checklist of the steps with the letters F, I, S, T down the side and their meaning next to each letter.

2. The steps in FIST are

First sentence is read
Indicate a question based on first sentence
Search for the answer to the question
Tie question and answer together through paraphrasing

Research Base

Allington & Cunningham, 2002

Cole, 1995

Dang et al., 2005

Derwinger et al., 2005

Ellis & Lenz, 1987

Moore et al., 2000

Odean, 1987

What to Watch for With ELL/CLD Students

1. Newcomers will need to have the FIST steps modeled and explained in their most proficient language before they can proceed independently.

2. Students can be paired with partners who are slightly more bilingual than they are to facilitate their learning this process.

236. MARKING TEXT

Purpose of the Strategy

1. Build reading comprehension

2. Develop note-taking skills

3. Reduce impulsivity

4. Develop reflection

5. Reduce distraction

6. Focus attention

How to Do It

1. At Tier 3, this strategy is done in individualized, focused, and intensive periods. Also called coding text (Davey, 1983), the students mark their text as a way to stay engaged in their reading.

2. The students use codes to indicate the type of thinking they are to use with particular passages. For example, if you want the students to make connections between their lives and the text, they might mark those passages with "REM" for "remember when." Students can also put "?" marks where they have questions about the text.

Research Base

Tovani 2000; see pages 29–30

What to Watch for With ELL/CLD Students

1. This is an easy strategy to assist students who are beginning to do more reading to organize and think about what they are reading.

2. This can be done in any language in which the students are literate.

237. READING COMPREHENSION—PQ4R

Purpose of the Strategy

1. Build transfer skills

2. Expand on learning foundation

3. Improve access to prior knowledge

4. Improve reading comprehension

How to Do It

At Tier 3, this strategy is done in individualized, focused, and intensive periods. PQ4R may assist students to become more-discriminating readers and retain more of what they are reading. The steps in PQ4R are

Preview
Question
Read
Reflect
Recite
Review

Research Base

Anderson, 2000

Hamachek, 1994

Pelow & Colvin, 1983

Sanacore, 1982

What to Watch for With ELL/CLD Students

1. Newcomers will need to have the PQ4R steps modeled and explained in their most proficient language before they can proceed independently.

2. Students can be paired with partners who are slightly more bilingual than they are to facilitate their learning this process.

238. SCAFFOLDING

Purpose of the Strategy

1. Build a foundation for learning

2. Facilitate steady growth in learning

3. Build confidence in learning process

4. Develop cognitive academic learning skills

5. Support students who are new to schooling

How to Do It

1. At Tier 3, this strategy is done in individualized, focused, and intensive periods. Scaffolding is a way to support, elaborate, and expand on students' language as they learn to read (and write).

2. Scaffolds are temporary frameworks that offer students immediate access to the meanings and pleasure of print.

Research Base

Opitz, 1998; see pages 150–157

Vygotsky, 1978

What to Watch for With ELL/CLD Students

1. Teachers will need to lay a foundation for learning and continue to support new learners through the process until they are ready to go on their own.

2. It is important to remember not to continue extensive scaffolding beyond the point of skill acquisition. The learners must become empowered to proceed independently.

3. Vygotsky (1978) discusses this in the context of the zone of proximal development.

239. WORDLESS PICTURE BOOKS

Purpose of the Strategy

1. Improve sequencing skills

2. Facilitate reading process

3. Improve vocabulary

How to Do It

At Tier 3, this strategy is done in individualized, focused, and intensive periods. Using wordless picture books with an emerging reader is very effective. It builds on the learners' oral language skills to develop the reading process. This allows for variations in phonology, syntax, vocabulary, intonation, and so on to be accommodated in an integrated classroom (i.e., students can participate in the activity regardless of reading level). The teacher selects a wordless picture book of high-interest content to the students. Wordless picture books are available at all age/grade levels. The students can "read" the pictures in small groups or individually, telling the "story" as they see it. The students can also make wordless picture books.

Research Base

Opitz, 1998; see pages 130–135

What to Watch for With ELL/CLD Students

1. Teachers may need to model how to go through a book and how to follow the sequence of the story through the pictures.

2. Begin with pictures the students recognize from experiences. Introduce new and unusual illustrations after the students understand what the process of reading is like in a wordless picture book.

3. Another variation on this is to use modern pop-up books to tell the story. Some of these are quite sophisticated and may be used in math and science lessons as well.

240. PROOFREADING—COPS

Purpose of the Strategy

1. Build review skills

2. Facilitate critical thinking

3. Expand writing and reading skills

How to Do It

At Tier 3, this strategy is done in individualized, focused, and intensive periods. This strategy provides a structure for proofreading written work prior to submitting it to the teacher. The steps in COPS are

Capitalization
Overall appearance
Punctuation
Spelling

Research Base

Cole, 1995; see pages 108–110

What to Watch for With ELL/CLD Students

1. Newcomers will need to have the COPS steps modeled and explained in their most proficient language before they can proceed independently.

2. Students can be paired with partners who are slightly more bilingual than they are to facilitate their learning this process.

241. GUIDED LECTURE PROCEDURE

Purpose of the Strategy

1. Build listening skills

2. Build study skills

3. Facilitate students taking control of learning

How to Do It

1. At Tier 3, this strategy is done in individualized, focused, and intensive periods. This strategy provides students with a structure for taking notes during lectures.

2. Active listening is involved to facilitate effective note taking. Students listen to the teacher's or the assistant's presentation. The speaker pauses periodically to allow the students to check their notes and fill in missing information.

Research Base

Kelly & Holmes, 1979

Kirschner et al., 2006

Toole, 2000

What to Watch for With ELL/CLD Students

1. This strategy is especially useful with upper-elementary and secondary students. The teacher may need to model how to listen and take notes appropriately.

2. Not all students will have prior educational experiences where they have listened to someone present and are then responsible for taking notes or developing commentary about what was said.

3. This can be paired with general guided practice in test preparation and test taking.

242. WRITING STRATEGY—PENS

Purpose of the Strategy

1. Expand language arts capabilities

2. Develop basic sentence structure

How to Do It

At Tier 3, this strategy is done in individualized, focused, and intensive periods. This strategy assists the students to write different types of sentences following formulas for sentence construction. The steps in PENS are

Pick a formula
Explore different words that fit the formula
Note the words selected
Subject and verb selections follow

Research Base

Derwinger et al., 2005

Eskritt & McLeod, 2008

What to Watch for With ELL/CLD Students

1. Newcomers will need to have the PENS steps modeled and explained in their most proficient language before they can proceed independently.

2. Students can be paired with partners who are slightly more bilingual than they are to facilitate their learning this process.

243. SOUND CLUES—SSCD

Purpose of the Strategy

1. Build awareness of learning

2. Build transfer skills

3. Develop personal control of situations

4. Develop thinking and planning skills

5. Improve access to prior knowledge

6. Reduce off-task behaviors

7. Strengthen language development

How to Do It

At Tier 3, this strategy is done in individualized, focused, and intensive periods. SSCD encourages the students to remember to use sound, structure, and context clues to address unfamiliar vocabulary. This strategy is followed by dictionary usage if necessary. The steps in SSCD are

Sound clues used
Structure clues used
Context clues used
Dictionary used

Research Base

Opitz,1998; see pages 82–83

What to Watch for With ELL/CLD Students

1. Newcomers will need to have the SSCD steps modeled and explained in their most proficient language before they can proceed independently.

2. Students can be paired with partners who are slightly more bilingual than they are to facilitate their learning this process.

BEHAVIOR ISSUES AT TIER 3

244. ACCOUNTABILITY

Purpose of the Strategy

1. Ensure that students are aware of and responsible for their actions

2. Develop awareness of the connection between their actions and the consequences of these actions

How to Do It

At Tier 3, this strategy is done in individualized, focused, and intensive periods. Establish rewards and consequences for completion of work and appropriate behavior, ensuring that these rewards and consequences are consistently implemented. For example, the teacher assists the students in setting up an agenda or plan of a personalized list of tasks that the student must complete in a specified time.

Research Base

C. A. Tomlinson, 1999; see pages 66–68

What to Watch for With ELL/CLD Students

Particular social groups and cultures have different expectations of adults and children when it comes to being accountable for task completion. This is a learned difference between cultures. The teacher needs to be aware that the expectations in an American school may need to be taught directly to CLD students and should not assume that they are understood.

245. ALTERNATE RESPONSE METHODS

Purpose of the Strategy

1. Facilitate learning

2. Accommodate diverse learning styles

3. Develop task completion

How to Do It

1. At Tier 3, this strategy is done in individualized, focused, and intensive periods. This strategy adapts the mode of response required of students.

2. The students respond to questions in a manner compatible with their needs. Allow students who have difficulty with writing activities to record their answers. Students are allowed to express understanding of a question or issue in varied ways. This ensures that the students have the best possible chance to show acquired and retained skills and knowledge.

3. For example, students may record oral responses to questions given in class. For the geography unit, provide the questions in writing for the students to take home and practice responding. Some names of American states are very difficult to pronounce; provide time for the student to work alone or with a peer to write the difficult state names on tag board cards that they can hold up during class discussion rather than say aloud.

Research Base

Bailey, 1993

Gardner, 1993a

Gardner, 1993b

Tannenbaum, 1996

What to Watch for With ELL/CLD Students

1. Some CLD students have had previous schooling in situations where students have no choice in their responses and teachers are authority figures who direct every action in the classroom.

2. When the teacher wishes to make student empowerment an instructional goal, this strategy is an excellent direction to take.

3. Demonstrate how the various responses can be made, including color, modeling, illustrating, and so on.

4. Some role-play in the process from initial choice to final task completion may be helpful.

246. CHOICES

Purpose of the Strategy

1. Facilitate learning

2. Accommodate diverse learning styles

3. Develop task completion

4. Alleviate power struggles between teacher and student

5. Reduce fears associated with assignments

How to Do It

1. At Tier 3, this strategy is done in individualized, focused, and intensive periods. Provide the student the opportunity to select one or more activities developed by the teacher

2. The teacher provides two different reading selections of interest to the student, both of which address the same desired objective. Allow the student to select one of the selections for the assignment. If student does not choose either of the selections, introduce a third selection or ask the student to choose a content-appropriate reading selection.

Research Base

Ainley, 2006

Cordova & Lepper, 1996

Flowerday & Schraw, 2003

Flowerday, Schraw, & Stevens, 2004

Kragler & Nolley, 1996

Sanacore, 1999

What to Watch for With ELL/CLD Students

1. Some CLD students have had previous schooling in situations where students have no choice and teachers are authority figures who direct every action in the classroom.

2. When the teacher wishes to make choice and student empowerment an instructional goal, this strategy is an excellent direction to take.

3. Demonstrate how the choice has to be made, including color coding or otherwise graphically illustrating the different choices.

4. Some role-play in the process from initial choice to final task completion may be helpful.

247. CONTENT MODIFICATION

Purpose of the Strategy

1. Adapt content to meet individual or unique student needs

2. Improve motivation and response

3. Reduce frustration

How to Do It

At Tier 3, this strategy is done in individualized, focused, and intensive periods. The teacher uses subject matter rather than specific linguistic skill exercises to teach English to the student with limited proficiency in English. Allow the students who have difficulty with writing activities to record their answers.

Research Base

Arkoudis, 2005

Brinton, Wesche, & Snow, 2003

Echevarria & Graves, 2006

McIntyre, Kyle, Chen, Kraemer, & Parr, 2009

Weisman & Hansen, 2007

What to Watch for With ELL/CLD Students

1. This can be done in any language and content lesson, but will need to be explained in students' most proficient language.

2. Provide lots of practice and modeling.

3. When presenting a topic, the teacher can ask students for what specifically they would like to learn about this topic.

248. CONTRACTING

Purpose of the Strategy

1. Improve motivation

2. Facilitate learner empowerment

3. Reduce distractibility

How to Do It

1. At Tier 3, this strategy is done in individualized, focused, and intensive periods. This strategy clarifies responsibilities, assignments, and rewards.

2. Establish a verbal or written mutual agreement between teacher and student.

3. For example, use a written document stating the agreement that the student will complete 20 math problems with 80% accuracy during the regular math period. The student will receive 10 minutes of extra free time if contract conditions are met.

Research Base

Harwell, 2001; see pages124–125

C. A. Tomlinson, 1999; see pages 66–68, 87–91

What to Watch for With ELL/CLD Students

1. Contracts will need to be explained in the students' most proficient language.

2. Examples should be provided from their family or community experience.

249. EXPECTATIONS AWARENESS/REVIEW

Purpose of the Strategy

1. Ensure that each student is familiar with specific academic and behavioral expectations

2. Reduce frustration in students because of unclear expectations

3. Minimize ambiguity in classroom

How to Do It

At Tier 3, this strategy is done in individualized, focused, and intensive periods. This strategy modifies or breaks downs general classroom rules into specific behavioral expectations to ensure that each student knows exactly what is meant by acceptable behaviors.

Research Base

Davis, 2005

J. R. Nelson, Martella, & Galand, 1998

Rubenstein, 2006

What to Watch for With ELL/CLD Students

1. Particular social groups and cultures have different expectations of adults and children when it comes to being accountable for task completion. This is a learned difference between cultures. The teacher needs to be aware that the expectations in an American school may need to be taught directly to CLD students and should not assume that they are understood.

2. One way to introduce the idea of your classroom rules is to ask students about any rules their parents have for them at home or rules they have learned about crossing the street or playing games. This can then be expanded to the idea of rules for completing tasks and acting appropriately in a classroom.

3. Demonstrate all of the desired behaviors and rules. Some role-play may be helpful. Examples of inappropriate behaviors may be used with caution.

250. PLANNED IGNORING

Purpose of the Strategy

1. Reduce confrontations over minor misbehaving

2. Eliminate inappropriate behavior after a few moments

How to Do It

1. At Tier 3, this strategy is done in individualized, focused, and intensive periods. This strategy purposely ignores certain behaviors exhibited by the students.

2. For example, the teacher elects to ignore some whispering by the target student during independent work time.

Research Base

Grossman, 2003

Hall & Hall, 1998

Rafferty, 2007

What to Watch for With ELL/CLD Students

1. Some ELL and CLD students may have limited experience with attending schools and not know what the rules are in classrooms.

2. In some cultures, students who understand some tasks are expected to assist their relative or friend with a task who may not be doing so well, so some quiet helping should be allowed as long as it appears to be on task.

251. PLANNED MOVEMENT

Purpose of the Strategy

1. Prevent inappropriate moving around the room

2. Minimize behavior problems in the classroom

How to Do It

1. At Tier 3, this strategy is done in individualized, focused, and intensive periods. Periodically, provide students opportunities to move about the classroom for appropriate reasons.

2. For example, the teacher allows students to move to a learning center or study booth for part of their independent work time instead of remaining seated at desk for the entire period.

Research Base

Evertson & Neal, 2006

Evertson & Weinstein, 2006

Kaufman, 2001

Williams, 2008

What to Watch for With ELL/CLD Students

1. Differences in mobility and movement by children are learned differences among cultures and social groups. In some families, children are expected to get up and move around whenever they want to; in other families, children are expected to remain seated or in one place unless and until they are given permission to move elsewhere.

2. Some children may have undiagnosed conditions that inhibit their sitting or standing in one place without moving occasionally. Using planned movement and making accommodations for opportunities for students to move facilitates learning for all students.

252. POSITIVE REINFORCEMENT

Purpose of the Strategy

1. Increase the frequency of appropriate responses or behaviors

2. Facilitate students' comfort with learning environment

How to Do It

1. At Tier 3, this strategy is done in individualized, focused, and intensive periods. This strategy provides feedback or rewards for completing appropriate tasks.

2. For example, the teacher provides students with extra free time when their math or reading assignment has been completed.

Research Base

Cole, 1995; *see pages 115–116*

Harwell, 2001; *see pages 126–127*

Opitz, 1998; *see page 61*

What to Watch for With ELL/CLD Students

1. What is rewarding to one person is not necessarily rewarding to another. This is another learned preference.

2. The teacher should use a variety of affirmatives, words, and phrases to denote reinforcement.

3. When using physical rewards, always do some research to identify cultural, developmental, and gender appropriate items.

4. When using extra time or a special activity as a reward, vary these depending on the students' interests.

253. PROXIMITY (PROXEMICS)

Purpose of the Strategy

1. Increase time spent on task

2. Reassure frustrated students

How to Do It

1. At Tier 3, this strategy is done in individualized, focused, and intensive periods. The teacher and/or other students are strategically positioned to provide support and to prevent or minimize misbehaviors by the target student.

2. For example, the teacher circulates throughout the classroom during group or independent activities, spending more time next to the particular student.

Research Base

Etscheidt, Stainback, S. B., & Stainback, W. C., 1984

Evertson & Weinstein, 2006

Gunter & Shores, 1995

Marable & Raimondi, 1995

Walters & Frei, 2007

What to Watch for With ELL/CLD Students

1. All cultures have guidelines about how close or how far away to stand or sit next to another person. These are mostly unspoken and learned through being raised in the culture and community where the proximity to another person is seen and remarked on by those around you.

2. These space relations are also affected by whether someone is standing over or sitting under another person. These relative positions convey power and control relationships, which vary from culture to culture.

3. Teachers must familiarize themselves with the proximity rules of the various cultures represented in their classrooms before expecting to use proxemics strategically to promote learning.

254. REDUCED STIMULI

Purpose of the Strategy

1. Enhance ability of students to focus on learning

2. Encourage questioning and exploration of new learning

3. Reduce response fatigue

4. Reduce culture shock

5. Develop personal control of situations

How to Do It

At Tier 3, this strategy is done in individualized, focused, and intensive periods. The teacher starts the room with relatively blank walls and empty spaces, also monitoring the use of music and other auditory materials. The teacher does not display or use visual/auditory materials until students have been introduced to the content or have produced the materials. Visual, tactile, and auditory experiences are introduced gradually and with demonstration.

Research Base

P. Nelson, Kohnert, Sabur, & Shaw, 2005

Wortham, 1996

What to Watch for With ELL/CLD Students

1. Newcomers may become overly stimulated by lots of bright, new, unfamiliar, and strange objects, signs, sounds, and miscellany in their new classroom. They do not know what is important to attend to and what is not important. It is all new and exciting.

2. This is also going to impact students with undiagnosed neurological conditions that they have not yet learned to accommodate.

3. It is better to start out with less and add more as students become comfortable and familiar with what is in the classroom.

255. REST AND RELAXATION TECHNIQUES

Purpose of the Strategy

1. Enhance ability of students to learn new things

2. Develop self-monitoring skills

3. Reduce anxiety and stress responses

4. Reduce culture shock side effects

How to Do It

At Tier 3, this strategy is conducted in individualized, focused, and intensive periods. Relaxation techniques are shown in video or demonstration form with an explanation in home and community language when possible. Students discuss when to use these techniques.

Research Base

Allen & Klein, 1997

Page & Page, 2003

Thomas, 2006

What to Watch for With ELL/CLD Students

1. Heightened anxiety, distractibility, and response fatigue are all common side effects of the acculturation process and attributes of culture shock.

2. ELL and CLD students need more time to process classroom activities and tasks. Building in rest periods will provide thinking and processing breaks in their day.

256. SELF-REINFORCEMENT

Purpose of the Strategy

1. Build awareness of learning

2. Develop personal control of situations

3. Develop thinking and planning skills

4. Facilitate access to prior knowledge

5. Facilitate language development

6. Improve motivation and response

7. Reduce off-task behaviors

How to Do It

At Tier 3, this strategy is conducted in individualized, focused, and intensive periods. Students reward themselves for appropriate behavior and performance by using a self-developed checklist.

Research Base

C. A. Tomlinson, 1999; see pages 66–68

What to Watch for With ELL/CLD Students

1. ELL students who are LEP may need the process explained in their most proficient language.

2. Points are not intrinsically reinforcing. What is rewarding to one person is not necessarily rewarding to another. This is a learned preference.

3. The points may initially be paired with some more directly rewarding action, and then gradually progress to use of only points.

257. SIGNALS

Purpose of the Strategy

1. Facilitate nondirective guidance of student misbehavior

2. Prevent minor inappropriate behaviors from escalating

3. Reduce specific attention to student misbehavior

How to Do It

1. At Tier 3, this strategy is conducted in individualized, focused, and intensive periods. The teacher uses nonverbal cues or signals to control inappropriate behavior by students.

2. For example, the teacher flicks the classroom lights or clicks a clicker to redirect students' attention to an assignment.

Research Base

Marable & Raimondi, 1995

Petrie, Lindauer, Bennett, & Gibson, 1998

Rogers, 2006

What to Watch for With ELL/CLD Students

1. Always introduce signals to ELL and CLD students by explaining them in their most proficient language.

2. ELL/CLD students who have had prior schooling might be asked what sort of signals they were familiar with and that could become part of the classroom routine.

258. SUCCESS

Purpose of the Strategy

1. Improve confidence and self-esteem

2. Facilitate student's view of him/herself as a successful person

3. Improve retention

4. Utilize prior knowledge

5. Develop thinking and planning skills

How to Do It

1. At Tier 3, this strategy is conducted in individualized, focused, and intensive periods. The teacher ensures that students successfully complete assigned tasks. The teacher initially reduces the level of difficulty of materials and gradually increases the level of difficulty as easier tasks are met with success. The teacher reduces the complexity level of vocabulary or concepts in written material to help the students complete a reading task. Through this strategy, learners may read material similar to others in the class without requiring an excessive amount of individual attention from the teacher.

2. For example, the teacher places a transparency over a page of written material, with a fine-point marker crosses out the more difficult words, and writes simpler equivalents of those words above or in the margin next to the crossed-out words. As the students read, they substitute the simpler words for those marked out.

Research Base

Gibbons, 2003

Krumenaker, Many, & Wang, 2008

Leki, 1995

C. A. Tomlinson, 1999

What to Watch for With ELL/CLD Students

1. The teacher needs information or professional development about all of the diverse learning styles, cultures, and languages in the classroom to design accessible learning activities for all students.

2. There is as much diversity within the ELL and CLD population as there is between the non-ELL and ELL population as a whole.

259. SURVIVAL STRATEGIES FOR STUDENTS

Purpose of the Strategy

1. Build awareness of appropriate behaviors for school language and rules

2. Build transfer skills

3. Develop confidence in school culture interactions

4. Develop personal control of situations

5. Reduce response fatigue

How to Do It

At Tier 3, this strategy is conducted in individualized, focused, and intensive periods. The teacher identifies basic rules of social and formal interaction that the student will need to know immediately. Students may identify situations where they made mistakes. The teacher, the assistant, and peers discuss situations and what interactions are expected. Students may need to practice these interactions.

Research Base

Ashworth & Wakefield, 2004

Felix-Brasdefer, 2008

Jackson, Boostrom, & Hansen, 1998

B. Johnson, Juhasz, Marken, & Ruiz, 1998

What to Watch for With ELL/CLD Students

1. Particular social groups and cultures have different expectations of adults and children when it comes to following rules. This is a learned difference between cultures. The teacher needs to be aware that the expectations in an American school may need to be taught directly to CLD students and not just assume that they are understood.

2. One way to introduce the idea of behavior and strategies specific to your classroom is to ask students about how their parents have them behave at home or how they learned playing games. This can then be expanded to the idea of acting appropriately in a classroom.

3. Demonstrate all of the desired behaviors and strategies. Some role-play may be helpful. Examples of inappropriate behaviors may be used with caution

260. TIME-OUT

Purpose of the Strategy

Facilitate student regaining control over self

How to Do It

1. At Tier 3, this strategy is conducted in individualized, focused, and intensive periods. The teacher structures opportunity for students to think about their behavior and behavioral expectations of the teacher.

2. Students are removed temporarily from the immediate environment to reduce external stimuli.

3. For example, the teacher removes a student to a quiet or time-out area for three to five minutes when the student is unable to respond to a situation in a nonaggressive manner.

Research Base

Harwell, 2001; see page 129

What to Watch for With ELL/CLD Students

1. Some ELL and CLD students have limited experience with public schools and the rules expected in the classroom.

2. Time-outs should be explained to the student in their most proficient language before using them or while taking them out of a situation.

261. TOUCH

Purpose of the Strategy

1. Increase time spent on task

2. Build student's self-awareness of behavior

How to Do It

1. At Tier 3, this strategy is conducted in individualized, focused, and intensive periods. The teacher uses touch to minimize misbehaviors and convey messages to students.

2. For example, if a student is looking around the room during independent work time, the teacher can walk up to the student and gently tap on the student's shoulder as a signal to focus on the assignment.

Research Base

Koenig, 2007

Little & Akin-Little, 2008

Marable & Raimondi, 1995

What to Watch for With ELL/CLD Students

1. All cultures have guidelines about how a person can touch another person. These are mostly unspoken and learned through being raised in the culture and community where touching another person is seen and remarked on by those around you.

2. These touch relations are also affected by whether someone is related to the other person. These relative positions convey power and control relationships, which vary from culture to culture.

3. Teachers must familiarize themselves with the touch rules of the various cultures represented in their classrooms before expecting to use touch strategically to promote learning.

262. GUIDED PRACTICE IN CROSS-CULTURAL CONFLICT-RESOLUTION STRATEGIES

Purpose of the Strategy

1. Develop personal control of situations

2. Enhance ability to resolve conflicts with others

3. Facilitate the school adaptation process

4. Reduce acting-out behaviors

5. Reduce number of conflicts with other students

How to Do It

At Tier 3, this strategy is done in individualized, focused, and intensive periods. A peer or a specialist demonstrates conflict-resolution techniques in a given school culture situation. The situation is explained in home and community language when possible, and each step is modeled. The student then practices each step of the resolution with familiar participants until comfortable and successful in appropriate behaviors.

Research Base

Aram & Shlak, 2008

Fitzell, 1997

Hafernik, Messerschmitt, & Vandrick, 2002

Ovando & Collier, 1998

What to Watch for With ELL/CLD Students

1. Particular social groups and cultures have different expectations of adults and children when it comes to conflict resolution. This is a learned difference between cultures. The teacher needs to be aware that the expectations in an American school may need to be taught directly to CLD students and not just assume that they are understood.

2. One way to introduce the idea of conflict-resolution behavior and strategies specific to your classroom is to ask students about how their parents have them behave at home when they disagree with their siblings. This can then be expanded to the idea of acting appropriately in a classroom.

3. Demonstrate all of the desired behaviors and strategies. Some role-play may be helpful. Examples of inappropriate behaviors may be used with caution.

263. SELF-MONITORING TECHNIQUES

Purpose of the Strategy

1. Develop confidence in cognitive academic interactions

2. Develop independence in learning situations

3. Develop personal control of situations

4. Increase time spent on task

5. Facilitate student assuming responsibility for learning

6. Reduce response fatigue

7. Reduce inappropriate behaviors

How to Do It

At Tier 3, this strategy is done in individualized, focused, and intensive periods. Students monitor their learning behaviors using teacher- or student-made checklists. For example, the students record a checkmark each time they catch themselves being distracted, tapping a pencil on their desk, or they complete a specified portion of an assignment.

Research Base

Borba, 2001; see pages 81–118

Strickland et al., 2002; see page 216

C. A. Tomlinson, 1999; see pages 66–68

What to Watch for With ELL/CLD Students

1. All cultures have expectations and rule' about the degree to which children are responsible for their actions. This is related to differences in cultural practices regarding locus of control.

2. Students can learn this strategy and benefit from it, but the teacher has to directly teach this process and not assume students automatically know about the purpose.

3. Use the students' most proficient language to explain what the process and purpose of the strategy.

4. Teachers must familiarize themselves with the self-control rules of the various cultures represented in their classrooms before expecting to use self-monitoring strategically to promote learning.

264. USE OF FIRST LANGUAGE

Purpose of the Strategy

1. Build transfer skills

2. Develop confidence in school language and rules for academic and social interactions

3. Develop cognitive academic language

4. Improve motivation

5. Minimize behavior problems

6. Reduce code-switching

How to Do It

At Tier 3, this strategy is done in individualized, focused, and intensive periods. The teacher directs advanced-fluency students to lead a guided activity in the home and/or community language. Students can retell parts of a story after the directed activity. Students then write summaries of what they have heard. Writing can be in either home or community language or English.

Research Base

Carrigan, 2001; see page 191

What to Watch for With ELL/CLD Students

1. The language helpers can prepare the ELL/LEP students for an English lesson by reviewing key vocabulary words, explaining what will be occurring, and discussing what the teacher's expectations will be for the students' performances. This would then be followed by the teacher presenting the lesson in English. Students would be given the opportunity to ask for specific clarification in their first language.

2. Students could work on their projects subsequent to the English lesson with the assistance of the bilingual helper as needed. Content discussion and clarification should be in the students' most proficient language while they are preparing their task or project for presentation in English with the rest of the class.

265. RETENTION STRATEGY—CAN DO

Purpose of the Strategy

1. Develop higher tolerance

2. Develop thinking and planning skills

3. Improve mnemonic retrieval

4. Improve retention

5. Utilize prior knowledge

How to Do It

At Tier 3, this strategy is done in individualized, focused, and intensive periods. This visualization technique may assist with memorization of lists of items. The steps in CAN-DO are

Create list of items to learn
Ask self if list is complete
Note details and main ideas
Describe components and their relationships
Overlearn main items followed by learning details

Research Base

Derwinger et al., 2005

Eskritt & McLeod, 2008

Jutras, 2008

S. W. Lee, 2005

What to Watch for With ELL/CLD Students

1. Newcomers will need to have the CAN-DO steps modeled and explained in their most proficient language before they can proceed independently.

2. Students can be paired with partners who are slightly more bilingual than they are to facilitate their learning this process.

266. CONSISTENT SEQUENCE

Purpose of the Strategy

1. Build academic transfer skills

2. Build awareness of appropriate academic behaviors

How to Do It

At Tier 3, this strategy is done in individualized, focused, and intensive periods. The teacher presents all content lessons with the same instructional language and direction sequence to the extent possible.

Expansion: Students can role-play giving the directions themselves.

Research Base

Mathes, Pollard-Durodola, Cárdenas-Hagan, Linan-Thompson, & Vaughn, 2007

Vaughn & Linan-Thompson, 2007

What to Watch for With ELL/CLD Students

1. This strategy is consistent with the Sheltered Instruction Observation Protocol (SIOP) model used in many ELL programs.

2. Newcomers who have never attended school may become confused if every lesson and activity occurs in seemingly random patterns. They do not know what is expected of them at various stages of the lesson. They do not know what to attend to and what is less important.

3. This is also going to impact students with undiagnosed attention deficit disorders that they have not yet learned to accommodate.

4. It is better to start out with simple, consistent steps and add to them as students become comfortable and familiar with what is going to happen in the classroom.

267. DEMONSTRATION

Purpose of the Strategy

1. Improve confidence in academic interactions
2. Reduce distractibility
3. Build academic transfer skills
4. Develop content knowledge foundation

How to Do It

At Tier 3, this strategy is done in individualized, focused, and intensive periods. The teacher, the assistant, or a peer demonstrates the content of the lesson. The content is explained in home and community language when possible, and each aspect of the lesson is demonstrated. Students demonstrate understanding of the lesson and content. Activities and assessment are designed to facilitate demonstration of understanding.

Research Base

Echevarria et al., 2007

Gibbons, 2006

What to Watch for With ELL/CLD Students

1. This strategy is consistent with both Sheltered Instruction Observation Protocol (SIOP) and the Guided Language Acquisition Design (GLAD) process used in many ELL programs.

2. Students who have never been schooled before will not know what is expected and will benefit from concrete, direct demonstrations of content elements and activity expectations.

268. STAR

Purpose of the Strategy

1. Build awareness of learning

2. Develop personal control of situations

3. Improve access to prior knowledge

4. Reduce off-task behaviors

5. Strengthen language development

How to Do It

At Tier 3, this strategy is done in individualized, focused, and intensive periods. This strategy can be used for all content areas and for behavior modification. Student can make cue cards for each step. The steps in STAR are

Stop
Think
Act
Review

Research Base

Agran, King-Sears, Wehmeyer, & Copeland, 2003

Carpenter, 2001

S.-H. Lee et al., 2006

What to Watch for With ELL/CLD Students

1. Newcomers will need to have the STAR steps modeled and explained in their most proficient language before they can proceed independently.

2. Students can be paired with partners who are slightly more bilingual than they are to facilitate their learning this process.

COGNITIVE ISSUES AT TIER 3

269. ADVANCED ORGANIZERS

Purpose of the Strategy

1. Build language transfer skills

2. Build awareness of appropriate content language for school language and rules

How to Do It

1. At Tier 3, this strategy is done in individualized, focused, and intensive periods. The teacher has the target students preview the lesson, outlining key issues, rehearsing vocabulary, and reviewing related prior knowledge. Advanced-fluency students help less-advanced students understand how to organize their reading and writing materials.

2. May use analogy strategy described here to teach one or more of the advanced organizer tools (e.g., KWL+, W-star, graphic organizer, mind map). Students implement strategy with a specific task or lesson.

3.   KWL+ is done by asking the student to discuss the following questions before beginning the lesson: What do you already know about this content? What do you want to know about this content? What will we learn about this? Why should we learn this? And how will we learn this content? This may be done on a chart and student answers posted on the chart.

4.   W-Star is done by asking the student to brainstorm before beginning a reading: Who do you think this story/event is about? Where do you think the story/event is located? When do you think the story/event occurs? How do you think the story/event turns out? The answers are written onto the points of a star diagram, each point of which represents one of the W questions.

5.   Mind mapping has various forms, but the basic idea is to put the central concept or vocabulary word related to what will be in the lesson in a circle on the board or on a piece of paper. Students then generate other words or concepts related to that main idea and connect them to the center like spokes on a wheel. For each of these ideas or words, another set of connections may be made outward from the center concept.

Research Base

C. Collier, 2003; see pages 130–142.

Harwell, 2001; see page 214

Heacox, 2002; see pages 91–98

Moore et al., 2000; see pages 143, 198–205

Opitz, 1998; see pages 115–121

What to Watch for With ELL/CLD Students

1.   There are cultural differences in cognitive/learning style, and some ELL/CLD students may not respond to the brainstorming construct behind most advanced organizers.

2.   By keeping the graphic design of the advanced organizer as close as possible to the illustrations in the text or some aspect of the lesson, the teacher can more tightly connect the concepts being studied with the W questioning that precedes the lesson.

3.   This is another activity that works best with preparation in the students' most proficient language and relevance to their culture before proceeding.

270. EVALUATION

Purpose of the Strategy

1.   Build awareness of learning process

2.   Develop categorization skills

3.   Develop extended time spent on task

4.   Develop personal control of situations

How to Do It

1.   At Tier 3, this strategy is done in individualized, focused, and intensive periods. Students use evaluation cards to cue themselves for each step. They select a specific problem or task and use the cards as mnemonics as they proceed through the assignment.

2.   The teacher introduces the student to the strategy by explaining that a strategy is a tool to help them learn and evaluation is one of these tools or strategies.

3. The teacher's goals in developing the student's evaluation strategy skills include increasing the students' awareness of what they need to do to complete a given task, providing the student with concrete guidelines for selecting and using appropriate specific strategies for achievement and guiding the student in comprehensive monitoring of the application of the strategy. These goals are accomplished through modeling, demonstrating, and describing the purpose or rationale for using the strategy. This, in turn, assists students to become aware of the types of tasks or situations where the strategy is most appropriate, the range of applications and transferability, the anticipated benefits from consistent use, and the amount of effort needed to successfully deploy the strategy

4. The teacher takes the students through the steps, pointing at a poster or diagram of the four steps. The first step is to think about how to identify what a problem consists of and how it can be measured and completed. The second step is to identify all the components of the problem and all the elements needed to solve it or to complete the task. The third step is to plan for difficulties and to identify where and how to get feedback and assistance. The fourth and final step is to think about ways to generalize the lesson learned and how to apply the information in other settings and contexts.

5. Steps for student to follow in implementing the strategy are listed here.

   a. How will I analyze the problem?

   b. What are the important elements of this problem?

   c. How will I get feedback?

   d. How can I generalize the information?

6. Steps for teaching evaluation

   a. *Inform* the students what evaluation is, how it operates, when to use it, and why it is useful. Begin by saying that evaluation is a way to help them analyze and monitor their learning. It works by asking and answering the series of five questions concerning a lesson they are working on. Once they learn how to use evaluation, they can use it anytime and with any content or lesson you give them to do.

   b. *Use cues,* metaphors, analogies, or other means of elaborating on a description of evaluation combined with visual cues. One way to do this is to have the student watch a panel discussion or other presentation on television where a group is analyzing a problem or evaluating a proposal to do something. Another is to show a video of scientists working in a laboratory to evaluate whether a substance works effectively. Show how everyone can analyze, monitor, and control learning when they go step by step.

   c. *Lead group discussions* about the use of evaluation. Have students start by talking about a science or math lesson they have just successfully solved. They can go back through the lesson or interaction stopping to show how each step of the lesson can be analyzed and monitored using the evaluation steps to see how they work and what is required. Encourage them to ask you anything about the learning process they want clarified.

   d. *Provide guided practice* in applying evaluation to particular tasks. Here is an example of guided practice as the teacher leads the student through the use of evaluation. Examples of both teacher and student comments are shown here.

Teacher: "First, you must analyze the task to determine what it requires. This includes items such as materials, time, space, or types of actions. What is the expected outcome of the task? What steps must you follow in order to complete the task? Review other completed assignments to determine possible steps you might take to complete this task."

Student: "What do I need to do to complete this task, and do I have all necessary materials and resources? What should the expected outcome look like? What steps must I follow to effectively achieve the expected outcome?"

Teacher: "Second, after you have analyzed the task, you must identify possible strategies that might be used to accomplish the task. Think about strategies you have used in the past to complete similar tasks. One or more of these may be necessary to complete this task."

Student: "What strategies do I know that might be appropriate for this particular task? Why might these be useful in this particular situation?"

Strategy Implementation

Teacher: "Third, prior to using a selected strategy, review the steps in that strategy. Remember that one strategy may be used in several different situations and different situations may require the use of more than one strategy."

Student: "I've selected these strategies for this task. I'll review the process associated with each strategy prior to implementation. I'll use these strategies while I complete this task."

Feedback

Teacher: "Fourth, you must become aware of how useful it is to use the strategies you have selected. They assist you to complete the task accurately and efficiently. Periodically, reflect on how you are doing and how effective the strategy is for completing the task at hand."

Student: "How useful is this strategy for this particular task? Is this strategy helping me to accurately and efficiently confront the assigned task? Do I need to use a different strategy?"

Teacher: "Finally, think of other previously completed tasks where the use of one or more of these strategies would have been beneficial to confronting the tasks. Could you have completed those tasks more efficiently had you used these strategies? Think of other types of tasks or future tasks where you might appropriately use one or more of these strategies."

Student: "Why were these strategies useful to this particular task? In what other types of situations would the use of these strategies be beneficial?"

e. *Provide feedback* on monitoring use and success of evaluation. While students use evaluation in small groups, you should move around the room listening and supplying encouragement for consistent use of the question and answer steps. As students get more comfortable using this strategy, you can have them monitor one another in the use of the strategy, encouraging one another to ask and/or answer the questions.

f. *Provide generalization* activities. Have your students use evaluation for a variety of lessons and tasks. You should be sure to identify the strategy by name and point to the poster or visual cues about the strategy whenever you have students use it. Hold enhanced cognitive discussions about the use of evaluation in these different lesson settings and encourage discussion of how useful or not useful students found this strategy in particular tasks.

Research Base

Brown & Palincsar, 1989

Cole, 1995; see pages 115–116

Opitz, 1998; see page 61

Pressley, Borkowski, & O'Sullivan, 1984

What to Watch for With ELL/CLD Students

1. If the student is limited in English proficiency, the monolingual, English-speaking teacher must increase the amount of demonstration and visual cues and rely less on verbal descriptions and cues. If available, bilingual assistance from peers or other education personnel may be useful in translating what is discussed in the classroom. This is especially

important in order to provide explicit information to students concerning the rationale and value of the strategy. In addition, analogy elaboration of the evaluation strategy may be drawn from the students' cultural and linguistic backgrounds. This reinforces the validity of the students' previous successful learning and increases the ability of the students to make associations that will strengthen their cognitive development.

2. Students who have never been in school before will not know what is expected and what measuring, analyzing, and evaluating look like.

3. Some translation and discussion in the ELL students' more proficient language may be necessary to clarify what is to be done and why.

271. TEST-TAKING STRATEGY—PIRATES

Purpose of the Strategy

1. Build cognitive academic language

2. Build learning strategies

3. Facilitate test-taking success

4. Reduce distractibility

5. Improve test-taking skills for typical achievement tests

How to Do It

1. At Tier 3, this strategy is done in individualized, focused, and intensive periods.

2. PIRATES may assist learners to complete tests more carefully and successfully. Students can create cue cards of the mnemonic and use them to work through each test and test item. The steps in PIRATES are

Prepare to succeed
Inspect instructions carefully
Read entire question, remember strategies, and reduce choices
Answer question or leave until later
Turn back to the abandoned items
Estimate unknown answers by avoiding absolutes and eliminating similar choices
Survey to ensure that all items have a response

Research Base

DeVries Guth & Stephens Pettengill, 2005

Hughes et al.,1993

Lebzelter & Nowacek, 1999

What to Watch for With ELL/CLD Students

1. Newcomers will need to have the PIRATES steps modeled and explained in their most proficient language before they can proceed independently.

2. Students can be paired with partners who are slightly more bilingual than they are to facilitate their learning this process.

272. INFORMATION ORGANIZATION—EASY

Purpose of the Strategy

Organize and prioritize information by focusing on questions designed to identify important content.

How to Do It

At Tier 3, this strategy is done in individualized, focused, and intensive periods. Students can create cue cards to remember each step. Students follow steps while reading passages or thematic elements. The steps in EASY are

Elicit questions (who, what, where, when, why)
Ask self which information is least difficult
Study easy content initially, followed by difficult
Yes! Provide self-reinforcement such as a pat on the back

Research Base

Lapp et al., 2007

Moore et al., 2000

What to Watch for With ELL/CLD Students

1. Much like the other mnemonics provided in these strategy lists, ELL/CLD students need bilingual explanations of the teacher's expectations and guided practice in implementing the steps in the strategy.

2. Newcomers will need to have the EASY steps modeled and explained in their most proficient language before they can proceed independently.

3. Students can be paired with partners who are slightly more bilingual than they are to facilitate their learning this process.

273. PROBLEM-SOLVING STRATEGY—COPING

Purpose of the Strategy

1. Build awareness of learning process

2. Develop extended time spent on task

3. Develop higher tolerance

4. Develop personal control of situations

5. Develop problem-solving skills

6. Lower anxiety levels

How to Do It

1. At Tier 3, this strategy is done in individualized, focused, and intensive periods. Have students identify specific problem(s) they want to solve as a group. The students follow the coping steps as they address a problem, writing down their answers and ideas for each stage of the problem solving.

2. Steps for students to follow in implementing the coping strategy are listed here.

    a. What is the problem?

    b. What are possible solutions?

c. What is my action plan?

d. Where can I go for help?

e. When should I start?

f. How will I deal with setbacks?

g. What is my outcome?

3. When applying the coping strategy, students work through problems or tasks using the sequence of self-monitoring questions. Let us suppose that you are about to have your students begin a new unit in social studies about your local community services and service people. You tend to enjoy challenges and usually teach these lessons by having students discover local resources and people on their own, but you have several students who are new to your community and from culturally and linguistically diverse backgrounds. You could modify your usual instructional approach by building in an opportunity for your students to examine what your expectations are and identify any problems they may have in meeting your expectations (Step 1 of coping, "What is the problem?"). The students would identify what they will need to do to successfully complete the lesson (Step 2 of coping, "What are my action steps?"), discussing ahead of time who they might see, where they might go, and what might happen. This might include identifying vocabulary words and discourse patterns they will need to use and possibly some practice ahead of time in speaking with adults from different speech communities from their own. They identify ahead of time where sources of information and assistance are available to them (Step 3 of coping, "Where can I go for help?") including people at the school, church, or other community groups. During this planning time, they also discuss what might happen to prevent them getting information or achieving parts of your outcomes. They come up with a supportive, group plan for dealing with barriers in accomplishing their tasks (Step 4 of coping, "How will I deal with setbacks?"). Finally, they create a clear idea of what exactly an acceptable outcome of this activity will be (Step 5 of coping, "What will my outcome be?"). By following these steps and keeping all of this in mind while working on the lesson you have for them, they will greatly reduce their anxiety level about the task and will increase their likelihood of completing the task successfully.

Research Base

McCain, 2005

Reid, Webster-Stratton, & Hammond, 2007

What to Watch for With ELL/CLD Students

The strategy preparation can be done in the native language or dialect of the students to assure their understanding of your expectations and their task prior to carrying the assignment out in English or other communication mode.

274. ORGANIZATION

Purpose of the Strategy

1. Develop analytical skills

2. Develop association skills

3. Develop categorization skills

4. Develop field independents kills

5. Improve mnemonic retrieval

How to Do It

1. At Tier 3, this strategy is done in individualized, focused, and intensive periods. The teacher directs students to empty out their backpacks. They go through the steps, sorting all the items in the piles. They make lists of the groups of items. Steps for student to follow in implementing this strategy are listed here.

  a. What elements go together and why?

  b. What do I call these groups?

  c. Can I remember the elements by the group?

  d. How can I generalize this information?

2. When applying the organization strategy, the student works through problems or tasks using the sequence of self-monitoring questions. For example, you are going to have a new unit about rocks and minerals (i.e., igneous, sedimentary, and conglomerate). Many of your students are unfamiliar with these ways of grouping natural materials that they consider generically as rocks. One group of students comes from a culture where rocks are grouped by hard versus soft; another comes from a culture that groups rocks by whether they can be used to produce something in the home. You might introduce your class to the lesson by having actual examples of the rocks to be studied present to handle or take the class on a field trip to the museum or a local mine or industrial area to observe them. You could also show pictures or videos of chemists interacting with the materials. Have the target students look for patterns in appearance, use, environment, chemical reactions, and the like. They could chart the attributes and characteristics of the rocks and minerals on a graph or in Venn diagrams (Step 1 of organization, "What elements go together?"). Now they should look for distinctive patterns of commonality between rocks and minerals that show whether they go together (Step 2 of organization, "What attribute of these am I using to group them?"). Ask the students what the group of rocks and minerals should be called based on the major attributes. Now introduce the common English name of the group (Step 3 of organization, "What name do I give to each group?"). Discuss how the materials in each group share certain common characteristics, and then discuss the characteristics that all rocks and minerals share in common as rocks and minerals (Step 4 of organization, "How are the groups similar to one another?"). Discuss how the rocks in each group might differ from one another, how each group of rocks and minerals differ from the other groups, and how rocks differ from nonrocks (Step 5 of organization, "How are the groups different from one another?"). Finish the unit with a discussion of how to find patterns in anything you are studying (Step 6 of organization, "What organization patterns do I see?").

3. You might now step back from the lesson and discuss the enhanced cognitive learning that you have provided the students, the learning to learn lesson that is represented by the strategy you had them use. At this point, you would discuss how everything in the world is composed of various elements that need to be identified to understand the whole thing being studied (field independence) and that when all the parts are put together the meaning of the whole thing results (field sensitive).

Research Base

  Ferris & Hedgcock, 2005

  Iachini, Borghi, & Senese, 2008

What to Watch for With ELL/CLD Students

1. The strategy preparation can be done in the native language or dialect of the students to assure their understanding of your expectations and their task prior to carrying the assignment out in English or other communication mode.

2. Understand that all cultures have different ways of thinking of common attributes of a group of similar objects. What constitutes the criteria to pay attention to will vary based on cultural values and learning practices. Although it seems obvious to one group that the predominant surface color of a set of objects is what links them together as a set of objects, to another group it might be that surface texture or size is more important as an attribute for sorting out similarity and difference.

275. CONSISTENT SEQUENCE

Purpose of the Strategy

1. Build academic transfer skills

2. Build awareness of appropriate academic behaviors

How to Do It

At Tier 3, this strategy is done in individualized, focused, and intensive periods. The teacher presents all content lessons with the same instructional language and direction sequence to the extent possible.

Expansion: Student can role-play giving the directions.

Research Base

Mathes et al., 2007

Vaughn & Linan-Thompson, 2007

What to Watch for With ELL/CLD Students

1. This strategy is consistent with the Sheltered Instruction Observation Protocol (SIOP) model used in many ELL programs.

2. Newcomers who have never attended school may become confused if every lesson and activity occurs in seemingly random patterns. They do not know what is expected of them at various stages of the lesson. They do not know what to attend to and what is less important.

3. This is also going to impact students with undiagnosed attention deficit disorders that they have not yet learned to accommodate.

4. It is better to start out with simple, consistent steps and add more as students become comfortable and familiar with what is going to happen in the classroom.

276. CONTEXT EMBEDDING

Purpose of the Strategy

1. Develop content knowledge foundation

2. Develop cognitive academic language proficiency

3. Develop content area skills

How to Do It

At Tier 3, this strategy is done in individualized, focused, and intensive periods. The teacher presents lessons with concrete, physical models and demonstrations of both content and expected performance. Language is simplified and content focused. Lessons address real-life situations and learning. Students are encouraged to work on content-focused activities and to discuss lessons in home and community language.

Research Base

Cummins, 1984

Cummins, Baker, & Hornberger, 2001

Donaldson, 1978

Roessingh et al., 2005

What to Watch for With ELL/CLD Students

1. Vocabulary may be previewed with fluent speakers in the students' most proficient language.

2. Some cultures may have strictures against children handling or being too close to certain objects. Always screen items ahead of time with knowledgeable community members.

277. ALTERNATE RESPONSE METHODS

Purpose of the Strategy

1. Facilitate learning

2. Accommodate diverse learning styles

3. Develop task completion

How to Do It

1. At Tier 3, this strategy is done in individualized, focused, and intensive periods. This strategy adapts the mode of response required of students.

2. Students respond to questions in a manner compatible with needs. Allow students who have difficulty with writing activities to record their answers. Students are allowed to express understanding of a question or issue in varied ways to meet individual needs. This practice ensures that students have the best possible chance to show that have acquired and retained skills and knowledge.

3. For example, students may record oral responses to questions given in class. For the geography unit, provide the questions in writing for the students to take home and practice responding. Some names of American states are very difficult to pronounce; provide time for the students to work alone or with a peer to write the difficult state names on tag board cards that they can hold up during class discussion rather than say the name aloud.

4. Keep in mind Howard Gardner's (1993a; 1993b) work on multiple intelligences. What other forms might be available to the students to express their understanding? If the topic is westward expansion, the students could find musical examples illustrating the various cultures that came into contact with one another and could make a mixed sound recording to demonstrate the culture clashes and consequences of expansion. The students could draw a map or other illustration supporting the musical representation and their understanding of the geographic concept of the movement of populations from one location to another.

Research Base

Bailey, 1993

Cole, 1995; see pages 34–35

Gardner, 1993a

Gardner, 1993b

Tannenbaum, 1996

What to Watch for With ELL/CLD Students

1. Some CLD students have had previous schooling in situations where students have no choice in their responses and teachers are authority figures who direct every action in the classroom.

2. When the teacher wishes to make student empowerment an instructional goal, this strategy is an excellent direction to take.

3. Demonstrate how the various responses can be made, including color, modeling, illustrating, and the like.

4. Some role-play in the process from initial choice to final task completion may be helpful.

278. PROMPTING

Purpose of the Strategy

1. Develop higher tolerance

2. Develop personal control of situations

3. Increase students' probability of generating a correct response

4. Utilize prior knowledge

How to Do It

At Tier 3, this strategy is done in individualized, focused, and intensive periods. This strategy provides students with clues or prompts as they complete a task (e.g., underline one letter of a pair of letters that a student is studying). Focus attention on characteristics of both letters to reduce confusion.

Research Base

Ferris & Hedgcock, 2005

Houghton & Bain, 1993

What to Watch for With ELL/CLD Students

1. All cultures have guidelines about how much help you should give to children or another person. Prompting is a kind of helping.

2. These are mostly unspoken and learned through being raised in the culture and community.

3. Find someone in the cultural community who can brief you about what is acceptable or expected regarding supporting and helping learners. It may well be that you are expected to help a great deal more than you think is appropriate. This will be your cue that your students will need a lot of guidance in how to use prompts appropriately.

Tier 4 Interventions

4

INTRODUCTION TO TIER 4 INSTRUCTIONAL FOCUS

Not all models consist of three tiers; some add a fourth tier. Generally, the fourth tier is considered referral and placement in special education. Some four-tier models are similar to the three-tier, problem-solving model with the fourth tier the individualized education plan (IEP) option. Some four-tier models are similar to three-tier standard protocol models where the fourth tier is proscribed as a result of poor student response to intervention (RTI).

Berkeley, Bender, Peaster, and Saunders (2009) state that in all three-tier models, special education placement is considered a separate process that occurs after RTI/RTII remediation interventions have been exhausted. However, they note inconsistencies regarding when the special education referral process can be initiated. Although most programs consider special education after students have progressed through Tier 3, some conduct special education referrals after Tier 2, and others allow special education referrals to be made at any point in the RTI/RTII process.

PROGRESS MONITORING AT TIER 4

Regular performance-based monitoring occurs at Tier 4 in the context of individualized, specially designed instructional programs. For example, suppose a student of concern has been identified as having an unusually high level of distractibility and failure with task completion, enough so that attention deficit disorder is suspected by some of the teachers working with the student. Before moving the student into a Tier 4 intervention, various interventions at Tier 1, Tier 2, and Tier 3 have been implemented in the general education classroom, small group settings, and in one-to-one sessions. None of the interventions have been successful in addressing the attention issue in a sustainable manner. By referring the student for consideration as eligible for Tier 4 of the RTI/RTII process, the team of instructional personnel is saying that the documentation they have collected over Tiers 1, 2, and 3 interventions indicates that the ELL/CLD student does not have the capacity to modify his or her attention to task without specific, intensive, and individualized special services. The instructional intervention team refers the student to the evaluation team based on evidence that the student may need special education services, individualized assistance, or other special intervention beyond support and intervention strategies provided in the general program.

After comprehensive evaluation (including medical, physical, psychological, and other examinations as appropriate), the team discusses the results of the evaluations and determines whether the English language learner (ELL)/culturally and linguistically diverse (CLD) student is eligible for placement in special education. Three hypotheses are tested during the meeting: (1) the ELL/CLD student's learning and behavior problems are primarily because of language learning and cultural factors, (2) the student's problems are primarily because of a disabling condition, or (3) the student's problems are primarily because of a combination of language/ culture factors and a disabling condition. The team shares and discusses the findings of its evaluations of the student, the results of the RTI/RTII problem-solving process implemented with the student, additional information provided during the formal referral, and any other information pertinent to each hypothesis. Analyzing hypotheses during the staffing meeting leads to placement decisions.

In summary, an ELL/CLD student formally referred for an evaluation and staffing for unresolved learning or behavior problems must be assured of equitable process and decision making. Under the Individuals with Disabilities Education Act (IDEA), there are specific areas of consideration related to ELL/CLD students in making decisions to place and serve ELL/CLD students in IEPs or other special services. Baca and Cervantes (2003) summarize pertinent recommendations related to these, including the following

1. Identification of students who need special education services must include the use of adequate bilingual resources.

2. Appropriate evaluation must include the establishment of school-based support teams to evaluate students in their environment using a bilingual, nondiscriminatory evaluation process.

3. Appropriate programs in the least restrictive environment must include a comprehensive continuum of services with the provision of appropriate bilingual programs at each place on the continuum for students with limited English proficiency.

4. Due process and parental and student rights must include a native language version of a parents' rights booklet, which explains all of the due process rights of students and parents. Also included is the hiring of neighborhood workers to facilitate parental involvement in the evaluation and development of the IEP.

5. Education personnel must conduct a language screening at the beginning of each school year to determine if the new students are exposed to or influenced by a language other than English.

6. If this initial language screening indicates the presence of a language other than English, school personnel must assess language dominance and proficiency.

7. School personnel must inform parents of all due process rights in their native or most proficient language. Schools must provide an interpreter at all meetings if parents cannot communicate effectively in English.

8. When analyzing evaluation data for placement decisions, education professionals must draw information from a variety of sources, including socioeconomic and cultural background and adaptive behavior.

9. Education professionals must develop an IEP that reflects the student's linguistic and cultural needs if it is determined that a diverse student is both disabled and has limited English proficiency.

The reauthorized Individuals with Disabilities Education Act of 2004 added several specific guidelines addressing language and culture issues when identifying, assessing, and developing instructional plans for limited English proficient (LEP) students with special needs. With its reauthorization, its name was changed to the Improving Education Results for Children with Disabilities Act (H. R. 1350) and includes the following provisions addressing LEP concerns.

1. The term native language, if used with reference to an individual of limited English proficiency, means

   a. The language normally used by that individual, or, in the case of a child, the language normally used by the parents of the child (except as provided here); and

   b. In all direct contact with a child (including his or her evaluation), the language normally used by the child in the home or learning environment (§300.19).

2. The definition of "native language" has been expanded to clarify that

   a. In all direct contact with a child (including his or her evaluation), communication would be in the language normally used by the child and not that of the parents, if there is a difference between the two; and

   b. For individuals with deafness or blindness or no written language, the mode of communication would be that normally used by the individual (such as sign language, Braille, or oral communication; (§300.19).

3. These changes should enhance the chances of school personnel being able to communicate effectively with an LEP child in all direct contact with the child, including evaluation of the child (§300.19).

4. The public agency shall take whatever action is necessary to ensure that the parent understands the proceedings of the IEP meeting, including arranging for an interpreter for parents with deafness or whose native language is other than English (§300.345).

5. With respect to a child with limited English proficiency, the IEP team shall consider the language needs of the child as those needs relate to the child's IEP, when

   a. The team develops the child's IEP, and

   b. The team conducts a meeting to review and, if appropriate, revise the child's IEP [§300.346(a)(2)(ii) and §300.346(b) and (c)].

6. In considering the child's language needs (as they relate to the child's IEP), if the IEP team determines that the child needs a particular device or service (including an intervention, accommodation, or other program modification) for the child to receive Free and Appropriate Education (FAPE), the IEP team must include a statement to that effect in the child's IEP [§300.346(a)(2)(ii) and §300.346(b) and (c)].

7. In developing an IEP for an LEP child with a disability, it is particularly important that the IEP team consider how the child's level of English proficiency affects the special education and related services that the child needs to receive FAPE [§300.346(a)(2)(ii) and §300.346(b) and (c)].

8. Under Title VI of the Civil Rights Act of 1964, school districts are required to provide LEP children with alternative language services

   a. To enable them to acquire proficiency in English, and

   b. To provide them with meaningful access to the content of the educational curriculum available to all students, including special education and related services [§300.346(a)(2)(ii) and §300.346(b) and (c)].

9. An LEP child with a disability may require special education and related services for those aspects of the educational program that address the development of English language skills and other aspects of the child's educational program [§300.346(a)(2)(ii) and §300.346(b) and (c)].

10. For an LEP child with a disability, the IEP must address whether the special education and related services that the child needs will be provided in a language other than English [§300.346(a)(2)(ii) and §300.346(b) and (c)].

11. Included in the meaning of "consent" is that the parent has been fully informed of all information relevant to the activity for which consent is sought in his or her native language or other mode of communication [§300.500(b)(1)].

12. Each public agency shall ensure that the parents of each child with a disability are members of any group that makes decisions on the educational placement of their child [§300.501(c)(5)].

13. The public agency shall make reasonable efforts to ensure that the parents understand and are able to participate in any group decisions relating to the educational placement of their child, including arranging for an interpreter for parents with deafness or whose native language is other than English [§300.501(c)(5)].

14. Written notice must be given to the parents of a child with a disability a reasonable time before the public agency proposes or refuses to initiate or change the identification, evaluation, educational placement of the child, or the provision of FAPE to the child. This written notice must be provided in the native language of the parent or other mode of communication used by the parent unless it is clearly not feasible to do so [§300.503(c)].

15. If the native language or other mode of communication of the parent is not a written language, the public agency must take steps to ensure

    a. That the notice is translated orally or by other means to the parent in his or her native language or other mode of communication;

    b. That the parent understands the content of the notice; and

    c. That there is written evidence that these two requirements have been met [§300.503(c)].

16. Each public agency must ensure that tests and other evaluation materials used to assess a child under Part B of IDEA

    a. Are selected and administered so as not to be discriminatory on a racial or cultural basis; and

    b. Are provided and administered in the child's native language or other mode of communication, unless it is clearly not feasible to do so [§300.532(a)].

17. Each public agency must also ensure that materials and procedures used to assess a child with limited English proficiency are selected and administered to ensure that they measure the extent to which the child has a disability and needs special education rather than measuring the child's English language skills [§300.532(a)].

18. Under Title VI of the Civil Rights Act of 1964

    a. To properly evaluate a child who may be limited English proficient, a public agency should assess the child's proficiency in English as well as in his or her native language to distinguish language proficiency from disability needs; and

b. An accurate assessment of the child's language proficiency should include objective assessment of reading, writing, speaking, and understanding [§300.534(b)(1)].

19. Even in situations where it is clearly not feasible to provide and administer tests in the child's native language or mode of communication for a child with limited English proficiency, the public agency must still obtain and consider accurate and reliable information that will enable the agency to make an informed decision as to

a. Whether the child has a disability; and
b. The effects of the disability on the child's educational needs [§300.534(b)(1)].

20. In some situations, there may be no one on the staff of the public agency who is able to administer a test or other evaluation in the child's native language, but an appropriate individual is available in the surrounding area (§300.345).

21. In that case, a public agency could identify an individual in the surrounding area who is able to administer a test or other evaluation in the child's native language, including contacting neighboring school districts, local universities, and professional organizations (§300.345).

22. Upon completing the administration of tests and other evaluation materials, a group of qualified professionals and the parents of the child must determine whether the child is a "child with a disability" [§300.534(b)(1)].

23. A child may not be determined to be eligible under Part B if the determinant factor for that eligibility determination is the child's lack of instruction in reading or math or the child's limited English proficiency and the child does not otherwise meet the eligibility criteria for a child with a disability [§300.534(b)(1)].

24. A public agency must ensure that a child who has a disability—as defined in §300.7—is not excluded from eligibility because the child also has limited English proficiency or has had a lack of instruction in reading or math.

25. The State Education Agency (SEA) shall give notice that is adequate to fully inform parents about §300.127, which requires the state to have on file in detail the policies and procedures that the state has undertaken to ensure protection of the confidentiality of any personally identifiable information collected, used, or maintained under Part B, including a description of the extent that the notice is given in the native languages of the various population groups in the state [§300.561(a)(1)].

The process for moving an ELL/CLD student into an IEP at Tier 4 includes the following.

• Review and analysis of the information gathered during the problem-solving RTI/RTII period to determine whether the student requires additional screening and assessment. The formal referral starts the legal requirements of special educational procedures outlined under U.S. federal and state law.

• During this stage, evaluation and assessment tools and procedures must be evaluated for bias and appropriateness with the student's particular culture and language community. An identified and trained team is responsible for making the decision to refer to evaluation based on documented and monitored interventions of sufficient duration.

• Documentation must be adequate and appropriate to terminate intervention and move to a formal referral. Documentation is used to certify that the learning or behavior problem is not because of the student's cultural or linguistic difference or level of acculturation. Documentation exists to identify the student's language and acculturation needs in addition to an unresolved learning or behavior problem. There is a process for documenting the results of the intervention period and how these were used to justify the formal referral to evaluation and staffing.

Once an ELL/CLD student is determined to be eligible for special education and related services at Tier 4, the education team develops a comprehensive IEP that includes target goals for the presenting problem as well as language and adaptation within the context of the presenting problem. The special education teacher works in conjunction with the general education staff to provide instruction and to implement interventions.

SO WHAT DO I DO WITH AN ELL STUDENT AT TIER 4?

Example From Classroom Practice

My five very challenging ELL/CLD students, Tommy, Mary, Justin, Clarence, and Irving, required me to use all possible instructional options, problem-solving strategies, and diverse interventions with progress monitoring. I was able to resolve most of Tommy's learning and behavior issues with specific differentiation of instruction at the Tier 1 level of intervention. He also benefited from more focused, small group intervention at Tier 2, and I recommended to his other teachers that small break-out discussion groups facilitated his learning as he continued successfully with his ELL/CLD peers in acquiring English and core content throughout his years at our school. Tommy graduated from high school with proficiency in both his home and school language. Mary also benefited from Tier 1 differentiation but needed extended intervention in small group, Tier 2 instruction to make sustainable progress in language and academic content areas. She learned enough English to continue through the school system but always did much better with bilingual helpers around her. She worked hard to complete assignments to the best of her ability. Justin was a real handful and a very active, bouncy student but always full of great energy and ideas for things to do, not necessarily related to our lessons. He did not get a grip on schooling until we had moved through Tier 1 differentiations and Tier 2 more focused interventions into individualized, Tier 3, intensive applications. But once he caught up and caught on, he made great progress and became very proficient in both his home and school language. He was always ready to take charge and help with setting up activities. He became a leader in the community after school.

After several years, Clarence learned to speak enough of both his home language and English to communicate his basic needs with teachers and bilingual school staff. He was always pleasant and enjoyed participating in class activities. However, it was clear after extended differentiation with Tier 1 instruction, focused pullouts and set-aside groups with Tier 2 interventions, and almost full-time individualized, one-on-one tutoring and assistance at Tier 3, that he was able to neither attain nor sustain near peer levels of achievement in school. By documenting Clarence's response and access to reading, math, and other content instruction and intervention at all three levels of RTI/RTII and monitoring his language acquisition and development across time, we established that Clarence's learning and behavior problems were not principally because of his limited English proficiency or access to research-based instruction. The decision was made that although language and culture differences contributed to his instructional needs, he had specific special needs to be addressed in an intensive, individually designed instruction. We designed an IEP for Clarence, and he attended special education classes. He was successful in a sheltered workshop after he left school.

Irving attended my special classroom the entire time I taught at the school in his community. My students and I learned to include Irving in every possible activity, and my students kept a friendly eye on him when outside the classroom. Irving learned to sing songs with English sounds/words and to make himself understood in the language of his community. He learned to speak English using single words with a few gestures to convey his intended message. He learned how to get his needs met at school without disrupting the entire classroom. He learned how to sit down when prompted and that there were rules to follow in school. This learning was achieved by every use of strategies from Tiers 1, 2, and 3 that I could muster, and they were "successful" as long as Irving had an assistant with him at all times. We asked specialists to assess his vision and hearing, which had to be done directly on the sense organs, as Irving would not respond to the standard prompts. We documented that the learning and behavior problems Irving was experiencing were not because of his limited English proficiency. We documented his response and access to reading, math, and other content instruction through specific instruction and intervention at all three levels of RTI/RTII. The decision was made that although language and culture differences contributed to his instructional needs, he had specific special needs to be addressed in an intensive, individually designed instruction. Irving was put on an IEP and came to my classroom for most of his instruction. (By this time I had added special education, learning disabilities certification to my K–8 license with English for Speakers of Other Languages (ESOL) certification.) A bilingual aide was assigned to be with him whenever he was on the school grounds. I worked with the family to set up home support structures for encouraging Irving to use whole words and phrases in the home language rather than just gestures and sounds to communicate. A community member told me recently that Irving is still living in the community and that everyone makes sure he is okay.

ADAPTING INTERVENTIONS FOR ELL/CLD STUDENTS IN INDIVIDUALIZED SPECIAL PROGRAMS

Almost all of the strategies described in this book may be adapted for use with ELL/CLD students with special needs, depending on their particular learning and behavior profiles. The individualized applications listed as interventions appropriate for Tier 3 may be used as part of an integrated service plan for ELL/CLD students found eligible for special services. To the extent possible, ELL/CLD students with special needs should receive most of their instruction in integrated classrooms. Successful inclusion in general education classrooms, in resource rooms, and special education classrooms can be achieved using a cross-categorical approach (Haager & Klingner, 2005). As described by Haager and Klingner, a cross-categorical approach considers students' instructional needs and not disability-specific needs. Students are grouped according to their instructional needs rather than their disability labels and teachers can focus on the instructionally relevant needs of their students. Many educational needs of ELL/CLD students who receive special education and educational needs of ELL/CLD students with learning problems who do not qualify for special education are similar (Haager & Klingner, 2005). With appropriate instructional support and prepared personnel, students with high-incidence disabilities (learning disabilities) and low-incidence disabilities (sensory differences) can be taught in general education classrooms. Coteaching and collaboration among special, ELL, and general education personnel in inclusive classrooms provides much needed direct support to ELL/CLD students with disabilities and support for teachers in terms of coplanning, coteaching, and coassessing.

Beirne-Smith, Patton, and Kim (2006) describe four forms of collaboration that facilitate RTI/RTII, as well as instruction of ELL/CLD students in special programs: (1) collaboration-consultation, (2) peer-support system, (3) teacher assistance teams, and (4) coteaching

- Collaboration-consultation for ELL/CLD students involves the general education teacher and requests the services of either or both the special education teacher and ELL teacher to help generate ideas for addressing an ongoing situation.

- ELL/CLD peer-support system involves pairs of general education teachers or ELL teachers working together to generate ideas.

- Teacher assistance teams include special educators and ELL teachers assisting general education teachers.

- Coteaching for ELL/CLD students involves general, ELL, and special education teachers working together to provide services to ELL/CLD students.

At Tier 4 and other individualized instructional service points, the language needs of the ELL/CLD student are to be integrated into the comprehensive instructional plan addressing the student's learning and behavior goals.

In Conclusion 5

Berkeley, Bender, Peaster, and Saunders (2009) point out that although there is almost universal agreement that the multiple tier approach should be used, there remain many questions and differences of opinion for how problem solving with progress monitoring should be implemented. In addition, lack of specificity in assessment, intervention implementation, selection of research-based practices, and fidelity raises concern about how consistently the eligibility process will be implemented both within and between states. This is particularly true with English language learner (ELL)/culturally and linguistically diverse (CLD) students where research is even more limited.

However, education professionals continue to deal daily with the challenge of finding ways to ensure the academic success of these ELL/CLD students whose educational backgrounds, home cultures, and languages are, in the overwhelming majority of cases, different from their own. Through the systematic process of gathering instructionally meaningful information about students' strengths and needs in cross-culturally competent and appropriate ways, teachers can make effective decisions about the education of all of their students. Teachers can make significant differences for diverse learners through fully participating in and implementing comprehensive and dynamic problem-solving intervention, including response to intervention (RTI) and response to instruction and intervention (RTII).

Teachers can make lifelong educational differences in the lives of children from CLD backgrounds. Consideration of students' cultural, linguistic, and experiential background; level of acculturation; sociolinguistic development; and cognitive learning styles must be built into educational process to begin to develop a valid picture of the students and their capabilities and achievement levels. Teacher-preparation programs must help ensure use of best practices necessary to differentiate instruction, problem solve, implement interventions, and monitor progress. Teacher educators need to prepare teachers for the four broader roles they may be asked to play involving the four forms of collaboration (Beirne-Smith, Patton, & Kim 2006). Learning how to differentiate and monitor instruction and intervention to meet the challenges of diversity in general, ELL, and special education classrooms will ensure schools in the United States can truly facilitate academic success for all students in our educational systems.

References

Agran, M., King-Sears, M., Wehmeyer, M., & Copeland, S. (2003). *Teachers' guides to inclusive practices*: *Student-directed learning*. Baltimore: Paul H. Brookes.

Ainley, M. (2006). Connecting with learning: Motivation, affect and cognition in interest processes. *Educational Psychological Review, 18*, 391–405.

Ajibade, Y., & Ndububa, K. (2008). Effects of world games, culturally relevant songs, and stories on students' motivation in a Nigerian English language class. *TESL Canada Journal, 25*(2), 27–48.

Allen, J. S., & Klein, R. J. (1997). *Ready, set, relax: A research-based program of relaxation, learning and self-esteem for children*. Watertown, WI: Inner Coaching.

Allington, R., & Cunningham, P. (2002). *Schools that work: Where all children read and write*. Boston: Allyn & Bacon.

Anderson, J. R. (2000). *Cognitive psychology and its implications*. New York: Worth.

Aram, D., & Shlak, M. (2008). The safe kindergarten: Promotion of communication and social skills among kindergartners. *Early Education and Development, 19*, 865–884.

Arkoudis, S. (2005). Fusing pedagogic horizons: Language and content teaching in the mainstream. *Linguistics and Education: An International Research Journal, 16*, 173–187.

Artis, A. (2008). Improving marketing students' reading comprehension with the SQ3R method. *Journal of Marketing Education, 30*, 130–137.

Asher, J. (1980). *Learning another language through actions: The complete teacher's guidebook*. Los Gatos, CA: Sky Oaks.

Ashworth, M., & Wakefield, P. (2004). *Teaching the world's children: ESL for ages three to seven* (2nd ed.). Toronto Ontario, Canada: Pippin.

Baca, L. M., & Cervantes, H. (Eds.). (2003). *The bilingual special education interface* (4th ed.). New York: Prentice Hall.

Bailey, L. (1993, April). *Inventing writing: How ESL writers use commonly taught prewriting techniques*. Paper presented at the annual meeting of the Teachers of English to Speakers of Other Languages, Atlanta, GA. (ERIC Document Reproduction Service No. ED363132).

Becker, H., & Hamayan, E. V. (2008). *Teaching ESL K–12: Views from the classroom*. Boston: Heinle & Heinle.

Beckett, G. H. (2002). Teacher and student evaluations of project-based instruction. *TESL Canada Journal, 19*(2), 52–66.

Beckett, G. H., & Miller, P. C. (Eds.). (2006). *Project-based second and foreign language education: Past, present, and future*. Charlotte, NC: Information Age.

Beckett, G. H., & Slater, T. (2005). The project framework: A tool for language, content, and skills integration. *ELT Journal, 59*, 108–116.

Beirne-Smith, M., Patton, J. R., & Kim, S. H. (2006). *Mental retardation* (7th ed.). Upper Saddle River, NJ: Merrill.

Bender, W. N., & Shores, C. (2007). *Response to intervention: A practical guide for every teacher*. Thousand Oaks, CA: Corwin.

Berkeley, S., Bender, W. N., Peaster, L. G., & Saunders, L. (2009). Implementation of response to intervention: A snapshot of progress. *Journal of Learning Disabilities, 42*, 85–95.

Bondi, W. (1988). *Designing interdisciplinary units*. Tampa, FL: Wiles Bondi and Associates.

Borba, M. (2001). *Building moral intelligence: The seven essential virtues that teach kids to do the right thing*. San Francisco: Jossey-Bass.

Bradley, R., Danielson, L., & Doolittle, J. (2005). Response to intervention: 1997. *Journal of Learning Disabilities, 38,* 485–486.

Brinton, D. M., Wesche, M., & Snow, M. A. (2003). *Content-based second-language instruction: Michigan Classics Edition.* Ann Arbor: University of Michigan Press.

Brown, A. L., & Palincsar, A. S. (1989). Guided, cooperative learning and individual knowledge acquisition. In L. B. Resnick (Ed.), *Knowing, learning, and instruction: Essays in honor of Robert Glaser* (pp. 393–452). Hillsdale, NJ: Lawrence Erlbaum.

Brownlie, F., & King, J. (2000). *Learning in safe schools: Creating classrooms where all students belong.* Markham, Ontario, Canada: Pembroke.

Buchanan, L. (1990). Some effects of culture in the ESL classroom and their implications for teaching. *MinneTESOL Journal, 8,* 73–87.

Burnham, J. J., Mantero, M., & Hooper, L. M. (2009). Experiential training: Connecting school counselors-in-training, English as a second language (ESL) teachers, and ESL students. *Journal of Multicultural Counseling and Development, 37*(1), 2–14.

Carpenter, L. B. (2001). Utilizing travel cards to increase productive student behavior, teacher collaboration, and parent-school communication. *Education and Training in Mental Retardation and Developmental Disabilities, 36,* 318–322.

Carrigan, T. (2001). *Canada: Who are we and where are we going? Immigration, multiculturalism, and the Canadian identity.* Vancouver, British Columbia, Canada: Hawthorn Educational Group.

Cloud, N., Genesee, F., & Hamayan, E. (2000). *Dual language instruction: A handbook for enriched education.* Boston: Heinle & Heinle.

Cochran-Smith, M., & Zeichner, K. M. (Eds.). (2005). *Studying teacher education: The report of the AERA panel on research and teacher education.* Mahwah, NJ: Lawrence Erlbaum.

Coelho, E., & Rivers, D. (2003). *Adding English: A guide to teaching in multilingual classrooms.* Toronto, Ontario, Canada: Pippin.

Cole, R. W. (Ed.). (1995). *Educating everybody's children: Diverse teaching strategies for diverse learners.* Alexandria, VA: Association for Supervision and Curriculum Development.

Collier, C. (2003). Curriculum materials for the bilingual exceptional child. In L. M. Baca & H. Cervantes (Eds.). *The bilingual special education interface* (4th ed.). New York: Prentice Hall.

Collier, C. (2009). *Separating difference from disability* (4th ed.). Ferndale, WA: CrossCultural Developmental Education Services.

Collier, C., Brice, A. E., & Oades-Sese, G. V. (2007). Assessment of acculturation. In G. B. Esquivel, E. C. Lopez, & S. Nahari, (Eds.), *Handbook of multicultural school psychology: An interdisciplinary perspective* (pp. 353–380). Mahwah NJ: Lawrence Erlbaum.

Collier, V. P., & Thomas, W. P. (2007). Predicting second-language academic success in English using the prism model. In C. Davison & J. Cummins (Eds.), *International handbook of English language teaching* (pp. 333–348). New York: Springer.

Collins Block, C., & Mangieri, J. N. (2003). *Exemplary literacy teachers: Promoting success for all children in grades K–5.* New York: Guilford.

Cordova, D. I., & Lepper, M. R. (1996). Intrinsic motivation and the process of learning: Beneficial effects of contextualization, personalization and choice. *Journal of Educational Psychology, 88,* 715–730.

Croom, L., & Davis, B. H. (2006). It's not polite to interrupt, and other rules of classroom etiquette. *Kappa Delta Pi Record, 42*(3), 109–113.

Cummins, J. (1984). *Bilingualism and special education: Issues in assessment and pedagogy.* San Diego, CA: College Hill Press.

Cummins, J., Baker, C., & Hornberger, N. H. (2001). *An introductory reader to the writings of Jim Cummins.* Clevedon, UK: Multilingual Matters.

Dang, T., Dang, P., & Ruiter, R. (2005). *Highway to E.S.L.: A user-friendly guide to teaching English as a second language.* Bloomington, IN: iUniverse.

Davey, B. (1983). Think aloud: Modeling the cognitive process of reading comprehension. *Journal of Reading, 27*(1), 44–47.

Davis, B. M. (2005). *How to teach students who don't look like you: Culturally relevant teaching strategies.* Thousand Oaks, CA: Corwin.

Delpit, L. (1995). *Other people's children: Cultural conflict in the classroom.* New York: The New Press.

Derwinger, A., Stigsdotter Neely, A., & Bäckman, L. (2005). Design your own memory strategies! Self-generated strategy training versus mnemonic training in old age: An 8-month follow-up. *Neuropsychological Rehabilitation, 15,* 37–54.

DeVries Guth, N., & Stephens Pettengill, S. (2005). *Leading a successful reading program: Administrators and reading specialists working together to make it happen.* Newark, DE: International Reading Association.

Donaldson, M. (1978). *Children's minds.* Glasgow: Collins.

Dooley, N. (1991). *Everybody cooks rice.* Minneapolis, MN: Lerner.

Echevarria, J. (1995). Sheltered instruction for students with learning disabilities who have limited English proficiency. *Intervention in School and Clinic, 30,* 302–305.

Echevarria, J., & Graves, A. (2006). *Sheltered content instruction: Teaching English language learners with diverse abilities* (3rd ed.). Old Tappan, NJ: Pearson.

Echevarria, J., Vogt, M. E., & Short, D. (2007). *Making content comprehensible for English learners: The SIOP model* (3rd ed.). Old Tappan, NJ: Pearson.

Elliot, J. L., & Thurlow, M. L. (2005). *Improving test performance of students with disabilities: On district and state assessments* (2nd ed.). Thousand Oaks, CA: Corwin.

Ellis, E. S., & Colvert, G. (1996). Writing strategy instruction. In D. D. Deshler, E. S. Ellis, & B. K. Lenz (Eds.), *Teaching adolescents with learning disabilities: Strategies and methods* (2nd ed., pp. 127–170). Denver: Love.

Ellis, E. S., & Lenz, B. K. (1987). A component analysis of effective learning strategies for LD students. *Learning Disabilities Focus, 2*(2), 94–107.

Eskritt, M., & McLeod, K. (2008). Children's note taking as a mnemonic tool. *Journal of Experimental Child Psychology, 101,* 52–74.

Esparza Brown, J., & Doolittle, J. (2008). *A cultural, linguistic, and ecological framework for response to intervention with English language learners.* Tempe, AZ: NCCRESt.

Etscheidt, S., Stainback, S. B., & Stainback, W. C. (1984). The effectiveness of teacher proximity as an initial technique of helping pupils control their behavior. *Pointer, 28*(4), 33–35.

Evertson, C. M., & Neal, K. W. (2006). *Looking into learning-centered classrooms implications for classroom management.* Washington DC: National Education Association.

Evertson, C. M., & Weinstein, C. S. (2006). *Handbook of classroom management: Research, practice, and contemporary issues.* New York: Routledge.

Felix-Brasdefer, J. C. (2008). *Politeness in Mexico and the United States: A contrastive study of the realization and perception of refusals.* Amsterdam: John Benjamins.

Ferris, D., & Hedgcock, J. (2005). *Teaching ESL composition: Purpose, process, and practice* (2nd ed.). New York: Routledge.

Feuerstein, R. (1986). Learning to learn: Mediated learning experiences and instrumental enrichment. *Special Services in the Schools, 3*(1–2), 49–82.

Feuerstein, R., & Hoffman, M. (1982). Intergenerational conflict of rights: Cultural imposition and self-realization. *Viewpoints in Teaching and Learning, 58*(1), 44–63.

Fisher, D., & Frey, N. (2004). *Improving adolescent literacy: Strategies at work.* Upper Saddle River, NJ: Pearson Prentice Hall.

Fitzell, S. G. (1997). *Free the children! Conflict education for strong and peaceful minds. Conflict resolution skills for pre-K through grade 12.* Gabriola Island, British Columbia, Canada: New Society.

Flowerday, T., & Schraw, G. (2003). Effect of choice on cognitive and affective engagement. *The Journal of Educational Research, 96,* 207–215.

Flowerday, T., Schraw, G., & Stevens, J. (2004). The role of choice and interest in reader engagement. *The Journal of Experimental Education, 72,* 93–114.

Flowerdew, J., & Peacock, M. (2001). *Research perspectives on English for academic purposes.* Cambridge, UK: Cambridge University Press.

Ford, A., Davaern, L., & Schnorr, R. (2001). Learners with significant disabilities: Curricular relevance in an era of standards-based reform. *Remedial and Special Education, 22,* 214–222.

Freeman, D. E., & Freeman Y. S. (2007). *English language learners: The essential guide.* New York: Scholastic.

Freire, P., & Macedo, D. (1987). *Literacy: Reading the word and the world.* New York: Bergin & Garvey.

Fuchs, D., Mock, D., Morgan, P. L., & Young, C. L. (2003). Responsiveness-to-intervention: Definition, evidence, and implications for the learning disabilities construct. *Learning Disabilities Research & Practice, 18,* 157–171.

Garber-Miller, K. (2006). Playful textbook previews: Letting go of familiar mustache monologues. *Journal of Adolescent & Adult Literacy, 50,* 284–288.

Garcia, D. C., Hasson, D. J., Hoffman, E., Paneque, O. M., & Pelaez, G. (1996). *Family centered learning. A program guide for linguistically and culturally diverse populations.* Miami: Florida International University.

Garcia, E. E. (2005). *Teaching and learning in two languages: Bilingualism and schooling in the United States.* New York: Teachers College Press.

Gardner, H. (1993a). *Frames of mind: The theory of multiple intelligences* (10th ed.). New York: Basic Books.

Gardner, H. (1993b). *Multiple intelligences: The theory in practice.* New York: Basic Books.

Gay, G. (1985). Curriculum development. In T. Husen & T. N. Postlethwaite (Eds.), *International encyclopedia of education* (pp. 1170–1179). New York: Pergamon Press.

Gibbons, P. (2002). *Scaffolding language, scaffolding learning: Teaching second language learners in the mainstream classroom.* Portsmouth, NH: Heinemann.

Gibbons, P. (2003). Mediating language learning: Teacher interactions with ESL students in a content-based classroom. *TESOL Quarterly, 37,* 247–273.

Gibbons, P. (2006). *Bridging discourses in the ESL classroom: Students, teachers and researchers.* New York: Continuum International.

Goldsworthy, C. L. (2003). *Developmental reading disabilities: A language-based treatment approach* (2nd ed.). Florence, KY: Cengage Learning.

Grahame, K. (1983). *The reluctant dragon.* New York: Henry Holt.

Grossman, H. (2003). *Classroom behavior management for diverse and inclusive schools* (3rd ed.). Lanham, MD: Rowman & Littlefield.

Gunter, P. L., & Shores, R. E. (1995). On the move: Using teacher/student proximity to improve student's behavior. *Teaching Exceptional Children, 28*(1), 12–14.

Haager, D., & Klingner, J. K. (2005). *Differentiating instruction in inclusive classrooms: The special educators' guide.* Boston: Allyn & Bacon.

Hafernik, J. J., Messerschmitt, D. S., & Vandrick, S. (2002). *Ethical issues for ESL faculty: Social justice in practice.* Philadelphia: Lawrence Erlbaum.

Hall, R. V., & Hall, M. C. (1998). *How to use planned ignoring (extinction)* (2nd ed.). Austin, TX: Pro-Ed.

Hamachek, D. E. (1994). *Psychology in teaching, learning, and growth: Learning and growth* (5th ed.). Old Tappan, NJ: Allyn & Bacon.

Haneda, M. (2008). Contexts for learning: English language learners in a U.S. middle school. *International Journal of Bilingual Education and Bilingualism, 11,* 57–74.

Hansen-Thomas, H. (2008). Sheltered instruction: Best practices for ELL/CLD in the mainstream, *Kappa Delta Pi Record, 44*(4), 165–169.

Harwell, J. M. (2001). *Complete learning disabilities handbook: Ready-to-use strategies & activities for teaching students with learning disabilities.* Paramus, NJ: The Center for Applied Research in Education.

Heacox, D. (2002). *Differentiating instruction in the regular classroom: How to reach and teach all learners, Grades 3–12.* Minneapolis, MN: Free Spirit.

Hitchcock, C., Meyer, A., Rose, D., & Jackson, R. (2002). Providing new access to the general curriculum: Universal design for learning. *Teaching Exceptional Children. 35*(2), 8–17.

Hoover, J. J., Baca, L. M., & Klingner, J. J. (2007). *Methods for teaching culturally and linguistically diverse exceptional learners.* Upper Saddle River, NJ: Prentice Hall.

Houghton, S., & Bain, A. (1993). Peer tutoring with ESL and below-average readers. *Journal of Behavioral Education, 3,* 125–142.

Hu, R., & Commeyras, M. (2008). A case study: Emergent biliteracy in English and Chinese of a 5-year-old Chinese child with wordless picture books. *Reading Psychology, 29,* 1–30.

Hughes, C. A., Deshler, D. D., Ruhl, K. L., & Schumaker, J. B. (1993). Test-taking strategy instruction for adolescents with emotional and behavioral disorders. *Journal of Emotional and Behavioral Disorders, 1,* 189–198.

Iachini, T., Borghi, A. M., & Senese, V. P. (2008). Categorization and sensorimotor interaction with objects. *Brain and Cognition, 67*, 31–43.

Irvin, J. L., & Rose, E. O. (1995). *Starting early with study skills: A week-by-week guide for elementary students.* Needham Heights, MA: Allyn & Bacon.

Jackson, P. W., Boostrom, R. E., & Hansen, D. T. (1998). *The moral life of schools.* San Francisco: Jossey-Bass.

Jitendra, A., Edwards, L., Choutka, C., & Treadway, P. (2002). A collaborative approach to planning in the content areas for students with disabilities: Accessing the general curriculum. *Learning Disabilities Research & Practice, 17*, 252–267.

Johnson, B., Juhasz, A., Marken, J., & Ruiz, B. R. (1998). The ESL teacher as moral agent. *Research in the Teaching of English, 32*, 161–181.

Johnson, E., Mellard, D. F., Fuchs, D., & McKnight, M. A. (2006). *Responsiveness to intervention (RTI): How to do it.* Lawrence, KS: National Research Center on Learning Disabilities.

Johnson, J. E., Christie, J. F., & Yawkey, T. D. (1999). *Play and early childhood development* (2nd ed.). New York: Addison Wesley Longman.

Johnson, R. (1995). ESL teacher education and intercultural communication: Discomfort as a learning tool. *TESL Canada Journal, 12*(2), 59–66.

Jutras, P. (2008). How do you teach students to practice memorization? *Keyboard Companion, 19*(1), 50.

Kamps, D., Abbott, M., Greenwood, C., Arreaga-Mayer, C., Wills, H., Longstaff, J., et al. (2007). Use of evidence-based, small-group reading instruction for English language learners in elementary grades: Secondary-tier intervention. *Learning Disability Quarterly, 30*, 153–169.

Kaufman, D. (2001). Organizing and managing the language arts workshop: A matter of motion. *Language Arts, 79*, 114–123.

Kavale, K. (2005). Identifying specific learning disability: Is responsiveness to intervention the answer? *Journal of Learning Disabilities, 38*, 553–562.

Kelly, B. W., & Holmes, J. (1979). The guided lecture procedure. *Journal of Reading, 22*, 602–604.

Kim, Y., & Kellogg, D. (2007). Rules out of roles: Differences in play language and their developmental significance. *Applied Linguistics, 28*, 25–45.

Kirschner, P. A., Sweller, J., & Clark, R. E. (2006). Why minimal guidance during instruction does not work: An analysis of the failure of constructivist, discovery, problem-based, experiential, and inquiry-based teaching. *Educational Psychologist, 41*, 75–86

Klingner, J. K., Vaughn, S., & Boardman, A. (2007). *Teaching reading comprehension to students with learning difficulties.* New York: Guilford.

Koenig, L. J. (2007). *Smart discipline for the classroom: Respect and cooperation restored* (4th ed.). Thousand Oaks, CA: Corwin.

Koskinen, P. A., & Blum, I. H. (1984). Paired repeated reading: A classroom strategy for developing fluent reading. *The Reading Teacher, 40*, 70–75.

Kovelman, I., Baker, S., & Petitto, L. (2008). Age of first bilingual language exposure as a new window into bilingual reading development. *Bilingualism: Language and Cognition, 11*, 203–223.

Kragler, S., & Nolley, C. (1996). Student choices: Book selection strategies of fourth graders. *Reading Horizons, 36*, 354–365.

Krumenaker, L., Many, J., & Wang, Y. (2008). Understanding the experiences and needs of mainstream teachers of ESL students: Reflections from a secondary studies teacher. *TESL Canada Journal, 25*(2), 66–84.

Landis, D., Bennett, J. M., & Bennett, M. J. (2004). *Handbook of intercultural training* (3rd ed.). Thousand Oaks, CA: Sage.

Lapp, D., Flood, J., Brock, C. H., & Fisher, D. (2007). *Teaching reading to every child.* New York: Routledge.

Law, B., & Eckes, M. (2000). *The more-than-just-surviving handbook: ESL for every classroom teacher.* Winnipeg, Manitoba, Canada: Portage & Main Press.

Leaf, M. (2000). *The story of Ferdinand.* New York: Grosset & Dunlap.

Lebzelter, S., & Nowacek, E. J. (1999). Reading strategies for secondary students with mild disabilities. *Intervention in School and Clinic, 34*, 212–219.

Lee, S. W., (Ed.). (2005). *Encyclopedia of school psychology.* Thousand Oaks, CA: Sage.

Lee, S.-H., Amos, B. A., Gragoudas, S., Lee, Y., Shogren, K. A., Theoharis, R., et al. (2006). Curriculum augmentation and adaptation strategies to promote access to the general curriculum for students with intellectual and developmental disabilities. *Education and Training in Developmental Disabilities, 41,* 199–212.

Leki, I. (1995). Coping strategies of ESL students in writing tasks across the curriculum. *TESOL Quarterly, 29,* 235–260.

Little, S. G., & Akin-Little, A. (2008). Psychology's contributions to classroom management. *Psychology in the Schools, 45,* 227–234.

Livingstone, C. (1983). *Role play in language learning.* New York: Longman.

Ma, J. (2008). Reading the word and the world: How mind and culture are mediated through the use of dual-language storybooks. *Education 3–13, 36,* 237–251.

Macedo, D., & Bartolomé, L. I. (1999). *Dancing with bigotry: Beyond the politics of tolerance.* New York: St. Martin's.

Magos, K., & Politi, F. (2008). The creative second-language lesson: The contribution of the role-play technique to the teaching of a second language in immigrant classes. *RELC Journal, 39,* 96–112.

Marable, M. A., & Raimondi, S. L. (1995). Managing surface behaviors. *LD Forum, 20*(2), 45–47.

Mathes, P. G., Pollard-Durodola, S. D., Cárdenas-Hagan, E., Linan-Thompson, S., & Vaughn, S. (2007). Teaching struggling readers who are native Spanish speakers: What do we know? *Language, Speech, and Hearing Services in Schools, 38,* 260–271.

McAllister, G., & Irvine, J. J. (2000). Cross cultural competency and multicultural teacher education. *Review of Educational Research, 70,* 3–24.

McCain, T. D. (2005). *Teaching for tomorrow: Teaching content and problem-solving skills.* Thousand Oaks, CA: Corwin.

McIntyre, E., Kyle, D., Chen, C., Kraemer, J., & Parr, J. (2009). *Six principles for teaching English language learners in all classrooms.* Thousand Oaks, CA: Corwin.

Moore, D. W., Alvermann, D. E., & Hinchmann, K. A. (Eds.). (2000), *Struggling adolescent readers: A collection of teaching strategies.* Washington DC: International Reading Association.

Movitz, A. P., & Holmes, K. P. (2007). Finding center: How learning centers evolved in a secondary student-centered classroom. *English Journal, 96*(3), 68–73.

Munsch, R., & Martchenko, M. (1982). *Murmel, murmel, murmel.* Toronto, Ontario, Canada: Annick Press.

Naughton, V. M. (2008). Picture it! *Reading Teacher, 62,* 65–68.

Nelson, J. R., Martella, R., & Galand, B. (1998). The effects of teaching school expectations and establishing a consistent consequence on formal office disciplinary actions. *Journal of Emotional and Behavioral Disorders, 6,* 153–161.

Nelson, P., Kohnert, K., Sabur, S., & Shaw, D. (2005). Classroom noise and children learning through a second language: Double jeopardy? *Language, Speech, and Hearing Services in Schools, 36,* 219–229.

Nessel, D. D., & Nixon, C. N. (2008). *Using the language experience approach with English language learners: Strategies for engaging students and developing literacy.* Thousand Oaks, CA: Corwin.

Odean, P. M. (1987). Teaching paraphrasing to ESL students. *MinneTESOL Journal, 6,* 15–27.

Opitz, M. F. (Ed.). (1998). *Literacy instruction for culturally and linguistically diverse students.* Newark, DE: International Reading Association.

Ovando, C. J., & Collier, V. P. (1998). *Bilingual and ESL classrooms: Teaching in multicultural contexts.* Columbus, OH: McGraw-Hill.

Padak, N., & Rasinski, T. (2008). The games children play. *Reading Teacher, 62,* 363–364.

Padilla, E. R., Padilla, A. M., Morales, A., Olmedo, E. L., & Ramirez, R. (1979). Inhalant, marijuana, and alcohol abuse among barrio children and adolescents. *International Journal of the Addictions, 14,* 945–964.

Page, R. M., & Page, T. S. (2003). *Fostering emotional well-being in the classroom* (3rd ed.). Sudbury, MA: Jones and Bartlett.

Pelow, R. A., & Colvin, H. M. (1983, spring). PQ4R as it affects comprehension of social studies reading material. *Social Studies Journal, 12,* 14–22.

Petrie, G., Lindauer, P., Bennett, B., & Gibson, S. (1998). Nonverbal cues: The key to classroom management. *Principal, 77*(3), 34–36.

Popp, M. S. (1997). *Learning journals in the K–8 classroom: Exploring ideas and information in the content areas.* Mahwah, NJ: Lawrence Erlbaum.

Prasad, J. (2005). *Audio-visual education: Teaching innovative techniques.* Delhi, India: Kanishka.

Pressley, M., Borkowski, J. G., & O'Sullivan, J. T. (1984). Memory strategy instruction is made of this: Metamemory and durable strategy use. *Educational Psychology, 19,* 94–107.

Rafferty, L. A. (2007). "They just won't listen to me": A teacher's guide to positive behavioral interventions. *Childhood Education, 84*(2), 102–104.

Reggy-Mamo, M. (2008). An experiential approach to intercultural education. *Christian Higher Education, 7,* 110–122.

Reid, M. J., Webster-Stratton, C., & Hammond, M. (2007). Enhancing a classroom social competence and problem-solving curriculum by offering parent training to families of moderate- to high-risk elementary school children. *Journal of Clinical Child & Adolescent Psychology, 36,* 605–620.

Reschly, D. J. (2005). Learning disabilities identification: Primary intervention, secondary intervention, then what? *Journal of Learning Disabilities, 38,* 510–515.

Riley, J. (2006). *Language and literacy 3–7: Creative approaches to teaching.* Thousand Oaks, CA: Sage.

Ritter, S., & Idol-Maestas, L. (1986). Teaching middle school students to use a test-taking strategy. *Journal of Educational Research, 79,* 350–357.

Robinson, F. P. (1946). *Effective study.* New York: Harper & Row.

Roessingh, H., Kover, P., & Watt, D. (2005). Developing cognitive academic language proficiency: The journey. *TESL Canada Journal, 23*(1), 1–27.

Rogers, B. (2006). *Classroom behaviour: A practical guide to effective teaching, behaviour management and colleague support.* London: Paul Chapman.

Ross, D. (1971). The modification of extreme social withdrawal by modeling with guided participation. *Journal of Behavior Therapy and Experimental Psychiatry, 2,* 273–279.

Rubenstein, I. Z. (2006). Educational expectations: How they differ around the world: Implications for teaching ESL college students. *Community College Journal of Research and Practice, 30,* 433–441.

Rymes, B., Cahnmann-Taylor, M., & Souto-Manning, M. (2008). Bilingual teachers' performances of power and conflict. *Teaching Education, 19,* 93–107.

Sakta, C. G. (1999). SQRC: A strategy for guiding reading and higher level thinking. *Journal of Adolescent & Adult Literacy, 42,* 265–269.

Sanacore, J. (1982). Transferring the PQ4R study procedure: Administrative concerns. *Clearing House, 55*(5), 234–236.

Sanacore, J. (1999). Encouraging children to make choices about their literacy learning. *Intervention in School and Clinic, 35,* 38–42.

Semrud-Clikeman, M. (2005). Neuropsychological aspects for evaluating learning disabilities. *Journal of Learning Disabilities, 38,*563–568.

Shores, C., & Chester, K. (2009). *Using RTI for school improvement: Raising every student's achievement scores.* Thousand Oaks, CA: Corwin.

Short, D., & Echevarria, J. (2004). Teacher skills to support English language learners. *Educational Leadership, 62*(4), 8–13.

Siegel, J., & Shaughnessy, F. M. (1994). Educating for understanding: An interview with Howard Garder. *Phi Delta Kappan, 76,* 563–566.

Sink, D. W., Jr., Parkhill, M. A., Marshall, R., Norwood, S., & Parkhill, M. (2005). Learning together: A family-centered literacy program. *Community College Journal of Research and Practice, 29,* 583–590.

Smith, C. B. (2000). *Reading to learn: How to study as you read.* Bloomington, IN: ERIC Clearinghouse on Reading English and Communication.

Stough, L. M. (2002). Teaching special education in Costa Rica: Using a learning strategy in an inclusive classroom. *Teaching Exceptional Children, 34*(5), 34–39.

Strickland, D. S., Ganske, K., & Monroe, J. K. (2002). *Supporting struggling readers and writers: Strategies for classroom intervention 3–6.* Newark, DE: International Reading Association.

Tannenbaum, J. (1996). *Practical ideas on alternative assessment for ESL students.* Washington DC: ERIC Clearinghouse on Languages and Linguistics.

Thomas, P. (2006). *Stress in early childhood: Helping children and their careers.* Watson, ACT, Australia: Early Childhood Australia.

Tomlinson, B. (Ed.). (1998). *Materials development in language teaching.* Cambridge, UK: Cambridge University Press.

Tomlinson, C. A. (1999). *The differentiated classroom: Responding to the needs of all learners.* Alexandria, VA: Association for Supervision and Curriculum Development.

Tomlinson, C. A. (2003). *Fulfilling the promise of the differentiated classroom: Strategies and tools for responsive teaching.* Alexandria, VA: Association for Supervision and Curriculum Development.

Tomsho, R. (2007, August 16). Is an early-help program shortchanging kids? *The Wall Street Journal,* p. B1 [Electronic version]. Retrieved from http://online.wsj.com/article/SB118721849477198989.html

Toole, R. (2000). An additional step in the guided lecture procedure. *Journal of Adolescent & Adult Literacy, 44,* 166–168.

Tovani, C. (2000). *I read it, but I don't get it: Comprehension strategies for adolescent readers.* Portland, ME: Stenhouse.

Trudeau, K., & Harle, A. Z. (2006). Using reflection to increase children's learning in kindergarten. *Young Children, 61*(4), 101–104.

U.S. Department of Education. (2007, July). *Special education and rehabilitation services: IDEA's impact.* Retrieved November 4, 2009, from http://www.ed.gov/policy/speced/leg/idea/history30.html

Vaughn, S., & Linan-Thompson, S. (2007). *Research-based methods of reading instruction for English language learners: Grades K–4.* Alexandria, VA: Association for Supervision and Curriculum Development.

Vaughn, S., Linan-Thompson, S., & Hickman, P. (2003). Response to treatment as a means of identifying students with reading/learning disabilities. *Exceptional Children, 69,* 391–409.

Vygotsky, L. S. (1978). *Mind in society: The development of higher psychological processes.* Cambridge, MA: Harvard University Press.

Walker, D., Carta, J. J., Greenwood, C. R., & Buzhardt, J. F. (2008). The use of individual growth and developmental indicators for progress monitoring and intervention decision making in early education. *Exceptionality, 16,* 33–47.

Walter, C. (2004). Transfer of reading comprehension skills to L2 is linked to mental representations of text and to L2 working memory. *Applied Linguistics, 25,* 315–339.

Walters, J., & Frei, S. (2007). *Managing classroom behavior and discipline.* Huntington Beach, CA: Shell Education.

Wasik, B. H. (2004). *Handbook of family literacy.* Florence, KY: Routledge.

Watson, S., & Houtz, L. (1998). Modifying science instruction: One strategy for achieving success and equity in inclusive settings. *Journal of Science Education for Students with Disabilities, 1*(1), 24–37.

Webster-Stratton, C., & Reid, M. J. (2004). Strengthening social and emotional competence in young children—The foundation for early school readiness and success: Incredible year's classroom social skills and problem-solving curriculum. *Infants & Young Children, 17,* 96–113.

Weisman, E., & Hansen, L. (2007). Strategies for teaching social studies to elementary level ELL/CLD. *Education Digest, 73*(4), 61–65.

Williams, K. C. (2008). *Elementary classroom management: A student-centered approach to leading and learning.* Thousand Oaks, CA: Sage.

Wood, K. D., & Algozzine, B. (1994). Using collaborative learning to meet the needs of high-risk learners. In K. D. Wood & B. Algozzine (Eds.), *Teaching reading to high-risk learners. An integrated approach* (pp. 315–333). Boston: Allyn & Bacon.

Wood, K. D., & Harmon, J. M. (2001). *Strategies for integrating reading and writing in middle and high school classrooms.* Westerville, OH: National Middle School Association.

Wortham, S. C. (1996). *The integrated classroom: The assessment-curriculum link in early childhood education.* Upper Saddle River, NJ: Prentice Hall Business.

Wright, A., Betteridge, D., & Buckby, M. (2006). *Games for language learning.* Cambridge, UK: Cambridge University Press.

Youb, K. (2008). The effects of integrated language-based instruction in elementary ESL learning. *Modern Language Journal, 92,* 431–451.

Zutell, J., & Rasinski, T. V. (1991). Training teachers to attend to their students' oral reading fluency. *Theory Into Practice, 30,* 211–217.

Index

CORWIN
A SAGE Company

The Corwin logo—a raven striding across an open book—represents the union of courage and learning. Corwin is committed to improving education for all learners by publishing books and other professional development resources for those serving the field of PreK–12 education. By providing practical, hands-on materials, Corwin continues to carry out the promise of its motto: **"Helping Educators Do Their Work Better."**